Reflective Practice

Education at SAGE

SAGE is a leading international publisher of journals, books, and electronic media for academic, educational, and professional markets.

Our education publishing includes:

- accessible and comprehensive texts for aspiring education professionals and practitioners looking to further their careers through continuing professional development

- inspirational advice and guidance for the classroom

- authoritative state of the art reference from the leading authors in the field.

Find out more at: **www.sagepub.co.uk/education**

FOURTH EDITION

Reflective Practice

Writing and Professional Development

GILLIE BOLTON

Los Angeles | London | New Delhi
Singapore | Washington DC

Los Angeles | London | New Delhi
Singapore | Washington DC

SAGE Publications Ltd
1 Oliver's Yard
55 City Road
London EC1Y 1SP

SAGE Publications Inc.
2455 Teller Road
Thousand Oaks, California 91320

SAGE Publications India Pvt Ltd
B 1/I 1 Mohan Cooperative Industrial Area
Mathura Road
New Delhi 110 044

SAGE Publications Asia-Pacific Pte Ltd
3 Church Street
#10-04 Samsung Hub
Singapore 049483

Editor: Marianne Lagrange
Assistant editor: Rachael Plant
Production editor: Nicola Marshall
Proofreader: Emily Ayers
Marketing manager: Lorna Patkai
Cover design: Naomi Robinson
Typeset by: C&M Digitals (P) Ltd, Chennai, India
Printed in Great Britain by Henry Ling Limited at
The Dorset Press, Dorchester, DT1 1HD

Library of Congress Control Number: 2014933844

British Library Cataloguing in Publication data

A catalogue record for this book is available from
the British Library

MIX
Paper from
responsible sources
FSC™ C013985

ISBN 978-1-4462-8234-2
ISBN 978-1-4462-8235-9 (pbk)

At SAGE we take sustainability seriously. Most of our products are printed in the UK using FSC papers and boards.
When we print overseas we ensure sustainable papers are used as measured by the Egmont grading system.
We undertake an annual audit to monitor our sustainability.

Dedicated to all who heal, care, and educate

Knowledge is limited. Imagination encircles the world. (Einstein, [1929] 2002)

Try to love the *questions themselves* like locked rooms and like books that are written in a very foreign tongue. Do not now seek the answers, which cannot be given to you. *Live the questions now.* (Rainer Maria Rilke, [1934]1993)

TABLE OF CONTENTS

FOREWORD

Few books make it to a second edition; rarer still are those that merit a fourth! This new edition of Gillie Bolton's *Reflective Practice: Writing and Professional Development* demonstrates its enduring relevance for practitioners. Reflecting on the meaning of events and constructing experience from these is as old as human thought and, I would argue, central to any attempt to lead a significant life. Indeed, as Habermas argues, the interesting question is not so much how this happens, but rather when it doesn't happen what political forces are preventing it?

Of course being reflective is not necessarily inherently accurate or valid. After all, we can live through any number of events and construct bizarre or harmful interpretations of these. In the USA right now, Tea Party Republicans are construing Barack Obama's second Presidential victory as meaning that the party needs to lurch further to the right and become more extreme before it can win an election. In my practice as, variously, a community developer, adult educator, university teacher and academic leader, I have reflected on how to respond to silence in multiple situations, only to discover later that my readings of its cause and meaning were wildly inaccurate. My personal life is full of misplaced reflection, such as thinking for many years that the way to deal with my depression was to tell myself to 'snap out of it', or my lifelong belief that I have successfully resisted any socialisation into the ideology of White supremacy.

We all make micro-decisions in the middle of meetings, case conferences, lesson units, consultations, ward 'rounds' and conversations. Clinicians call the quick scan of situational cues, and the decisions and actions that are framed by these, the process of clinical reasoning. All of us do this constantly and we often rely on posing a mental checklist to ourselves to ensure we have done it well. Are my assumptions about why this is the right thing to do accurate? Have I missed a perspective on this situation that would reframe it differently? How can I draw on lessons I've learned from previous similar situations I've negotiated?

Gillie argues forcefully and persuasively that conducting these kinds of internal dialogues is not enough and that an essential component of reflective analysis is writing. Individual introspection and talking to colleagues and comparing notes are certainly crucial but there is something fundamentally different about writing down your understanding of, and reaction to, a situation. As you see the words appear on the screen or page in front of you, you are confronted almost with a second self and you often learn both pleasurable and disturbing things about that self that take you wholly by surprise.

In clear and lively prose Gillie builds her case for the importance of writing and provides numerous examples of helpful activities and exercises, not only in this book but also in the website constructed to accompany it. Narrative and story are powerful tools in multiple human contexts, conveying the essence of what we are trying to accomplish. We remember stories far more readily than we do mission or goal statements. Similarly, metaphors can galvanise a group, communicating in a shorthand way a vision of where we wish to go in a project. When we write our reflections on events we not only create meanings for ourselves, we produce a version that can be communicated to others.

Of course stories are constructs and change in the telling, often by eliminating inconvenient information that reveals our shortcomings, or giving us a heroic power of agency that, in truth, never really existed. As Gillie points out, we all have internal supervisors, justifiers and saboteurs who undermine and distort our versions of events. Writing a story down, however, is an act imbued with a sense of permanence and seriousness. I have found that when I write a story of some pedagogic event I am made far more aware of my tendency to edit out troublesome details or contradictions. When I speak it, on the other hand, the reactions of listeners embolden me to forget these inconveniences. There is something about writing your version of events that brings home to you the editorial power of the narrator.

Gillie deals with the ethical issues involved in narrative writing and provides numerous examples that illustrate its variety. She is also not afraid to confront the ways we sometimes become stuck in our stories. When the narrative we have constructed to explain our situation becomes self-evidently clear and unchallengeable in our eyes it often serves to confirm for us the validity of the self-destructive path we journey.

This is a book that travels across multiple territories and terrains. You will be provoked and impressed by the breadth of authors and concepts Gillie invokes and the variety of narrative forms she explores. I was challenged by this book to experiment with poetry and metaphor in a far more intentional way. It has always surprised me that the books I have written that have had most impact, and the parts of those books that people remember most clearly, have pretty much always featured narrative. Gillie has helped me understand better why this is the case and also why the power of narrative is sensed, and sometimes avoided, by students. Through poems, six minutes' writing, and rewriting the story of an event in a different genre (such as sci-fi, children's adventure, romance and so on) Gillie suggests ways we, and those we work with, can get past the intimidating and stifling sense of actually committing something to the page or screen, and thereby making the inside narrative of our life a public document.

Reflective Practice: Writing and Professional Development is packed with examples of activities, exercises and instructions that can be adapted in multiple contexts. Although theoretically well grounded, the book tackles head on matters of practice, particularly the thorny question of assessment. But it is the stories of contradiction, loss, and perplexity, as well as those of self-insight, transformation and change, that you will remember the most.

Stephen Brookfield,
John Ireland Endowed Chair,
University of St. Thomas,
Minneapolis-St. Paul, USA

ACKNOWLEDGEMENTS

Many practitioners and colleagues have enabled *Reflective Practice: Writing and Professional Development*, generously giving time, enthusiasm and insight into your experience, knowledge and feelings, and – perhaps most vitally – warmth. Heartfelt thanks is all I can offer for our adventures, your sensitivity, and permission to be quoted. I thank Sheffield University Institute of General Practice Master in Medical Science and Master in Education graduates, Institute of Public Health in Ireland Leadership Programme graduates, Nottingham Community Health nurses, participants in medical, nursing, social work, counselling/therapy, education, and management development programmes.

There are some without whom I could not even have laced my boots. Robert Hamberger has danced through the mud with me, Kate Billingham laughingly pointed out contours I had missed, and Amanda Howe lakes. I can't sufficiently value the company along the way of Stephen Brookfield, David Boud, Jonathan Knight, Lucy Henshall, Joyce Scaife, David McCormack, David Megginson, Julie Hughes, Kathleen Russell, Moira Brimacombe, Jo Cannon, Helen Drucquer, David Gelipter, Charles Heatley, Martin McShane, Bob Purdy, Caroline Walton, Jane Searle, Helen Starkey, Rosie Welch, Shirley Brierley, Clare Connolly, Naomi Dixon, Maggie Eisner, Seth Jenkinson, Sheena McMain, Mark Purvis, Becky Ship, Bev Hargreaves, Di Moss, Janet Hargreaves, Tom Heller, John Goodwin, Lindsay Buckell, Leslie Boydell, Kate Milne, Jane Calne, Brendan Boyle, Clare Shephard, Angela Mohtashemi, Sonya Yates, Ken Martin, Andrew Eastaugh, Jeannie Wright. I also sincerely thank Jo Turner, Claire Collins, Kirsten Jack, Kevin Marsden, Kostas Magos, Keith Collett, Judy Clinton, Erika Mansnerus, Eimear Allen, Miriam Landor, Olwen Summerscales, David McLaggan, Elaine Trevitt, Carol Wood, Mavis Kirkham, Mark Jones, Mairi Wilson, Susanna Gladwin, Margaret Meyer, Sam Kyeremateng, Chris Banks, Meryl Marger Picard, Ruth Segal, Janet Tipper, John McAuley, Caroline Ridley, Sally Jane Shaw, Russell Delderfield, Linda Garbutt, Caroline Hadley, Teresa Smith, Sue McDonald, Chris Neanon, Martin Stone, Derek Snaith, Maria Garner, Carry Gorney, Joolz Mclay.

Dan Rowland says 'Oh Gillie!' but helps me again to click, and discusses everything important and unimportant. Alice Rowland advises on colours and coats, and how not to slip on mud.

Particular thanks go to Marianne Lagrange who is a fearsomely wonderful editorial guide in velvet gloves. And Rachael Plant who has picked up pieces of me dropped on the track.

Stephen Rowland has travelled this and many other roads with me so closely I am no longer sure if it is his journey or mine. This fourth edition is another milestone in our shared adventure. He not only makes sure I have warm jerseys, compass, whistle, the right map, and right words, but fills my rucksack with endless goodies.

PREFACE: ABOUT THIS BOOK

This fourth edition explains why reflection and reflexivity are essential: clearly and straightforwardly demonstrating how to start and develop, with whom, when and where. Practical and theorised methods for understanding and grasping authority over actions, thoughts, feelings, beliefs, values and professional identity in professional, cultural and political contexts, are described, and examples offered. This book supports you in creating your own questions about your life and work; it does not give answers, because the process of reflective practice is one of developing our own enquiries. As Van Manen said:

> A pedagogical text like this one should not be composed and studied as if it were a technical handbook that specifies effective procedures... Rather, [it] needs to possess an inspirational quality together with a narrative structure that invites critical reflection and possibilities for insight and that leads to a personal appropriation of a moral intuition (1991, p. 9).

This introduction to critical reflective practice using writing arises from my experience of years of teaching and research with a wide range of professions. It gives a powerful method of reflective and reflexive enquiry, based on firm theoretical foundations created by the great reflective practice theorists and researchers (such as Schön and Brookfield). It is also based on my own enquiry into scholarly and practical work from a wide range of appropriate disciplines.

Reflective practice, and advice on it, has changed significantly since my first edition in 2000. On my shelf are 25 textbooks published in the last three years. These contain good advice, discussion of relevant theories, and questions which would be useful to answer reflectively and reflexively.

Yet, when I meet young trainees or professionals, they nearly always say they found reflective practice boring, a waste of time, too difficult, or too exposing; and in my reading I perceive others have similar experience (e.g. Hargreaves and Page, 2013). What's going on?

My experience tells me that reflection and reflexivity only develop when people are facilitated to gain a powerful process which takes them to the heart of what's significant to them, enables them to explore it, and then supports them making changes which develop practice based on their learning. So often professionals/students are exhorted to reflect; the benefits are enumerated; the areas upon which they need to reflect are listed. Perhaps it's not by chance that there are five question openers beginning with w, and only one beginning with another letter: HOW.

HOW TO REFLECT is a major focus of this book. And like all the best solutions in life: it is simple. We write. We write as a process of exploration and expression. We write to find out and examine and question. We don't write to report or write up reflection. The writing IS the reflection, exploration of the wide and rather perplexing other side of the mirror, questioning everything, turning our world inside out, outside in and back to front. A Masters (Medical Science) student wrote the advice below on how to reflect by writing:

The aha moment

Rowing is a precise art. You must have confidence in your boat and oars, but also confidence in your ability to let go and trust your natural instincts.

I will let you into a secret. The best way of introducing this feeling is to take away for a moment the crew's vision. To get them to shut their eyes. This lifts outside interference and pushes back those constraints of *how it ought to be* to *how it is*.

Shutting your eyes and letting those natural instincts take over can be daunting but liberating.

SEE HOW IT CAN BE DONE IF YOU JUST LET GO... (Jo Turner)

If we can trust the process of reflective writing, if we can let go of fears and inhibitions, if we can 'let those natural instincts take over', then we will find it exhilarating and dynamic. We will engage critically and learn; we will be empowered to change our practice (and perhaps also our institution). The process Jo and I ask you to trust is completely trustworthy.

Background information is clear, as is detailed guidance and advice, with plenty of illuminative examples from practitioners and students. It assumes nothing, and explains clearly, approachably and engagingly. Knots are untied, and the complexity of reflective practice clarified.

This fourth edition starts with an in-depth introduction to reflective practice, its personal, social and political responsibility, and what reflection and reflexivity are. How to discover what each of us needs to reflect upon, and common blocks, are examined. Reflective practice is a moral and principled process based upon ethical values: these are discussed, as well as many of the theories, frameworks and models of reflection which have been developed by others, and advice on how to make good use of them. Reflective practice is facilitated in many contexts, such as e-learning and video, and within other developmental processes such as supervision and mentoring: these are described.

The ways narrative, perspective and metaphor are foundational to reflective practice are described and illustrated. And then the processes of reflective and reflexive writing, including the reflective practice journal – why, how, what, with and for whom, when, where – are fully examined, particularly why and how.

Assessment of reflective practice is a problematic, contested area. Many views and experiences are discussed, and some solutions offered. We then turn from benefits to individuals, to benefits to teams. Graphic examples are given of how reflective practice writing can powerfully support team development. Finally, two experienced reflective writers present pictures of the reflective practice writing process at work.

This book is supported by a Sage Companion Website, containing additional free materials. Significant amongst these are two full chapters on teaching reflective practice: one on pedagogical models, values and principles; the other describing exactly how to run a reflective practice writing course. The full contents are listed on the website (www.sagepub.co.uk/bolton).

'"What is the use of a book," thought Alice, "without pictures or conversation?"' (Carroll, [1865] 1954, p. 1). Wise Alice knew texts have to capture heart, imagination and spirit, as well as mind, to communicate. This text is fully illustrated and exemplified throughout with original writings from colleagues, students and publications. These are first-hand accounts of practice, discussions about writings, reflections upon the usefulness of the reflection and reflexivity, and a range of descriptions of methods and their effectiveness. Reflective and reflexive processes are as old as thinking people: ancient wise texts offer simple windows on understanding.

A suggested criterion for my Master's students' final assessment was *evidence of enjoyment* (as well as *evidence of substantive reading*, and so on). My involvement in marking was increased when students' enjoyment oozed off the page. We only learn effectively when doing what we want to do. Stefano's research conclusions at the Neurosciences Research Institute, New York State University, include: 'pleasure is our brain's way of subconsciously and continuously ranking what is most important to us: pleasure leads to pure rationality' (2004). This book concerns critical, enjoyable, always challenging reflexivity and reflective practice.

Oars are 'wings that make ships fly', according to Odysseus (Homer 1996, p. 464). I hope *Reflective Practice* will enable you, reflective practitioner reader, to fly, and find 'goodness there':

> Just halfway through this journey of our life
>
> I reawoke to find myself inside
>
> A dark wood, way off course, the right road lost.
>
> How difficult a task it is to tell
>
> What this wild, harsh, forbidding wood was like
>
> The merest thought of which brings back my fear;
>
> For only death exceeds its bitterness.
>
> But I found goodness there. (Dante, 1988, Canto 1, ll 1–8)

Read to Learn

Howatson-Jones, L. (2013) *Reflective Practice in Nursing*. 2nd edn. London: Sage.
A helpful beginning text for students.

Knott, C. and Scragg, T. (2013) *Reflective Practice in Social Work*. 2nd edn. London: Sage.
This is a useful introduction for social work students.

Tarrant, P. (2013) *Reflective Practice and Professional Development*. London: Sage.
A useful introduction for teachers. Tarrant devotes an interesting chapter (6) to peer learning.

 Write to Learn

We all go through patches of 'dark wood' on our life's journey. Think of yours, write what 'goodness' you've 'found there'.

KEY TERMS (GLOSSARY)

The specific ways in which *key terms* are used in *Reflective Practice* are explained below. Some are from other disciplines and can seem foreign. Many are explained more extensively in the following chapters: please refer to the index.

Authority: specific areas of knowledge or experience justifying action.

Boundaries: the means by which proper separation is kept between, for example, my emotional states and those of my clients.

Critical: a questioning approach investigating how political and social forces shape values, assumptions, judgements, and beliefs.

(To) critique: the process of being critical. A *critique* is the product.

Critical incidents: events which are subject matter for critique or critical investigation.

Description: an accurate account of events, places or persons, including feelings, thoughts, beliefs, values.

Empathy: use of the imagination to enable sensitive perception of others' perspectives, enabling support of clients' feelings without involvement of professionals' personal emotions.

Espoused values: values that are claimed.

Ethical: behaviour (or values) which aim to optimise human wellbeing.

Ideologies: sets of beliefs underpinning social customs and identity, explained by theories, and maintained by institutions; commonsense and 'true' (assumptions) to insiders, they can seem strange or oppressive to others.

Inclusivity: respecting and wishing to include people with different cultural ways of being and knowing, who are often marginal due to having different values and sense of identity to the mainstream.

Metaphor: a figure of speech in which something otherwise unrelated stands in place of another: 'my work is a Christmas tree hung with lights and gifts'.

Mindfulness: complete focus upon present action (whether physical, or psychological such as reflecting upon the past) in which we make choices about how we respond to experience rather than being driven by habit.

Models: representations of the relationships between theoretical principles which underlie practice.

Narrative: an account given to describe or explain an event.

Observation: the act of watching carefully to ascertain something's essential qualities; generally followed by description.

Perspective: how things appear from a specific viewpoint.

Phronesis: application of knowledge in a wise and reasoned way, based on values and in relation to context.

Principles: general laws or rules adopted or professed to guide action; the value of respect for others might, for example, lead to the principle of welcoming diversity of faith, race and gender.

Professional: one who has authority arising from training, education and experience in a specific field.

Reflection: in-depth focused attention.

Reflective practice: the development of insight and practice through critical attention to practical values, theories, principles, assumptions, and the relationship between theory and practice which inform everyday actions.

Reflexivity: focused in-depth reflection upon one's own perspective, values and assumptions.

Responsibility: accountability for actions.

Values: the ethical bases of actions and beliefs, requiring no justification.

Values-in-practice: values embedded in practice, which may or may not be claimed.

CHAPTER 1

REFLECTIVE PRACTICE: AN INTRODUCTION

Reflective practice is introduced and described, its social and political responsibility outlined. Donald Schön's theory that reflection-in, and -on-action are essential to inform us how to work in conditions of uncertainty is outlined. Reflection and reflexivity, common blocks to them, and how to discover just what each practitioner needs to reflect upon, are defined and explained.

By three methods we may learn wisdom: first, by reflection, which is noblest; second, by imitation, which is easiest; and third by experience, which is the bitterest. (Confucius, quoted in Hinett, 2002, p. v)

There are in our existence spots of time /… whence… our minds

Are nourished and invisibly repaired; /… Such moments

Are scattered everywhere. (Wordsworth, [1880] 2004, p. 208)

How can we develop the practitioner from the practice? (GB)

How can we know the dancer from the dance? (Yeats, 1962, p. 128)

Reflective practice is a state of mind, an ongoing attitude to life and work, the pearl grit in the oyster of practice and education; danger lies in it being a separate curriculum element with a set of exercises. Brookfield calls it 'a reflexive habit… second nature' (2009). It enables us to make illuminative sense of where we are in our own practice, and our relation to our profession and our institution: we don't travel far with it. Yet it makes the difference between 20 years of experience and merely one year of experience repeated 20 times (Beaty, 1997, p. 8).

Reflective practice can enable professionals to learn from experience about: themselves; their work; the way they relate to home and work, significant others and wider society and culture; the way social and cultural structures (e.g. institutions) are formed and control us. Professionals face complex and unpredictable situations; they need complex and diverse reflective and reflexive processes. Engaging in these critically will be reflected in the quality of their work (see Whelan and Gent, 2013). It brings greater unity and wholeness of experience to the practitioner and greater empathy between them and their client. Job satisfaction will increase, and work-related stress decrease (Alarcon and Lyons, 2011).

> Perhaps the most accessible form of freedom, the most subjectively enjoyed, and the most useful to human society consists of being good at your job and therefore taking pleasure in doing it – I really believe that to live happily you have to have something to do, but it shouldn't be too easy, or else something to wish for, but not just any old wish; something there's a hope of achieving. (Levi, 1988, p. 139)

> If it wasn't for reflective practice, [stuff] would undoubtedly go around and around in my mind.

> It is much more helpful to get it out of my head and onto the paper and look back.

> I feel I can genuinely ask my clients, 'unpick unpick unpick, cry, open up'… because I have done it, I know what I am asking you to do is really difficult, but I also know that it is a really helpful.

> You relate the clinical work to the theory in reflective practice, and that gives you that 360° knowing, 'now I understand what the book is talking about'.

> (Reflective practitioners quoted in Collins, 2013, pp. 54, 83, 84, 88)

Reflective practice can give strategies to bring things out into the open, and frame appropriate and searching questions never asked before. It can provide relatively safe and confidential ways to explore and express experiences otherwise difficult or impossible to communicate. It can challenge assumptions, ideological illusions, damaging social and cultural biases, inequalities; and it questions personal behaviours which perhaps silence the voices of others or otherwise marginalise them. This book consistently enables enquiry into:

- what we know and wish or need to explore further
- what we know but do not know we know
- what we do not know and want to know
- what we think, feel, believe, value, understand about our role and boundaries
- how our actions match up with what we believe
- how to value and take into account personal feelings.

Practitioners explore and experiment with difficult areas of experience, such as:

- how to perceive from others' perspective
- how to value others' perspective, however different they are from us

- what we can change in our context; how to work with what we cannot change
- how others perceive us, and their feelings and thoughts about events, and our actions
- why we become stressed, and its impact on life and practice
- how to counteract seemingly *given* social, cultural and political structures.

We know a great deal more than we are aware, absorbing information unwittingly. We have challenging material shoved into boxes mentally labelled *do not open*. We have not celebrated and learned from positive experiences (Ghaye, 2011).

Donald Schön's Swampy Lowlands

Schön described professional practice as being in a flat place where we can't see very far (1987). Everyone would love to work on a high place from which all the near valleys and far hills are in view. Everyday life and work rarely has signposts, definitive maps, or friendly police to help with directions. The teacher in the classroom, clinician in the consulting room, healthcare professional with a patient, social worker in the client's home, lawyer with a tricky issue, member of the clergy, or the police officer themselves, relies on knowledge, skills and experience, and what they can glean quickly from immediate sources. Each one is rarely certain what is needed now. We cannot stand outside ourselves and our work (from the cliff), in order to be objective and clear. We work in the 'swampy lowlands' (Schön, 1987) by trial and error, learning from our mistakes. Everyone gets it wrong sometimes and has to live and work with the consequences.

Reflective practice makes maps. Everyone needs thorough methods to sort through *and learn from* muddles, uncertainties, unclarities, mistakes and anxieties. All need to perceive hitherto unnoticed issues, which will otherwise cause greater and greater problems. How do we know which way to go, to avoid sinking into Schön's bog? How do we know which unclear path to take at a junction as they all seem to lead further into the swamp?

I remind us of Schön's powerful image because we cannot climb out of the lowland, but do the best we can down here. There often seems no clear reason for choosing this path through tussocks or that one over a muddy stream. What and who can we trust here? That bright green grass looks inviting, but I sink up to my knees in water. What is my compass?

We do have compasses and maps: Schön (in Schön and Argyris, 1974) called them our *theories-in-use*, which he said we develop within our practice as 'a conversation with the situation' (1983, p. 76). But these maps are indistinct because they are tacitly rather than consciously used: our actions are governed by habitual patterns and ways of being. We use our *theories-in-use* unwittingly. If I were questioned about an action I would respond with *espoused theory* which I have thought out, but is possibly at variance with what I actually do.

So to develop my practice, gain greater effectiveness, I need to observe and understand my *theories-in-use*, what I actually do, alongside my *espoused theories*, what I believe I do. And as far as is practically possible I need to bring these into congruence (close to being the same thing). What equipment can I rely upon in this foggy swamp? Where, when and how do I begin?

I begin with reflective practice. We really are thrown onto our own resources in the everyday work environment, and have to trust what equipment we have: reflective practice can provide the very best. Schön said the process of trial and error and learning from mistakes is artistry. The reliable map and accurate compass are reflection and reflexivity.

Schön gave us the *swamp* image because he knew that all education requires entering a place of not-knowing, of having to ask significant questions to find out. The traveller on the educative journey through difficult terrain has to trust their few pieces of equipment. They might have helpers along the way, but no definitive guide. Being guided with certainty through the swamp would not be educative.

We learn by doing, through the very struggle to make our own judgements, not by being told where, when and how to turn, who to trust, and what is the correct path. The reflective educative process is one of each individual constantly asking *why* of everything from the individual case to the running of the whole organisation. Albert Einstein ([1929] 2002) was successful partly because he doggedly and constantly asked questions with seemingly obvious answers. Childlike, he asked why?, how?, what?, rather than accepting givens or assumptions. He had the confidence to stay with and be open to: 'love[ing] the *questions themselves* like locked rooms', and certainly '*liv[ing]* the questions' (Rilke, [1934] 1993, p. 35).

There are no single answers to 'How could I have done better?' Yet more questions arise instead, such as 'If I had done this, which I think would have been better, what would the patient/doctor have felt?' Answers tend to put a stop to the enquiring process; more and more pertinent questions take us deeper (see David, Clutterbuck and Megginson, 2013). As Master's student Ann commented: 'No wonder it all takes so much time!' Exploring issues in depth and width can take time. Though enlightenment can arrive after 15 minutes' writing.

Seeking a Route

Route-finding equipment or information can only help when the traveller knows their destination. One cannot find the solution without having identified the problem accurately and precisely. This is the conundrum of reflective practice. We want to become good experienced practitioners. But to do this, we have to discover which specific areas of practice we need to improve, and why. We find out by exploring, experimenting and discovering, with uncertainty as the central paradox. Dewey (1933a) said doubt and uncertainty is an essential element of effective reflection.

Focusing upon personal beliefs, theories, values-in-use, and reflecting upon them, is tricky. So much we have always thought or believed is taken for granted – 'everyone in my workplace thinks this way'. The very structure of language creates assumptions about things being immutable: this is how they are. Yet we only have to widen our perspective to perceive that other cultures do it differently, believe differently.

We all know colleagues who cannot say 'I don't know', believing they act the 'right way'. Their effectiveness is severely diminished by their inflexible need to be right. Schön called these people *Technical Rationalists*, who assume they work on the cliff-top where they see widely and can know what's going on, what the outcomes will be, and that everyone agrees with them (or should do). We neither respect them nor trust their judgement, knowing (even if they do not) that they are indeed in the lowlands with us.

Reflective practice helps us accept uncertainty which is the route to effective learning and professional artistry. It enables us to say 'I don't know what's going on here, and I want to find out'. We find what kind of practitioner we are, and connect ourselves with our practitioner-selves (Brookfield, 1995). All this gives confidence and strength to:

- let go of certainty, in a safe enough environment
- look for direction without knowing where we need to go
- begin to act without knowing how.

This essential uncertainty is hard for many; practice and organisational contexts influence the effectiveness of reflection (Wilson, 2013). I found some senior practitioners heavily defended, using self-protective reasoning as proof against uncertainty and doubt. Their sense of themselves in their role was paradoxically too uncertain for them to lay it open to doubt and enquiry. This uncertainty is also difficult for students. 'Pre-service teachers want answers and methods. They want to be certain, to know: but certainty does not generate the flexibly enquiring attitude required by learning. In [professional] education, working towards habits of uncertainty and puzzlement is need[ed]… [In fact] certainty goes down as experiential knowledge goes up…' (Phillion and Connelly, 2004, p. 468).

Our technologically and digitally based culture has not valued reflection and still less reflexivity, where market place, machine, and computer metaphors are paramount. They have been ghettoised as *soft and fluffy* (feminine), a waste of valuable professional time, because they are unmalleable by masculine processes of commodification, nor can they be reduced to component mechanical parts, or tested by tick boxes. Reflection and reflexivity are sophisticated human processes, requiring sophisticated educative support:

> The goal of education, if we are to survive, is the *facilitation of change and learning*. The only person who is educated is the person who has learned how to learn; the person who has learned how to adapt and change; the person who has realised that no knowledge is secure, that only the process of seeking knowledge gives a basis for security. Changingness, a reliance on process rather than on static knowledge, is the only thing that makes any sense as a goal for education. (Rogers, 1969, p. 152)

Reflective practice can increase:

- acceptance of, and confidence with, the essential complexity, uncertainty and perspectival nature of professional life
- reflexive critique of personal values, ethics, prejudices, boundaries, assumptions about roles and identity, decision-making processes, taken-for-granted structures
- reflexive critique of professional environments and workplaces
- awareness of diversity, and struggle against misuse of institutional power and managerialism
- willingness to explore the interrelatedness of the professional and the personal
- sensitive, fruitful review of 'forgotten' areas of practice
- analysis of hesitations, skill and knowledge gaps
- respect for, and trust in, others' and own feelings and emotions
- development of observation and communication abilities
- constructive awareness of collegial relationships
- relief of stress by facing problematic or painful episodes
- identification of learning needs
- communication of experience and expertise with a wide range of colleagues.

Reflection In- and On-practice: Our Map for the Swampy Lowlands

Schön divided reflective practice into *reflection-in-action* and *reflection-on-action*.

Reflection-in-action is the hovering hawk in the mind, enabling us to bring remembered skills, experience and knowledge into play at the right time. We have to act immediately and cannot normally say to a student (patient/client/parishioner etc.) 'sorry but I've got to stop and think how to do this'. The hawk enables us to draw on our *theory and knowledge in use* as we go along. With more experience, we have more to draw upon; reflection-in-action can work more swiftly to bring appropriate values, knowledge, skill or theory into use.

Experienced practice relies on reflection-in-action, rather than working from automatic assumptions. This latter can lead to actions at variance with our own espoused values, and even those of the profession. Copley (2011), a police trainer, highlights police value assumptions about race, in, for example, the Stephen Lawrence case. Actions based on skilful, experienced assessment, including awareness of appropriate values, might lead to completely different policing outcomes.

Reflection-on-action is reflection after event, and increases the effectiveness of reflection-in-action. The artistry of practice is when our knowledge, skill and theory base becomes:

- large and diverse appropriate to our practice
- more and more available when needed.

Reflection and Reflexivity: Demystification

> Reflection and reflexivity are the essential elements of reflective practice. Perceiving the difference makes it less of an 'ill-defined process' (Bleakley, 1999, p. 317).

Reflection is in-depth review of events, either alone – say, in a journal – or with critical support with a supervisor or group. The reflector attempts to work out what happened, what they thought or felt about it, who was involved, when and where, what these others might have experienced and thought and felt about it from their own perspective. Most significantly, the reflector considers WHY?, and studies significant theory and texts from the wider sphere. It is to bring experiences into focus from as many angles as possible: people, place, relationships, timing, chronology, causality, connections, the social and political context, and so on. Seemingly innocent details might prove to be key; seemingly vital details may be irrelevant. Reflection might prove something thought to be vital to be insignificant, or lead to insight about something unnoticed at the time, pinpointing perhaps when the seemingly innocent detail was missed.

Reflexivity is finding strategies to question our own attitudes, theories-in-use, values, assumptions, prejudices and habitual actions; to understand our complex roles in relation to others. It develops responsible and ethical action, such as becoming aware of how much our ways of being are culturally determined; other peoples have very different expectations and norms (Bager-Charleson, 2010). To be reflexive is to examine, for example, the limits of our knowledge, of how our own behaviour plays into organisational structures counter to our own personal and professional values, and why such practices might marginalise groups or exclude individuals. It is questioning how congruent our actions are with our espoused values and theories (e.g. about religion or gender).

Thus, we recognise we are active in shaping our surroundings, ways of relating to others and communicating. We begin asking critical questions, rather than merely accepting or reacting; we help review and revise ethical ways of being and relating (Cunliffe, 2009b). Reflexivity means we might point out inconsistencies (e.g. between espoused and values-in-action) in political, social or cultural structures (e.g. my employing organisation).

To be reflexive involves thinking from within experiences, or as the *Oxford English Dictionary* puts it, 'turned or reflected back upon the mind itself', and 'the effect of the personality on what is being investigated'. This is complex artistry, working out how our presence influences knowledge and actions. Reflexivity involves innovative dynamic methods, rather than coming from *reflex*, 'an action performed independently of the will, as an automatic response to a stimulus' (OED). A reflexive-minded practitioner might ask themselves:

- why did this pass me by?
- what were my assumptions which made me not notice?

- what are the organisational etc. pressures or ideologies which obstructed my perception?
- how and in what way were my actions perceived by others?

Such deep questioning can enable development, much more than problem solving questions such as 'what happened?', 'what did I think and feel about it?', 'how can I do it better next time?'

Reflexivity is the near-impossible adventure of making aspects of the self strange: attempting to stand back from belief and value systems and observe habitual ways of thinking and relating to others, structures of understanding ourselves, our relationship to the world, and the way we are experienced and perceived by others and their assumptions about the way that the world impinges upon them. Questioning assumptions is a struggle against a sense of immutability – 'it's just how things are', or 'it's common sense' – so significant it's 'like laying down charges of psychological dynamite... educators who foster transformative learning are rather like psychological and cultural demolition experts' (Brookfield, 1990, p. 178).

Looking at ourselves thus can feel 'embarrassing' (Bager-Charleson 2010, p. x); it requires bravery in staying with uncertainty, finding out others' perceptions, flexibility to change deeply held ways of being, and willingness to be noticed (perhaps as 'whistle-blowers', Hargreaves and Page, 2013, p.160) – all of which are highly responsible social and political activities.

Strategies are required such as internal dialogue, and the support of trusted others such as supervisor or peer-reader of an account. Hibbert (2012) describes effective teaching methods for developing reflexivity from reflection, and Hanson (2013) explores deepening pedagogical practices around critical reflection and reflexivity.

Reflective practice enables us to wonder at our own world, work, and indeed ourselves, because 'problems do not present themselves to the practitioner as givens... he must make sense of an uncertain situation that initially makes no sense' (Schön 1983, p. 40). It is looking at everyday taken-for-granteds, perceiving them as (possibly shockingly) unfamiliar and open to change. It 'is designed to facilitate identification, examination, and modification of the theories-in-use that shape behaviour, [a process of professional development which] requires change in deeply held action theories' (Osterman and Kottkamp, 2004, pp. 13–14). Such deep change can involve 'loss... of an element that made a part of what you were' (Roffey-Barentsen and Malthouse, 2013, p. 20). Reflective practice helps us to meet this in the spirit of discovery rather than defensively (Schön, 1987) in and about our workplace (Matsuo, 2012).

Many writing suggestions begin with one of the querying words, or *tin-openers*. Between them they can set us off on a journey of asking more and more significant questions.

> I keep six honest serving men
>
> (They taught me all I knew);

Their names are What and Why and When

And How and Where and Who. (Kipling, 1902, p. 83)

These servants have served me well for years, too. As well as starting reflective and reflexive questions, they also can create checklists for planning and writing, helping ensure we have covered everything. Eimear Allen (see example in Chapter 3) said 'I think it is a method which will help me explore future problems I might face in reflective writing by challenging them with these questions'.

Here is a seemingly simple, obvious reflection, yet its significance to Kirsten Jack's practice was profound: 'it was a very big and complex thing and I still feel that I was coming to terms with it only years later. It didn't have a "start" and "finish". Maybe the initial understanding of what was going on was there, but the actual thinking and feeling processes continued and might never end.'

The man in the green pyjamas

A first year student nurse on my first hospital placement, I met 'Harry' who was confused and trying to get out of bed to go home. Unable to eat, he repeatedly tried to pull out his naso-gastric tube, making his nose bleed, so the registered nurses decided to bandage his hands.

I found the image of this agitated man extremely distressing. Tall and thin, in ill-fitting green pyjamas with frequently exposed genitalia, he had lost his dignity. I felt very sad and helpless to do anything to assist, apart from speaking to him quietly and soothingly.

I could not get Harry out of my mind and spent the night crying, feeling a grief I had not felt for a long time. I realised that Harry reminded me of my own father who had died when I was ten. The same build as Harry, my dad died in the same hospital in circumstances which remained a mystery to me. My sadness was for my dad; I was grieving as a daughter, not as Harry's nurse.

Through reflection I was able to make sense of my feelings of fear, anxiety and real heartbreak, and come to an understanding of how my grief as a daughter differed to that of student nurse. The reflective process led to emotional awareness and the beginning of my journey to manage my feelings, so that they did not overwhelm me when in practice. My emotions had been tangled; reflection helped me to unravel my grief, so that I could continue to nurse Harry without feeling overwhelmed.

Kirsten Jack

Many professionals never realise certain individuals distress them because they remind of them of someone else in their life. Kirsten asked the critical question, why did this man so distress her? She wasn't satisfied with: it's a very sad case, of course I'm distressed. I myself took years to learn that I responded defensively and weakly to bullying male senior colleagues because they reminded me of my brother. My career would have been immeasurably enhanced if I could have learned this as early as Kirsten's reflection began to help her. Like Kirsten, I bear burdens of past events which colour how I perceive the present. We all 'relive' (Bruce, 2013) past emotions in present events, processes called projection or transference in psychology (Humphrey, 2011). Reflective practice can significantly prevent these inhibiting or skewing our present abilities and empathy. Understanding these past experiences can enhance present practice. Reflection upon my past experience enables me to offer better support to those who are bullied, as well as help bullies tackle their essential weakness. And Dr Mark Purvis was able to treat extremely sick children once he had reflected upon his little brother's death (Chapter 2).

Reflective Practice: a Political and Social Responsibility

There is much in life we are genuinely not in control of, such as birth, death, illness, accidents, and obeying the law of the land. We may not even fully control our feelings and thoughts; we are surely responsible for our actions. Reflective practitioners take their share of responsibility for the political, social and cultural situations within which they live and work, as well as for their own actions and values. We can't say: 'I did that because my senior instructed me to', 'it was in the protocol', 'everyone does that!', or even 'oh, I've never thought about why, or if I should'.

Questioning and changing work assumptions and attitudes is demanding. Our professional and personal roles, values and everyday actions are embedded in complex and volatile structures. Power is subtle and slippery; its location is often different from how it appears. Reflective practice for genuine development involves each individual:

- recognising, taking *authority* over and *responsibility* for their own personal and professional actions, identity, values, feelings
- *contesting* lack of diversity, imbalance of power, the way managerialism can block development
- *asking questions* and being willing to stay with *uncertainty*, unpredictability, doubt. This is the only way to discover our assumptions and do something about them.

Reflective practice can enable discovery of who and what we are, why we act as we do, and how we can be much more effective. The educative process is perceiving and developing our own searching questions, rather than responding to given questions. The search for solutions, leading to yet more pertinent questions and more learning, leads to unsettling uncertainty: the foundation of all education. In learning and understanding about human rights, for example, law students need to learn 'not only the practice of law. Rather... the practice of people, their lives and the values, needs, beliefs that people hold and wish to protect, or promote, or advocate' (Williams, 2002, p. 134).

The route is through spirited enquiry leading to constructive developmental change and personal and professional integrity based on deep understandings. Despite questioning all assumptions and strongly held beliefs, the process is self-affirming and illuminative: people only learn and develop when happy and benefiting personally.

The reflective/reflexive attitude is similar to Winnicott's (1965) creative *transitional space* (or *play space* [1971]), the realm of the artist. The *transitional space* is part way between our inner psychological experience, and culture outside the self: a place of exploration just beyond the boundaries. Because it is betwixt and between, that which is created comes from both the artist's private self (or psyche) as well as from culture. It fosters activities which are not tidy and safe (it wouldn't be artistic if it was). So it is likely to come up with dynamic possibilities, and startling solutions.

Being able to enter the *transitional (play) space* with the wisdom of the child, being able to venture outside the firmly boundaried inner self into a place of exploration and letting go of assumptions and certainties to develop new ways of being and understanding, can ultimately enable us to relate to others in non-judgemental, unprejudiced ways.

Reflective practice can sometimes fall into the trap of becoming only *confession*. 'Confession' can be a conforming mechanism, despite sounding liberating, freeing from a burden of doubt, guilt and anxiety (Bleakley, 2000b). Confession has a seductive quality because it passes responsibility to others.

The desire is strong to confess and tell, like the ancient mariner (Coleridge, [1834] 1978). Nias and Aspinwall (1992), noted with surprise that all their research interviewees were keen to tell their autobiographies. People always are, but *they do not want their confessions questioned*: *this* is the role of reflective practice.

Reflective practice is more than an examination of personal experience, it is located in the political and social structures which increasingly hedge professionals (Goodson, 2004). The right of professionals in the west to moral and professional judgements is eroded; they are being reduced to technicians, their skills to mere technical competencies. Yet they are also increasingly under pressure to have 'strong and stable personalities and to be able to tolerate complexity', and they are 'pushed destructively and distortingly by obsessive goals and targets in a masculine culture of assertiveness and competitiveness' (Garvey et al., 2014, pp. 112, 249). They are also pushed to work according to a scientifically derived evidence base. 'Since the seventeenth century, Western science has excluded certain expressive modes from its legitimate repertoire: rhetoric (in the name of "plain" transparent signification), fiction (in the name of fact), and subjectivity (in the name of objectivity). The qualities eliminated from science were localised in the category of "literature"' (Clifford, 1986, p. 102).

The assumption that an objective view of the world is 'grown-up', that we should shed our subjective view along with sand and water play, is being questioned (see also Sacks, 1985, pp. 1–21). 'We are impoverished if out of touch with any part of ourselves. The dominant culture is scientific, but the scientist who concentrates on this side of themselves exclusively is as impoverished as the musician or writer who concentrates only on the artistic' (Paul Robertson, director, Medici String Quartet, 1999).

Goodson creates a distinction between *life stories* and *life history*. The latter is the former plus appropriate and challenging data from a wide range of sources, and evidence of vital discussion with colleagues. 'The life history pushes the question of whether private issues are also public matters. The life story individualises and personalises; the life history contextualises and politicises' (1998, p. 11).

An ethnographer can no longer stand on a mountain top to map authoritatively (Clifford, 1986). Clinicians cannot confidently diagnose and dictate from an objective professional or scientific standpoint; teachers do not know answers; lawyers do not necessarily know what is right and what wrong. The enmeshment of culture and environment is total: no one is objective. Ideal professionals, gathering data on which to base their pedagogy, diagnosis or care, are like social anthropologists. Successful ethnographers create a 'thick description': a web of 'sort of piled-up structures of inference and implication through which the ethnographer is continually trying to pick his way' (Geertz, [1973] 1993, p. 7).

A critical reflective practitioner attempts to understand the heart of their practice. Understandings gained in this way, however, are always partial; the deeper the enquiry, the enquirer realises the less they know and understand: *the more you know, the more you know you do not know.*

A supported process, such as recommended in this book, which encourages doubt and uncertainty, paradoxically gives practitioners strength in the face of such contradictory expectations and attempts to control. Where enquiry into practice is undertaken alongside open discussions with peers on pertinent issues, an examination of texts from the larger field of work and politics, and discussions with colleagues from outside practitioners' own milieu, reflective practice can then be critical: a life-changing enquiry into the assumptions which underpin our practice, rather than mere confession.

Training and education curricula need shaking up, and more enquiry-based reflective methods introduced. *Curriculum* is Latin for race course (Rome's oval Piazza Navona was one): perhaps we need to progress from chasing each other and ourselves round a set track. 'Unearthing and questioning assumptions is often risky' (Brookfield, 2013, p. 23): let's take the risk.

Valuing diversity

Reflection and reflexivity support appreciation of diversity, which 'should be engraved on every teacher's heart' (Brookfield, 1990). Theories, values and practices vary between cultures, affecting how clients and others respond to professionals and their practice. For example, the West has a strong ethic of individualism, deriving from ancient Greece, which is very different from Eastern (particularly Chinese and Japanese) understandings of the self. Eastern thinking discourages abstraction (unlike Western), and focuses upon social harmony and a sense of constant change (Sellars, 2014). Culture is an iceberg: we are aware of differences, but they are even greater and more significant than they appear (Sellars, 2014).

An awareness of how groups can be marginalised or individuals excluded (Cunliffe, 2009a), of inclusivity and empathetic supportiveness with regard to, for example, non-traditional students and widening access and participation, are essential elements. Wright's (2005) study found reflective journals written in English, despite this not being their writers' mother tongue; their learning from the process would have been negated: this should not happen. Collins et al. (2010) developed a strategy for enhancing multicultural elements in reflective practice in counselling.

Making Sense of Experience

A closely observed event (Wordsworth's 'spot of time'), written about, rigorously reflected upon, discussed critically and re-explored through further writings can stand metonymically for that professional's practice. Stories and poems are slices, metonymically revealing the rest of practice.

Knowing what incident to reflect upon is not straightforward. Significant issues become elusive, and can become like looking for Piglet: 'It was still snowing as [Pooh Bear] stumped over the white forest track, and he expected to find Piglet warming his toes in front of the fire, but to his surprise he found that the door was open, and the more he looked inside the more Piglet wasn't there' (Milne, [1928] 1958, p. 163). Only with the courage to stop *looking* and trust the reflective and reflexive processes, will we begin to perceive what needs tackling. Mark Purvis (*The Death of Simon*, see Chapter 2) did not seek consciously for his 'critical' incident: he put his hand on the page and started writing.

Writings often focus on seemingly unimportant incidents. The 'right' one might be a seemingly-simple daily habitual action, or incidents ignored because they are problematic, often for unexamined reasons, or those which have been 'forgotten' or unconsidered (because they appear not to belong in the realm of practice but in personal life). 'Critical' incidents, described by Brookfield (1990, p. 84) as 'vividly remembered events', such as giving the wrong vaccine because they had been stored higgledy-piggledy in the fridge, will inevitably be examined. Events we 'forget' are often those needing reflection, and can give rise to the deepest reflexivity: 'we need to attend to the untold' (Sharkey, 2004). 'A passionate, almost religious belief... is that it is in the negligible that the considerable is to be found... The unconsidered is deeply considerable' (Miller, 2009, p. 12). A human resource development exercise is writing what you *do not* remember (Joy-Matthews et al., 2004). Plato, who said 'the life without examination is no life' (Plato, 2000, p. 315), reckoned education is finding pathways to what we do not know we know.

A critical incident is an incident we are critical about. We do need to be critical *about* incidents. Kevin Marsden wrote a special-school experience:

Malcolm was struggling to recognise sets of two in number work, and sat slumped on an elbow.

I had one of those 'bright ideas' teachers tend to get. Let's make it more practical. 'Malcolm, look at Darren. How many eyes has he got?'

Malcolm looked at Darren. Pointing with his finger he slowly counted in his deep voice, 'One... two'.

'Good, well done,' I said. 'Now look at Debbie, how many eyes has she got?'

Pointing carefully again Malcolm intoned slowly, 'One... two'.

'That's great, Malcolm, now look at Tony, count his eyes.'

'One... two.' Let's take this a step further, I said smugly to myself.

'Now Malcolm, look at Matthew. Without counting can you tell me how many eyes he has got?'

Malcolm looked at me as if I had gone mad. 'OK that's fine Malcolm, count them like you did the others.'

Relieved he slowly repeated: 'One... two'.

There is a magical moment in teaching, when the penny drops, the light goes on, the doors open. Success is achieved. I was starting to worry. We weren't getting there!

'Malcolm, how many eyes has Naheeda got?' Malcolm counted slowly, as if it was the first pair of eyes he had ever seen.

'Good, you're doing really well.'

We carried on round the class. Eager faces looked up to have their eyes counted. I was growing desperate as we ran out of children. Was I leading Malcolm on an educational wild-goose chase? Were we pursuing an idea that was not yet ready to be caught?

The last pair of eyes was counted. 'One... two.' There was only me left. 'Malcolm,' I said, trying to hide my desperation, 'How many eyes have I got?' Malcolm studied my face carefully. He looked long and hard at my eyes. I waited expectantly in the silence. His brow furrowed. Finally he spoke.

'Take your glasses off.'

Kevin Marsden

Kevin read this to his established sub-group of five Masters in Education teachers. They trusted and felt confidence and respect for each other's professional abilities and views. Kevin was able to share his frustrations and sense of failure; the group learned about the methods, joys and problems of special-school teaching. They were able to explore the probability that Malcolm had had a different understanding of his task than did Kevin. Possibly Malcolm thought he was to count the eyes, rather than 'guess' how many each had. To do this he would have had to ask for spectacles to be removed so he could see clearly. The situation of a mismatch between a teacher's intentions and a child's understanding must happen so often. In order to gain a grasp of what might be going on, Kevin had to examine and question his assumptions.

Blocks and Limitations to Reflection

- Inexperience at imagining another's experience
- Not knowing how to create a dynamic reflective narrative (see Chapter 4)
- Fearing incompetence, fearing ridicule
- Tiredness/overwork/lack of time/too many other things to do
- Lack of motivation
- Seeing it just as a way of passing the exam
- Too painful and revealing

Reflection and reflexivity are essential for responsible and ethical practice, yet there are arguments against it. Some consider it challenges position or status in organisations where professionals are expected to do as they are told: managerialism is a significant block (Heel et al., 2006; Redmond, 2006); some that it is a luxury within packed curricula taught by demotivated, over-stretched tutors who use risk-averse and evidence-based approaches fostering disengagement and negativity (Munro, 2010).

Yet the busier we are, the more vital reflection and reflexivity are to prevent us missing significant issues and making mistakes (Hedberg, 2009), and losing authority by becoming uncritically conformist. Reflection is personally demanding, and needs to be undertaken at the individuals' own pace and to their taste (Smith, 2011).

Without confident, experienced support (Standal and Moe, 2013; Chi, 2013) and advice, such as provided by this book, practitioners may experience feelings of helplessness, frustration and eventual burnout (Gray, 2007), anxiety and antagonism (Livtack et al., 2010), resistance (Bulpitt and Martin, 2005), blocking negativity (Hobbs, 2007; Smith, 2011), or feel 'angry, challenged, threatened, demoralized, shocked, and put off by the *leap into the unknown*' (Trelfa, 2005, p. 206), focus merely on technical skills merely to meet academic requirements (Collins, 2013), or write abstractly rather than about specific experiences. Inamdar and Roldan (2013) tell us that 'the ability to face, frame, and build solutions to ambiguous, highly uncertain situations is [essential] in rapidly evolving and globalizing business settings... Yet our findings showed that reflection is the least taught skill in business schools... and the most challenging for students' (p. 766). Tutors focus upon the least challenging and easiest to teach.

Dialogue with students to ascertain feelings and needs could lead to more informed tuition (Schmidt and Adkins, 2012). Creating an educative environment where practitioners and students challenge themselves as practitioners, the very roots of their practice, and significantly critique their organisations, can be complex and perplexing. Instruction resulting in neatly written competencies is less demanding and easer to mark, but is not reflective practice.

A paradox is that organisations or courses require reflective practice as curricula or professional development elements. Since the very nature of reflective practice is essentially personally, politically and socially unsettling, it does not allow anything to be taken for granted; everything has to be questioned. Enquiry-based education, education for creativity, innovativeness, adaptability, is education for instability.

Smooth-running social, political and professional systems run on the well-oiled cogs of stories we construct, and connive at being constructed around us. Welcoming of diversity can be mere window dressing. Effective reflective practice and reflexivity are transgressive of stable and controlling orders; they lead cogs to decide to change shape, change place, even reconfigure whole systems. Change and development take time, energy and commitment. Critical reflective practice leading to dynamic change is the result of tough practitioner (or student) exploration and self-examination.

Understanding the Name: *Reflective Practice*

A mirror reflection is merely the image of an object directly in front of it, faithfully reproduced back to front. What is the reflection of shit? Shit. The word reflection has static connotations, meaning 'the action of turning [back] or fixing the thoughts on some subject' (OED).

A mirror image suggests *me out there* practising in the big world, and reflected *me in my head,* an unhelpful opposing duality: *this* as opposed to *that, in* and *out, here* and *there*:

> You must first forsake the dualities of: self and others, interior and exterior, small and large, good and bad, delusion and enlightenment, life and death, being and nothingness. (Tsai Chi Chung, 1994, p. 95)

Reflective practice is purposeful, not the musing one slips into while driving home, or rumination which can suppress emotions and create distressing yet absorbing negative thoughts (Fogel, 2009), leading to depression, anxiety, hostility and vulnerability. *'It's easy to end up thinking and thinking and ruminating but not getting anywhere'* (cited in Claire Collins, 2013, p.72, see also Farber, 2005). Rumination is a sheep or goat chewing smelly cud. Lindsay Buckell (see Chapter 7) sent me a cartoon of a sheep, nose to nose with her mirrored reflection and meadow, saying:

'I'm sure the grass is greener in the mirror, but whenever I try to reach it, this ugly ewe bars the way and butts me on the nose.' The 'ugly ewe' is of course herself reflected. We need intensive explorative and expressive methods in order not just to be confronted by our own 'ugly ewe'.

We need to throw out a sense that reflection is merely self-indulgent. Narcissus fell in love with his own reflection: this is self-indulgence. Reflective practice is not narcissistic because rather than falling in love with our own beauty, we bravely face the discomfort and uncertainty of attempting to perceive how things are. We seek to uncover dark corners by asking difficult questions. We reflect in order to try to perceive ourselves with others' eyes (employers, clients, colleagues), to gain a clearer picture. Perhaps this approach should be called flexive. Flexion means 'alteration, change, modification', and 'a bend, curve, and a joint' (OED).

Let me explain with another picture. In London's Covent Garden Opera House, we share the magic of world-class performance in the crimson and gold auditorium. We cannot part the red curtain, however, and go onto the stage and beyond. Yet there are acres and acres of stage, rehearsal space, offices, canteens, costume and set stores, etc. Fabulous opera and ballet could not take place without this invisible space and activity. We live our lives in the auditorium of our minds – excitingly and dramatically playing different characters (parent, colleague, lecturer, lover…) – but without realising what's beyond the curtain. Reflective practice writing enables exploration of areas we didn't know we knew, had forgotten, never bothered to develop, never really noticed, etc. Beyond the curtain we remove our masks and props and become vulnerable and uncertain. This is education and learning.

Being reflectively aware is like Einstein's 'appreciation of the mysterious [which] is the fundamental emotion which stands at the cradle of true art and true science' (1973, p. 80), and Socrates' 'wonder is the beginning of wisdom', because wonder is an open enquiring state of mind when anything might be possible, when startling inspiration appears as a result of no cognitive logical thought. The sculptor Juan Muñoz spoke of an aim of his art 'to make [viewers] trust for a second that what he wishes to believe is true. And maybe you can spin that into another reality and make him wonder'. This reality spinning can involve imaginatively entering others' consciousness, empathetically and ethically:

> There would seem to be a need for some special intuitive faculty which allows me to range beyond my own sense-data, transport myself into your emotional innards and empathise with what you are feeling. This is known as the imagination. It makes up for our natural state of isolation from one another [each in their own separate auditorium]. The moral and the aesthetic [imaginative] lie close together, since to be moral is to be able to feel what others are feeling. (Eagleton, 2008, p. 19)

Reflective practice is here seen as complex, fascinating, and unstraightforward as life and practice itself.

'Reflection is the central dynamic in intentional learning, problem-solving and validity testing through rational discourse' (Mezirow, 1981, p. 4); but there is more than just the 'rational'. We can be enabled to reflect beyond Mezirow's 'rational' using the methods outlined in the following chapters. First, to develop our understanding of reflective practice, we consider some of its vital foundations.

 Read to Learn

Bruce, L. (2013) *Reflective Practice for Social Workers.* Maidenhead: Open University Press.
The first four chapters are a thorough, wise study of what reflective practice is and should be, and analysis of such issues as emotional intelligence, and what it is to be a professional. I recommend them to all readers, not just social work practitioners and students.

Fook, J. (2012) *Social Work: A Critical Approach to Practice.* London: Sage.
Jan Fook is a reliable, lucid guide to critical postmodern, poststructuralist practice. This book concerns social work, but I heartily recommend readers to turn to her for her wisdom, depth of research, and clarity.

Scaife, J. (2010) *Supervising the Reflective Practitioner.* Hove: Routledge.
Joyce Scaife is a reliable, intelligent and critically informed guide to reflective practice and supervision, both theory and practice. She clarifies and enlightens some of the dense issues with cartoons and light verse. I recommend this book to a wider readership than Scaife's field of psychology.

 Write to Learn

Each chapter ends with *Write to Learn*. These exercises can take very different lengths of time. Some are very affirming, some challenging; all result in positive writing. Each can be done individually or by a facilitated group: many are useful for initial group forming. See Chapter 8 for more advice on starting writing. For now:

- This is unplanned, off-the-top-of-the-head writing; try to allow yourself to write anything.
- Whatever you write will be right; there is no critic, red pen poised.
- All that matters here is the writing's content; if you need to adjust grammar and so on, you can – later.
- Ignore the *Inner Saboteur* who niggles about proper form and grammar, or says your writing is rubbish.
- This writing is private, belongs to the writer who will be its first reader.

- No one else need ever read it, unless the writer decides to share it with trusted confidential other(s).
- Before doing any of the exercises here, or in other chapters, do a *six-minute-write* about anything to limber up before starting (see Chapter 8).
- Reread all the writing with care and attention before reading it out to anyone.
- Writing can then be shared fruitfully with another or group, if this seems appropriate.

Advice for facilitators

It helps the process if:

- each writer reads silently back to themselves before reading to group or partner
- each person knows at the start they will be invited to read out
- everyone is offered the option of not reading if it feels inappropriate
- you know that many exercises occasion laughter, some tears: both are fine
- a facilitator gives instructions in numbered order
- participants finish writing each section before hearing the next
- minimal explanations are given: people usually 'play the game' if they trust the facilitator.

1.1 Names

1. Write anything about your name: memories, impressions, likes, hates, what people have said, your nicknames over the years: anything.
2. Write a selection of names you might have preferred to your own.
3. Write a letter to yourself from one of these chosen names.

1.2 Milestones

1. List the milestones of your life and/or career, do it quickly without thinking much.
2. Delete or add, clarify or expand as you wish.
3. Add some divergent things (e.g. when you first really squared up to your CEO).
4. Choose one. Write a short piece about it. If you wish, continue and write about others.

1.3 Insights

1. Quickly write a list of 20 words or phrases about your work.
2. Allow yourself to write anything; everything is relevant, even the seeming insignificant.

(Continued)

(Continued)

3. Reread; underline words or phrases which seem to stick out.
4. Choose one. Write it at the top of a fresh page. Write anything which occurs to you about it.
5. NOBODY else need read this ever, so allow yourself to write anything.
6. You might write a poem, or an account remembering a particular occasion, or muse ramblingly. Whatever you write will be right.
7. Choose another word from your list, if you wish, and continue writing.
8. Add to your list if more occur to you.

1.4 Significant clothes

1. Describe in detail favourite work clothes, including features such as mends.
2. Describe acquiring these clothes (was any part a gift?).
3. How do these clothes make you feel?
4. Describe your least favourite work clothes.
5. When do you wear these and why? Why do you dislike them?
6. Tell the detailed story of an occasion when you wore them.

1.5 A spot of time (Wordsworth: see beginning of this chapter)

1. Jot down a very quick list of occasions when you felt nourished, content, affirmed.
2. Choose one, write about it with as much detail as you can remember.
3. Give it a title as if it were a film; write the brief paragraph of film advertising blurb.
4. Read it back to yourself with care, adding or altering positively.
5. Write about another one if you have time.

 Visit **www.sagepub.co.uk/bolton** for additional useful resources including writing examples, exercises and videos.

CHAPTER 2

VALUES AND PRINCIPLES OF REFLECTIVE PRACTICE

Reflection and reflexivity are moral and principled practices based upon ethical values. Such firm foundations are essential in order to develop our work, and ourselves. We therefore now consider values, principles, and the ethics of requiring students to reflect, of reflecting upon clients, and sharing confidential material with colleagues. A range of emotions, such as anger, which reflective practitioners encounter are discussed, as well as some of the qualities required or engendered by the process: responsibility, authority, mindfulness, forgiveness, risk and safety.

A disciple became frustrated at never being taught anything, and never knowing how long meditation would last. The master always rang a bell: sometimes after five minutes, sometimes five hours. The disciple became so infuriated that one day she grabbed and rang the bell when *she* wanted meditation to end. The master bowed to her. She had unwittingly learned what she had needed to learn. (Ancient Zen story)

You understand how to act from knowledge, but you have not yet seen how to act from not-knowing. (Chuang Tsu, 1974, p. 68)

I'm no longer uncertain about being uncertain: uncertainty is now my mantra. (Reflective practice student)

The sage offered her disciple tea, but did not stop pouring. 'Master, the cup is full!' 'You are just like this cup: overflowing,' the sage replied, 'there is no space for you to learn.' (Story from Chuang Tsu)

Reflective practice and reflexivity, approaches which support critique of any aspect of professional life, are founded upon strong coherent ethical principles and values.

They are undertaken by practitioners in moral roles, relying on the quality of ethical attitude and actions; this chapter addresses these and discusses forgiveness, safety and risk.

What are Ethical Values?

Values are the ethical bases of our actions and beliefs, requiring no justification. We know we hold certain values, such as respect for others, and assume we live and work according to them: these are *espoused*. *Values-in-practice* are those we actually unwittingly live and work by; they are sometimes at variance with those we espouse. Values vary from culture to culture, as well as between individuals, often significantly. Writing from the perspective of someone from another culture, empathising with their values, can help a great deal with understanding differences (walking in their shoes to perceive what it's like to be them).

How do we discover our own values-in-practice? More crucially, how do we appraise and develop them? Values-in-practice, along with technical knowledge and skill, are foundations of living and working, according to the ancient Greek philosopher Aristotle. They are, however, rarely analysed or questioned. *Espoused values* (those we are aware are foundational to our practice) are recognised and routinely stated. Yet we are what we do; actions speak louder than words: values have significance only in practice. 'If we had asked people... about their values in abstract terms, we would have received generalised responses [espoused values]. By asking them to tell stories about important experiences, we were able to see... how values reveal themselves in a complex, varied and shifting way in practice' (Pattison et al., 1999b, p. 6).

Professional integrity can be defined as having values-in-practice as close to the same as espoused values as possible. Senge theorised the inevitable gap between our vision (espoused) and our practice (2006) as having creative tension, the one always pulling towards the other. Practice can be brought closer to our ideal, causing vision to move further to retain tension and encourage us to develop always further: just as a walker is encouraged to climb higher as a further peak comes into view ahead. Or we can lower our vision nearer to how things are. The tension is creative, it is the artistry of Schön, the creativity of reflective writing.

We intuitively base our actions upon *implicit* knowledge and values, hitherto unexamined, 'a collection of information, intuitions and interpretation' (Epstein, 1999, p. 834) gained initially from experience, observation, or study (Belenky et al., 1997; Eraut, 1994). This does not necessarily mean it is right, any more than is knowledge gained from randomised control trial research (explicit).

Critical reflective practice enables professionals to perceive their own implicit knowledge and values-in-practice and recognise possible dissonance between these and their explicit knowledge and espoused values, or those of their organisation. Reflection can then support them to clarify and develop their espoused values, and/or alter their practice. This might not be easy, particularly if they realise an action, or an aspect of their organisation has been (or is) against their own ethical code, or that they are in an untenable but unalterable situation (Rowland, 2000). Examining such fundamental areas requires a supportive, confidential, carefully facilitated environment.

> Reflecting on my practice in a meaningful way, key to improving it, involved articulating and reflecting on my values (espoused and practised) in ways that I had not done before. This process has led to… a richer understanding about who 'I' am, and how the values I bring to work affect my role. A necessary part of this process has been to explicitly surface my values as a way of ensuring I practice honestly and congruently. The result has been to create more appropriate strategies of intervention that are *acceptable* and *workable* to my [business consultancy] clients, which has in turn – by means of their own reflective processes – helped them create a more resilient organization (Shepherd, 2006, p. 346).

> Writing to explore professional values underlying practice is not easy. Such values are always difficult to express. Their articulation needs to be retraced as they become questioned and new experience [is] brought to bear. Thus we expect participants to refine ideas in one portfolio which may initially have been raised earlier, pursuing themes of enquiry across consecutive portfolios. (Rowland and Barton 1994, p. 371)

Branch tells us of a reflective learning programme using writing in safe supported group processes with young medical faculty which resulted in development of values such as empathy, compassion, fairness, and courage, and success in teachings, mentoring and leadership (2005, Branch et al., 2009, 2011). Reflection was facilitated upon shameful incidents such as a failure to act when faced by breaches of personal values; feeling humiliated by a superior; feeling confused about an assessment of a situation as 'wrong'; feeling inadequate when wishing to take responsibility for a patient; expressing compassion to a patient who had irritated teammates. Medical practitioner values are also developed by music, drama, fabric arts, drawing (McLean, 2014). Conversely, researchers found medical students to be less morally developed at the end of their training than the beginning (Patenaude et al. 2003): they clearly needed Branch's programmes. And reflective writing develops family therapy trainees to stay connected with their clients (Lutz and Irizarry, 2009), and business leadership students to empathise with their clients, to realise they are people (Lawrence, 2013).

Values and Principles of Reflective Practice

Critical reflective practice requires:

Trust in the processes of our practice and reflection upon it. This trust enables us to examine, question, explore and experiment: to be critical. We are the primary authority on our own experience; believing this requires trust, at least initially. It is in letting go that we find our direction.

Self-respect for our beliefs, actions, feelings, values, identity. This is the know-ledge that we have something vital to express and share with ourselves and others, and can do it well. We therefore communicate respectfully with ourselves, tackling inevitable fears, hesitations, and the voice of destructive inner critics. With the certainty gained from learning to respect ourselves, we can be creatively uncertain where we are going.

Responsibility for all our actions, including those of reflective practice. It is in taking full responsibility for our actions that we gain freedom to understand, explore and experiment with inspirational playful creativity.

Generosity and genuineness. We willingly give energy, time and commitment to personal and professional development in a focused spirit of enquiry. This giving enables us to receive inspiration and experience from others, and from our own enhanced self-understanding.

Positive regard and empathy. Reflecting upon incidents involving clients is respectful, even if the experiences were negative. Any feeling or thought can be explored within the privacy of reflective practice, both for cathartic release and in order to understand how and why an incident happened, and develop practice. These feelings, rather than being directed towards the individuals, are safely contained within the reflective process: unconditional positive regard (Rogers, 1969) can be maintained. Empathy is an imaginative process of leaving our own feelings and exploring others' perspectives. Negative memories, thoughts and feelings can facilitate learning from them; celebrating positive ones can be life and work enhancing.

Certain Uncertainty; Serious Playfulness; Unquestioning Questioning

The principles which underlie critical reflective practice enable practitioners and students to become meaningfully involved. I express them as paradoxes or oxymorons (two words together which *appear* to have opposite meanings), because critical reflective practice can *seem* essentially paradoxical.

Certain uncertainty: the one certainty is uncertainty (Chapter 1, Schön's swampy lowland). We begin to act when we do not know how we should act. Dynamic and creative interim goals arise, rather than one predetermined goal. Uncertainty is the essential educative state of mind, Barnett's 'bungee jumping', leaping into a void and opening up educative spaces (2007). Employees or students, used to being told what to do and the constraining but safe-seeming certainty of structure, may express nervousness or anger born out of anxiety, wishing superiors or tutors to take responsibility. Staying with uncertainty is uncomfortable, until the excitement of discovery takes hold. We bravely 'abandon previous "truths" and sit with *not knowing*' (Gerber, 1994, p. 290). Those who think they know are bound to be wrong. To people willing to 'not know', all sorts of things are possible.

For me reflexive writing was a way to express and manage doubt. I learned a narrative style that allowed for uncertainty, for tentative conclusions and contested views from which a more confident individual voice emerged.

What strikes me about doctoral students is the number of times they use the word 'doubt'. They doubt their ability to stay the course, make time to study, gain ethical approval, and above all, to write. I try to understand what doubt means to me, about doing research and the ways, as a supervisor, I can now help students overcome what is a painful and often debilitating barrier.

A doctoral thesis gets under your skin, permeating all areas of your life, stealing your evenings and weekends, swamping the kitchen table or office with books and waking you up in the early hours. My reflection suggested that maybe the doubt is located in the fear that by writing up the research for examination, you share it with others and thus expose a very intimate aspect of your intellect to scrutiny. As long as it's unwritten, you are safe from criticism.

On reflection, I realise that I can now help students to experiment with and develop this important skill.

Janet Hargreaves

Serious playfulness: willingness to experiment and adventure, makes uncertainty a positive force. Looking for something without knowing what it is uncovers pertinent questions. An adventurous spirit leads to that trackless moorland which education has come to be, rather than a walled or hedged field (Usher et al., 1997). There is, however, only so much we can do to alter our own situation, that of others, and the wider political one: we recognise our power is *unlimitedly limited*. This playfulness is essentially serious, taking place within a safe-enough educational environment in which people can feel confident to take risks. Listen to Kathleen, Episcopalian priest and USA lecturer in ministry, playing with alternative images:

Self-doubt about starting on my doctorate of ministry came from my old history of not pulling off final writing. So I made a list of **100** words to describe 'my doctoral project'.

Starting with 'arduous, challenging, complicated', going onto 'a gift to me, a gift to others, and adventure, exploration, the other side', finishing with 'blessing, gift, ME, MINE, my handwork—a basket, a quilt, a clutter of abundance, cornucopia'.

(Continued)

(Continued)

I became clear my list wasn't so much about the project itself, but about what it meant to me, my relationship with <u>it</u>. Three images came up: a tinker trying to sell a wagon of wares; Merlin who conjures a new world and gives others (students) entry into something new and fulfilling; and the Mad Hatter (or was I the white rabbit?).

So many were not fear of failure, confusion, or being out of control. Most were inviting, hopeful and meaningful. I was able to embrace being tinker and Merlin – even the Mad Hatter, who is a little dangerous: he just shows up – like a lot of good learning – it's in the surprises. Through this process of writing and reflection, my relationship with my project changed from one of anxiety and self-doubt to one of trust, ownership and hope.

Kathleen Russell

Unquestioning questioning: we accept, unquestioningly, the questioning spirit about anything and everything, leaving no room for self-importance. Questions determine directions, and what might be discovered, rather than destinations. Findings beget more questions. This *non-judgemental critical* process is active and enquiring, rather like the wise child's eternal *Why?* We find out about ourselves by letting go of everyday assumptions about who we are, in order to be open to the discovery of other possible selves. I discover the myselves of whom I am not habitually aware, the myself I might be, and the selves I am becoming, joining up the dots between these selves.

Kostas Magos runs a course exploring *Otherness* using narrative methods, at Thessaly University, Greece. Dina, a young pre-school teacher trainee, was vehemently anti-immigrant. Through narrative, journal-writing, and discussion in an environment of trust and security Dina questioned and re-questioned her views so intensely she suffered headaches and other symptoms. The group was finally asked to share personal experiences of *otherness*; she spoke up about her father's illiteracy:

'My father was like… immigrants who don't know the language. But in my father's case…, he spent an entire lifetime as an immigrant in the land where he was born…

I vented my anger [for foreigners, immigrants, all of them] and then had acquired the composure to talk and listen, especially listen, because in the past I did not listen.' (Magos, 2011, pp. 676, 678)

Those who don't listen, can't question. Only when 'the cup is empty' (Chuang Tsu) can we receive, hear what is being said, perceive what is happening and begin to question critically (see Hallet, 2013 for more on pre-school teaching reflection).

These oxymorons underpin an ethical and aesthetic (Schön's 'artistry', 1983) approach, rather than logical or instrumental. Practitioners and students have a responsibility to tell and retell their stories in ways appropriate to them: they are the authorities. They create narratives in relation to the stories of others and their social, cultural, professional contexts. Socrates' pedagogic method was based on just such oxymorons; here is Meno struggling with Socrates' ruthless method of enquiry into the nature of 'virtue':

Meno: Socrates, even before I met you they told me that in plain truth you are a perplexed man yourself and reduce others to perplexity...

Socrates: It isn't that knowing the answers myself, I perplex other people. The truth is rather that I infect them also with the perplexity I feel myself... So with virtue now. I don't know what it is. You may have known before you came into contact with me, but now you look as if you don't. Nevertheless I am ready to carry out, together with you, a joint investigation and inquiry into what it is.

Meno: But how will you look for something when you don't in the least know what it is? How on earth are you going to set up something you don't know as the object of your search? To put it another way, even if you come right up against it, how will you know that what you have found is the thing you didn't know? (Plato, 1958, pp. 127–8)

Dewey (1933b), an early proponent of reflection, said it requires 'open-mindedness, responsibility, wholeheartedness'. Open-mindedness being 'an active desire to listen to more sides than one, to give heed to facts from whatever source they come, to give full attention to alternative possibilities, to recognise the possibility of error even in the beliefs which are dearest to us'; wholeheartedness is 'genuine enthusiasm, an attitude that operates as an intellectual force' (pp. 29–30).

> We must first know and understand ourselves before we are at peace internally. We must be at peace internally to participate in our world in an effective manner. When we are at peace we naturally exhibit characteristics of integrity, honesty, openness, and trustworthiness. (Cunliffe, 2004, p. 22)

Ethical Relationships

Ethics and Students

Reflective practice raises significant ethical considerations concerning professionals, the populations with whom they practice, and their organisations. Practitioners may find distressing issues arise, or that they become unexpectedly angry (for example). 'This really made me realise the learner is not in control when exploring new ideas' (John, Master's student). Sutton et al. (2007) report students feeling they had been unsupportedly required 'to splurge out guts' (p. 396). Pre-service students are considered by some to be vulnerable, though this is not my experience: I've found they tumble in and out of being emotional. I have known experienced doctors break down and need support. Undergraduates make definite personal statements; 'I'm the sort of person who...', 'that's just like you, you always...'. Young adults explore who they are, and where their boundaries are. Hargreaves examined the ethics of requiring nurses to undertake this activity (1997).

> My feelings are private – yet I am expected to frame them in prose and submit them to my university. I don't know my lecturers or personal tutor intimately. What right has anyone to ask for such personal information, let alone ask that it be graded by a faceless lecturer? As nurses we respect patients' rights not to disclose their personal feelings. Yet no such right is afforded to students. (Sinclair-Penwarden, 2006, p. 12)

Practitioners bring their whole selves to reflective practice; and that whole person has vulnerabilities: this is part of the work. Experienced and knowledgeable facilitation (see the companion website) and appropriate levels of assessment (see Chapter 10) enable students and practitioners to find reflection and reflexivity valuable rather than intrusive. An understanding of therapeutic principles and practices can offer empathetic and facilitative understanding, and confidence with emotive situations; learning from other disciplines is appropriate to all experienced practice. Appropriate outside support may be sought for emergent therapeutic needs. Inexperienced facilitators may find students' reflections unexpectedly raise issues or emotions in themselves, needing support.

Checks and balances in facilitation can be provided by supervisors/mentors or co-peer mentors, or co-facilitating group sessions. Periods of group reflexivity and an awareness of Rowland's 'shared context' (2000, see the companion website) are invaluable. The group can be facilitated to take responsibility for its own processes, to observe if a member needs extra support or to be handled sensitively and will alert the facilitator if necessary. Each participant has responsibility for sharing distress or anxiety before it becomes too big for the group to handle. Clear and agreed ground rules of boundaries and confidentiality are valuable.

Ethics and Clients etc.

Confidential material about practitioners' clients is exposed, even when names and details are altered: specific issues need to be addressed rather than generalities. As a user of services myself, I would rather be reflected upon and discussed appropriately.

Practitioners do discuss cases with respect. Sometimes the need to release feelings overtakes: a group of doctors fell about laughing about a dropped corpse being unpickupable in snow and ice, I remember. No disrespect was intended, but the situation was too horrific to be countenanced until some emotion had been released. Paramedics and police officers release emotion in similar natural ways (gallows humour).

Narratives of practice are used to teach 'narrative ethics', offering 'richer ethical discourse for all' (Jones, 1998, p. 223): studying one's own stories and reading literature are ideal for development of ethical practice.

> The diary sessions are in-depth critical discussions and comparisons of clinical situations where logical and rigorous analysis of moral and ethical concepts takes place. Through this analytical process, assumptions made by health care professionals, patients and relatives are uncovered and examined. This leads to the revelation of attitudes, stereotyping, prejudices, preconceptions, philosophical ethics, frames of references, cultural influences, and the nurse's predisposition to act in a certain way: 'reflecting on clinical situations made me aware of my beliefs… and the assumptions I make… the uniqueness of people and their rights'. (Durgahee, 1997, p. 143)

This fully rounded reflective process involves feelings, as well as the 'logical and rigorous'. Reflective writing can support students to clarify their spiritual and ethical position, to strengthen relationships with clients (Briggs and Lovan, 2014).

Ethical dilemmas may arise concerning confidentiality and a colleague's faulty practice: should it be reported? What would I have done had my teacher-student (Chapter 4) not said his school was dealing with another teacher's sexual relationship with a pupil? There can be no rules: careful one-to-one discussion is the starting point. Self-respect is needed, while opening up to close observation, uncertainty and questioning previously taken-for-granted areas:

actions: what you and others did

ideas: what you thought; what others might have thought

feelings: what you felt, and what others might have felt.

Challenging Emotions

> We live in deeds not years; in thoughts, not breaths;
>
> In feelings, not in figures on a dial.
>
> We should count time by heart throbs. He most lives
>
> Who thinks most – feels the noblest – acts the best. (P.J. Bailey, *Festus*)

'Between feeling and action there is thought' (Sophocles, 1982). Effective actions arise from both feelings and thoughts. All learning, including reflection, involves emotion as well as cognitive engagement (Dirkx, 2008; Gully, 2004; Jordi, 2011; Schwind et al., 2013). Emotion is often the first reaction to significant situations, often associated with 'forgotten' memories, sometimes from long ago. Such emotions can seem to come from nowhere, although extremely personally significant.

Responding constructively, instead of crushing feelings, is part of reflection-in- and on-action. It took me years to realise my emotionally dysfunctional response to certain situations and places was their likeness to my hated and feared boarding school. Dr Mark Purvis recalled the death of his little brother to enable him to treat very sick children (see pp. 39–41). If we can be sensitively aware of and accepting of our own feelings, then we are likely to be able to form respectful helping relationships with others (Rogers, 1967).

> The idea that my emotions are a source of understanding has an exciting and novel ring for me. Exciting because it opens up the possibility… that the emotional part of me has a value outside my own personal attachment to it… It is novel because my experience of the world of learning has been that emotions are, at best, merely the icing on top of the cake, for decoration, self-indulgence and treats, but not the real substance. (Eastaugh, 1998, p. 48)

Reflecting upon emotional situations can help discover ethical values in practice. Emotions are aroused when values are transgressed, opposed or affirmed. People from cultures and religions different from our own might well have very different, and equally strong, values.

Recognising and working with emotions through reflexivity can significantly develop practice. The death of Victoria Climbié (Laming, 2003) indicates a failure of practice. Climbié's social workers failed to respond to clear indications of abuse because they protected themselves against the psychological and emotional stresses of working with violent clients (Ferguson, 2005). Professionals increasingly have an instrumental role in the delivery of services rather than being agents of change, support and care (Ruch, 2009). MacIntyre (1985) says managers' activities have become value neutral, concerned with rationality, efficiency and confidence, rather than moral debate or awareness. People are viewed as costs, effects or benefits, rather than feeling humans.

These metaphors can lead professionals to perceive service users in terms of specific problems or as theoretical constructs rather than unique people with unique needs (Redmond, 2006). Another issue concerning violent clients is that workers can *mirror* them, and become aggressive themselves (Knott and Scragg, 2013).

Anger is often viewed as inappropriate, beyond the professional boundary. Reflective practice is an appropriate locus for exploring it, and other seemingly dangerous emotions.

> As a result of reflecting upon these incidents I now understand how I felt unable to express anger because I was afraid of making a fool of myself, afraid of losing control, that if I get angry with someone they will not like me. I therefore tend to push my anger down inside. I had not been consciously aware of this and therefore not aware of how much anger I was carrying. I was therefore unable to explain unpleasant feelings when it began to rise to the surface.

> I now know it is not possible (or necessarily good) to please everybody all the time. I know the difference between telling someone I am angry and expressing the anger itself. I am able to recognise when I am angry, when I am suppressing it and the feelings that this causes. I feel more able to tell people when I am angry articulately. (Rod)

A doctor said of his vehement long-term 'diary' about his relationship with his health authority: 'I am much less emotionally reactive in management meetings, and certainly not as nervous!' (See also Lindsay Buckell's 'passionate hatred of the current climate of fear and blame' in Chapter 7). Dr Keith Collett, senior trainer and supervisor, encourages the writing of drafts of medical reports, responses to complaints and so on, so that they can be discussed, reflected upon and redrafted:

> This is incredibly useful to prevent registrars [interns] overstating support or condemnation for a patient… They have a chance to reflect on how it will be received by patient, relatives, or solicitor… I feel the first splenic draft is healing and calming. Too often dictaphones are used and the resultant text signed and sent without reflective reading. (Keith Collett)

Paula Salvio supports teachers in *empathetic enquiry*, a deeper understanding of ethnic minority students: teachers must 'travel into our own worlds' in order to 'travel to those of others'. This involves feelings, as 'emotional whiteout' will disable this travel (1998, p. 49). Cixous described this as feminine writing:

> All the feminine texts I've read are very close to the voice, very close to the flesh of language, much more so than masculine texts… perhaps because there's something in them that's freely given, perhaps because they don't rush into meaning, but are straightway at the threshold of feeling. There's tactility in the feminine text, there's touch, and this touch passes through the ear. (1995, p. 175)

Psychologist Oliver Sacks studied 'Dr P.' who could see, but had lost 'visual perception, visual imagination and memory, the fundamental powers of visual representation… insofar as they pertained to the personal, the familiar, the concrete', concluding:

> If we delete feeling and judging, the personal, from the cognitive sciences, we reduce *them* to something as defective as Dr P. – and we reduce *our* apprehension of the concrete and real… Our cognitive sciences are themselves suffering from an agnosia essentially similar to Dr P.'s. Dr P. may therefore serve as a warning and parable – of what happens to a science which eschews the judgmental, the particular, the personal, and becomes entirely abstract and computational. (Sacks, 1985, p. 19)

Reflective practice can learn from Sacks's 'warning and parable' to avoid agnosia.

> There is something rather odd about trying to get help from health workers who have not worked out their own feelings, or who deny them to themselves and others. Where do all those spontaneous feelings go and who is to say what damage they might be

doing to the delicate internal workings of our minds if we continue to repress and suppress them... The key insights and changes in the way I view myself and my professional work have come through self-reflective work. (Heller, 1996, pp. 365, 368)

I feel, I think, I believe are appropriate when writing about reflectively personal actions, decisions or responses (although less appropriate in academic writing founded on evidence from scholarly literature).

> I note my feelings being very different working with these women than with the men. I felt very maternal towards the men and they related to me with a mixture of respect and even affection that seemed a reciprocation of my feelings. I haven't had daughters or sisters, these women do still press the buttons of my school-day bullying by girls, which I'm aware makes me wary: I have to work much harder to feel warm towards them. This makes me less immediately empathetic, but also perhaps makes me more objective in how I hear them – provided I can keep being alert to my buttons being pressed!
>
> Judy Clinton

Critical reflective practice involves emotion; it therefore needs confident experienced teaching and facilitating (Standal and Moe 2013; Chi, 2013; Livtack et al., 2010). 'Academic programmes often neglect to support students with the affective aspects of learning' (Campbell 1999, p. 45).

Reflective Awareness: Responsibility, Authority and Boundaries

The critically reflective practitioner is responsible for all their reflective work and the outcomes. Some come to professional learning assuming that tutors take responsibility. The slowness of reflective learning frustrates them, with its constant reflexive involvement.

Reflective practice aims to give greater authority over professional principles, values and actions. The only route is to take responsibility and authority over the learning processes which get us there. Recognising, and taking responsibility for actions is part of reflexivity. When addressing the very stuff of our lives, only the individual practitioner can tackle it from the inside, with the help of outside perspectives of peers, and expert support of tutors. In order to take responsibility for professional actions, and some of the actions of others, we need a clearer perception of how we build our world, and how others build it around us: its narrative and metaphoric structures and content. This perception will enable, necessitate even, development and change. Many life constraints are constructed around and by us, rather than being bars we can only beat against. Sartre suggested that unperceived choices always face us, although we rarely perceive our freedom to choose ([1938] 1963).

Facilitators' roles include creation of safe-enough educational environments with clear boundaries. In this space practitioners can be brave enough to stay with uncertainty and self-doubt, gain confidence in their own strength and intelligence to develop significant questions, as well as meet and tackle challenges creatively and insightfully. This learning environment is secure enough for enquirers to take risks, beginning to realise, and wield, the full extent of their responsibility. It is like a window through which sunlight can enter (Chapter 11), an empty cup with room for new contents such as 'aha' or 'epiphanies'.

Critical reflection enables practitioners to explore experience, values and professional identities, and express aspects within certain personal and professional bounds which they expect to be respected. They are open to having understandings challenged, willing to have beliefs questioned, and courageous in discovering aspects underlying and affecting daily behaviour, of which they were hitherto unaware. They are open, willing and courageous *enough*: too much can be a recipe for disaster, as can self-protective closedness. None of this would be possible if the practitioner did not take full responsibility.

Entering this space, realising the necessity of taking ownership of learning, can feel uncomfortable. Here is a typical senior practitioner at the end of a reflective practice writing course:

> I felt to begin with that the course was slightly wacky and flaky – surreal... I felt uncomfortable and a bit insecure at first... But now I feel this process is empowering. I was initially afraid it was too self-indulgent.

She had expected structure and analysis, but was strong enough for these assumptions not to block her from responding to a totally new educational environment. Participants, whose senior roles involve telling others what to do, often try to block educative uncertainty due to their fear of insecurity. Nine senior doctors initially resembled naughty infant lads recently, using delaying and warding-off tactics. They did not want to be challenged to question the foundation of their responsibility and power. They would happily have given me, their tutor, authority and responsibility to tell them what to do and think. They would rather I artificially structured their learning with little scope for the uncomfortable uncertainty of critical learning.

Mindfulness

Mindfulness is complete focus upon present action. Senses and awareness are tuned: the opposite of multi-tasking. A focused non-judgemental state of mind, it also crucially means making 'choices in how you respond to your experience rather than being driven by habitual reactions' (Burch, 2008, p.55). Being mindfully aware develops accurate observation, communication, ability to use implicit knowledge in association with explicit knowledge, and insight into others' perceptions.

The term *sati* which is generally translated as *mindfulness*, can literally be translated as recollection, memory, recalling to mind (Gethin, 2011). So it is awareness of the present imbued with the values and ethics learned through life experience. Being consistently mindful can bring us to practical wisdom, which Aristotle called phronesis: 'the opposite of acting on the basis of scripts and protocols; those are for beginners, and continuing reliance on them can doom actors to remain beginners' (Frank, 2004, p. 221). Kinsella's study shows how reflective practice can enable health and social care students to practice with phronesis (2010).

The observation skills and awareness required of a reflective writer develop mindfulness, and are developed by it. Both require an acute focus upon what is happening at any time. Being fully conscious of actions can also enable awareness of their likely or possible outcomes, and therefore the appropriateness of the intended action. Mindfulness resembles reflection-before-action (Wilson, 2008): for example it might have prevented the abuse and death of Victoria Climbié (Knott and Scragg, 2013).

The positive impact of mindfulness practice on physical and psychological health is researched at Bangor University (www.bangor.ac.uk/mindfulness [accessed 29 November 2013]), and the University of Massachesetts Medical School (www.umassmed.edu/cfm [accessed 29 November 2013]).

Ours is an age of anxiety, tension, hyperactivity (multi-tasking, hot-desking, hitting the ground running), an era of inflated public emotion (a sea of flowers for a dead princess, road rage, televised war-torn victims). There is little reflective, reflexive, or simply mentally absent space allowed: 'A poor life this if, full of care, /We have no time to stand and stare' (William Henry Davies). We have lost even more than Davies's everyday consciousness of 'squirrels' and 'streams full of stars, like skies at night'. It is loss of professional agency and responsibility, because we are unaware of things of which we so need to be aware. The Buddhist meaning of mindfulness contains also an awareness of memory. Mark Purvis allowed himself to focus mindfully upon a very old recollection, in a doctors' reflective writing group (pp. 39–41).

Forgiveness

Reflective practice can enable a shift in attitude to events, relationships and values; forgiving others and oneself can become possible. Mercy has been marginalised as soppy and/or religious. Blake's description of mercy as having a 'human heart' (1958, p. 33) and Portia's powerful plea (Shakespeare's *Merchant of Venice*) are often forgotten. 'It is no wonder that people are flocking to various mental health practitioners with chronic guilt, shame, resentment, disease, and feelings of estrangement'

(Rowe and Halling, 1998, p. 227). The ancient Greek playwright Aeschylus made the goddess Athene say of forgiveness:

> Let your rage pass into understanding
>
> As into the coloured clouds of a sunset,
>
> Promising a fair tomorrow.
>
> Do not let it fall
>
> As a rain of sterility and anguish. (1999, p. 184)

The inability to forgive binds people to negative memories, thoughts and feelings and to vain hopes for the future (see also Rowe et al., 1989). Yet forgiveness, found through reflective practice, is like dropping a burden, carried often for years. Forgiveness of oneself and others go hand in hand. The letting go of remorse and hatred or anger with another cannot, however, be planned for or directed by a facilitator. Forgiveness is a gift coming with increased understanding (see Munno, 2006; Mark Purvis below).

Risk and Safety

> I have come to realise through the process of writing about this incident that reflection is not a cosy process of quiet contemplation. It is an active, dynamic, often threatening process which demands total involvement of self and a commitment to action. In reflective practice there is nowhere to hide. (Susan)

This kind of work can cause anxieties, doubts, fears, and fear of risk. One is that a pile of unperceived problems might appear ('the can of worms is safer left unopened'), another that an unknown aspect of oneself might surface, like bestial Mr Hyde taking the place of Dr Jekyll (Stevenson, [1886] 1984), or a murderous self step out of the mirror (*The Student of Prague*, 1926 Conrad Veidt film).

Reflexive questioning, which seeks to take apart assumptions, rethink previously accepted structures and relationships, can feel risky. Insight is gained into the motives, thoughts and feelings of people and organisations, and actions never before envisaged become possible, previously taken for granted structures and strategies cannot be tolerated any longer. This is likely to change practice, and the relationship of the practitioner to their practice, dynamically (Bay and Macfarlane, 2011). As well as generating energy, commitment to change and greatly enhanced practitioner knowledge, skills, and abilities, reflexivity can be politically and personally unsettling, even 'psychological dynamite' (Brookfield, 1990, p.178), 'an intensely threatening emotional experience' (Mezirow, 2000, pp. 6–7).

To provoke critical thinking, lecturers as well as students face risk, uncertainty, and doubt; this can take humility (Mackay and Tymon, 2013). Participants get what they pay for: those willing to express and explore deeply receive the most.

Practitioners involve themselves according to strengths, wants and needs. Those not so ready only go as far as they can: the choice is theirs, whether conscious or not. This risky venture can lead to greater emotional strength, agency and transformative learning, if it is undertaken in a safe-enough facilitated environment (Winnicott, 1971; Hunt, 2013).

Safety, Risk and Boundaries on a Master's Course

This section describes a course in detail in order to show how a specific group tackled risk, and found sufficient safety to be reflective and reflexive about their practice. The description of the course could be used as a model for facilitating reflective practice (substantial further information on the website).

A Master's in Medical Science group (Bolton, 1999) started reflective writing. It is one thing to say something tentatively in discussion, and then develop or alter it as the subject evolves and mutates. It is one thing to sit silent, or only venturing the odd expression while the more verbal and confident develop their ideas through discussion. It is quite another to stand by your written words. The group members knew I would ask them to write without forethought, not merely as rational discourse (Mezirow, 1991), but from intuitive knowledge, understanding, and memory of experience.

One asked: 'How do I know which incident to choose?' I replied I would facilitate, with every step carefully explained and agreed to. There was a sigh of relief. Developing confidence and trust in writing and sharing reflectively needs supportive, clear, interactive facilitation for it not to feel unsafe and confusing. Celia Hunt discusses similar apprehensions (2013). Writers need to feel whatever they write is right for them, and will be respected by listeners, as will seeming contradictions and changes of mind. We also pulled apart my facilitation style and skills, for the sake of their educational understandings; that is not the story here.

The group understood this would be hot writing (improvised, rather than cool from pre-planned ideas). They still needed me to explain how to allow words to flow from their pens; after all their heads were empty of ideas, or full of apprehension. They had to trust themselves to write without prior thought: the breath of creative life to poets, novelists, playwrights, autobiographers, but missed out by academic writers. Everyone wrote for six minutes without stopping, putting on the paper whatever was in their heads (like stream of consciousness). This was not for sharing (but could be if the writer so wished): it was to clear our heads; or capture whatever floating thoughts and ideas were there; and to get the pen flowing untroubled (or perhaps feverishly fast) over the page.

> Pierre has just left the room, obviously upset, and I think that emphasises just how powerful this can be. How does this 'power' get dealt with without leaving more scars? (Liz)

Risk, the students rightly discerned, is the power of this writing. Writing is also well paced: people do not normally write more than they are able to cope with. Writers need sufficient time to read and acquaint themselves with their own writing before sharing.

> The facilitation allowing the group to respond to the writings primarily and giving permission not to disclose any part of the writing made the group safe and gave responsibility to its members. (Elaine)

In talk-based discussion groups it is easy to blurt, and regret. Sonya (NHS Senior Nurse Manager) commented in her journal on her own six-minutes' writing:

> This seemed to spring from nowhere and resulted in me actively seeking a new job!! All based on a few minutes' thought!

We then wrote about 'a time when I learned something vital at work'. Ann (an experienced educator) wrote about a disastrous session with young disadvantaged mothers which she facilitated years previously:

> I started this critical incident with descriptive words, mostly relating to emotions, both mine and those I had felt from other people involved. As I began to write the story I was unsure why I had chosen this incident. Having happened some years ago and been discussed with a number of people, I had understood and analysed it. Perhaps I felt I had the answers ready to be neatly inserted into the story. I had been instructed to write about the first incident which came to mind and this was it.
>
> As I wrote, I could see the room, feel the atmosphere, although some details were hazy. What hit me again was the emotional force, both those of the women, but more particularly my own feelings. I couldn't believe how much there was to put down. I had to force myself to stop after all the others had finished. When I read the piece to the group I was overwhelmed by the emotional force and couldn't read. All those emotions. And I thought I had 'dealt with' this incident. (Ann)

Reflective practice writing can enable attention to less dominant sides of ourselves. This can feel risky because certainties which once felt comfortably secure, are now experienced as professional straitjackets. Issues previously buried as un-faceable arise to be faced; writers begin to doubt, become confused (how will I know who I am if I bring my basic practice into question?), need drastically to alter their practice, their world, even the worlds of others.

Later they feel exhilaration and increase in self-confidence and self-determination. Facilitators ensure this happens at a pace and depth, and with sufficiently created boundaries, so 'this "power" gets dealt with without leaving more scars' (Liz, above).

The next stage was to read and discuss writings. I contribute verbally only when appropriate and after everyone else has spoken (and I rarely wasted group time by reading my writing). Discussions were carefully facilitated towards reflectivity and reflexivity, within clear guidelines and boundaries set by the group.

Jessica's story concerned a knotty, ongoing work situation unflinchingly shared, implementing her fresh understandings immediately: 'I don't believe I could have done it without these learning opportunities'.

The group also worked in co-peer mentoring pairs, without tutors; one commented this enabled sharing which would have been impossible with the group. Creative, original, helpful suggestions were made to develop core stories.

> I surprised myself with both the subject and the power of emotions my writing provoked: so many unresolved feelings about the incident despite having talked about it many times. On reflection I feel that Gillie is right: there is something in the writing that gives another dimension. Seeing the words on the page gives an added intensity to the power of the feelings. There was a lot of honesty in the group, although some people understandably chose far less problematic incidents. I have learned a lot from hearing the others talk through their incidents. I have learned about the power of the written word. I have thought about trying to do sharing of critical incidents with primary health care teams and feel it could be very valuable. I'm sure every group finds its level of exposure. (Ann)

Ann felt the group were not sufficiently critical in supporting her to feel she had acted out of the best intentions. She wanted to face the possibility that having just good intentions was not enough. She noted six weeks later, however:

> I can see that I had still not been able to put this incident behind me and therefore was cross with others for trying to help me to do that. I feel rather embarrassed now by my reactions to the group. It was, of course, not about them but about me... I can now forgive myself for this incident, understand it and accept that everyone gets it wrong sometimes. (Ann)

Ann later commented how discussions developed and reflection deepened as the group gained confidence. Such groups need to begin sensitively and be gingerly supportive.

Liz rewrote her piece as a series of thought bubbles, fictional thoughts of various people unexpressed in the initial writing. Elaine's concerned a frustrating consultation with a client, which left her anxious and responsible. Initially she wanted never to reread the writing, nor think about that client. The group suggested, however, she rewrite the event twice fictionally: from the client's point of view, and as an occasion when both client and nurse felt in positive agreement.

> I was amazed at the reduction of anger when I wrote the win:win situation. I was also struck by the lack of centrality of my position in the clinic compared to the wide complex circumstances of the client's life... Writing a win:win situation enormously reduced the overall anxiety and power which caused both myself and the client to OVERACT and OVER-REACT. (Elaine)

Elaine and Liz stressed in their journals how writing, rewriting and discussion helped them become more objective. Both realised their inappropriately felt guilt: some responsibility belonged to the client. Writing and discussion: 'helped change my emotional response to the situations and be more mentally open to all options rather than solving it in a specific way' (Elaine's journal).

Focus on Reflection

The grown-ups stand around watching.
Grown-ups know what to do.
The grown-ups stand around watching.

Is that Simon lying on the pavement?
He has got blondie hair like Simon's.
The grown-ups stand around watching.

A boy has been run over, another kid says.
Is that Simon lying on the pavement? He *was* walking in front of me.
The grown-ups stand around watching.

Mrs Bailey puts a blanket over him – but I can still see his blondie hair.
She looks at me but before she can turn quickly to the other grown-ups,
I can see she's scared.
'Send Mark away.'
What have I done wrong?

The grown-ups know what to do.
They send me away.

I run ahead alone.
Trying to find Simon.
I might not recognise him.
Pulling kids by their shoulders – no that's not him.
I speed up when I hear the ambulance siren.

'Simon's been run over.' Pete Williams said.
I run away, trying hard not to believe him.

How can Pete Williams tell who is lying there,
anyhow I saw *him* looking for *his* brother too.

(Continued)

(Continued)

Surely I would have recognised my own brother.

My teacher says 'Simon will be in his classroom'.

But he isn't, so she smiles and cuddles me, warm and soft.

'It's alright Mark, they call ambulances for sprained ankles these days.'

When he came into the classroom everyone stopped and looked.

He didn't have to tell me.

I said 'Simon's dead,' and he nodded, unable to speak.

Mark Purvis

Mark (a GP trainer) needed to write about his little brother's death in a professional development situation to free himself from the way the unexplored memory inhibited his ability as a doctor to cope with child deaths. After he had read the poem to the group and we had discussed it, he wrote this:

I had never talked about what I was feeling when Simon died. Now I have written about it I can and do talk about it.

Simon and I had had an argument about a fortnight before he died. I'd asked Simon not to walk with me to school. You know what it's like, an older brother wants to be with his own friends and doesn't want to be seen taking care of his little brother. Until I did this writing I felt guilty about Simon's death – that it was my fault for not allowing him to walk with me.

In the past my feeling about Simon's death disabled me for dealing with the death of child patients. Everyone finds it difficult; but for me they used to bring all sorts of things to the surface. I remember one child who died, I was totally disabled and unable to cope with consultations with the parents. I cried with them, and told them about Simon and that I was crying for him.

The writing has made me feel completely different about Simon's death, has made me deal with it in a different way. I can now see I wasn't responsible; though my mother still feels very guilty that she didn't drive him to school that day. The time was right for me to write.

I didn't know I was carrying so much guilt. Now I know I don't need to carry it. I will cope differently now when a child patient dies. (Mark Purvis)

Mark Purvis created the character of 9-year-old Mark in his poem. This enabled revisiting that so painful scene, observing this bewildered little boy. The poem is so authentic: the voice of the child so consistently, movingly clear, drawing forth empathy in readers. Yet it is fiction, written by a senior and well respected doctor, not a 9-year-old child. Can you imagine Mark being able to *talk* about Simon with anything like this power? Writing enabled a private quiet space for this memory to be revisited.

Stories are a lens through which I view the world to make sense of my experiences and those of my colleagues and patients. In writing some of these stories I am able to focus on complex issues that have previously appeared distorted by time and emotions. Metaphors shed light on subjects that I had been unaware of before, patterns stand out in ways that I had not hitherto understood. (Mark Purvis)

Poetic form is an enabling device (see Chapter 14), being at a remove and clearly not 'true' even when it tells of life events (as poems usually do, one way or another). Poetry draws on a range of devices – such as repetition ('grown-ups'), and cutting away unnecessary words, as in the taut final stanza – which enable deeply painful events to be communicated. Marilyn Pietroni suggests the 'nature and aims of professional education' provide:

- a containing environment where individuals can recover or establish creative individual thought
- partnerships in learning between educators and learners
- a learning environment where messy details of day-to-day practice can be faced and scrutinised
- continuous workshop environments (Schön's practicum) where new ideas and approaches can be explored before and after their use (double-feedback loop)
- a place to examine the nature of organisational structures, defences and assumptions
- education for continuous change and development.

(1995, p. 48)

We have had privileged access, in this chapter, to significant foundations of reflective practice, through the experience of many practitioners. Next we turn to understanding some of the many theories, models and strategies, to help with building a strong form of reflective practice, appropriate to each of our needs and specific professional requirements.

 Read to Learn

Bager-Charleson, S. (2010) *Reflective Practice in Counselling and Psychotherapy.* London: Sage.
The first part of this book is a clear introduction, useful to all helping professions. Being Swedish, she brings a valuable non-English-speaking analysis of how our culture forms our assumptions and norms.

(Continued)

(Continued)

Brookfield, S.D. (2012) *Teaching for Critical Thinking: Tools and Techniques to Help Students Question their Assumptions.* San Francisco, CA: John Wiley.
This is an excellent clear introduction to critical thinking, and how to develop it. Chapter 1 particularly, 'What is Critical Thinking?', will set readers on the right path. Stephen Brookfield talks to his reader in straightforward language, yet packs huge amounts of information into small spaces.

Copley, S. (2011) *Reflective Practice for Policing Students.* London: Sage/Learning Matters.
A useful introduction, especially valuable within police training. Other students will also find Chapter 6 on values and beliefs useful.

Hibbert, P. (2012) Approaching reflexivity through reflection: issues for critical management education, *Journal of Management Education,* **37**(6), 803–27.
Paul Hibbert offers clear practical strategies for developing reflexivity.

 Write to Learn

For *How To* do this writing, please see *Write to Learn,* Chapter 1 (Chapter 8 for fuller advice). Do a *six-minute-write* about anything to limber up, before starting on the exercises below. Writings can be shared fruitfully afterwards with a group or confidential trusted other, if this seems appropriate once the writer has read and reflected on it first.

2.1 Who am I?

1. Complete these sentences: all or as many as you wish, and writing as much as you wish.

I am...   I believe...   I want...   I know...   I think...   I understand...
I wish...   I hope...   I wonder... I imagine... I'm surprised that...
I dream... If I were not a (my profession), I would be a...

2. Reread with care. Choose one to write more about.

2.2 Who thought what?

1. A newspaper is devoted to a specific work issue.
2. Create pages with the headlines, and columns written as if by OTHERS involved.
3. Write the Editorial by YOU.

2.3 Why and what and when, where and who and how?

1. Think of your work, a particular aspect, or in general.
2. Respond to these, in whatever way occurs to you (you cannot get this wrong):

What do I do?   Why do I do it?   How do I do it best?   For whom do I do it?
When?   Where?   What might I rather do?

3. Reread with care. Choose one to write about at greater length.

2.4 My work...

1. List 20 things you like about your work.
2. List 20 things you don't like about your work.
3. Now write a reflective piece: *Wouldn't it be nice if...*

 Visit **www.sagepub.co.uk/bolton** for additional useful resources including writing examples, exercises and videos.

CHAPTER 3

THEORIES AND CONTEXTS OF REFLECTIVE PRACTICE

Many theories, models and strategies have been devised to structure, describe, and ensure the effectiveness of reflective practice. This chapter examines many and gives support on understanding and working out how to use them to develop practice effectively, ethically and critically. Reflective practice is facilitated in a range of contexts also discussed here, such as e-learning, video, action learning/research and methods from the arts. It is also a strong element of other developmental processes such as supervision, mentoring and co-peer mentoring, all of which are described.

Socrates: It isn't that knowing the answers myself, I perplex other people. The truth is rather that I infect them also with the perplexity I feel myself. (Plato, 1958, p. 128)

No man can reveal to you aught but that which already lies half asleep in the dawning of your knowledge… If he is indeed wise he does not bid you enter the house of his wisdom, but rather leads you to the threshold of your own mind. (Gibran, [1926] 1994, p. 67)

Try to love the *questions themselves* like locked rooms and like books that are written in a very foreign tongue. Do not now seek the answers, which cannot be given to you. *Live* the questions now. (Rilke, [1934] 1993, p. 35)

Reflective practice has been theorised and analysed in many different ways. Reflection and reflexivity is grounded in and springs from individual practice, however, rather than from theories. Each individual practitioner has to develop strategies for their own reflection and reflexivity. Although its effects are ethical and can ultimately have political consequences affecting many, the activity of reflective practice is personal, undertaken initially in private, shared with few, and affecting individuals.

We are all different, and so we all respond best to different specific approaches. 'I used to be a "slave" to theory, that I had to "get it right"… now the crucial question is… whether and how it can enact critical possibilities…, and that multiple perspectives are taken into account in formulating a sound and complex approach' (Fook, 2012, p. 15).

Each of the many theories and models for reflective practice could have the focus of enabling practitioners to learn from their own experience, and develop practice, when based on the values and principles outlined in Chapter 2. This chapter outlines the major theories and models (Schön has already been discussed in Chapter 1). Readers can consider all these and take what is useful to them. 'There are no reflective activities guaranteed to lead to learning, and no learning activities guaranteed to lead to reflection (Boud and Walker, 1998, p. 193).

This chapter gives advice on how to relate to these theories. For example, some are based on a list of questions, which are excellent if used to remind beginning writers to include these areas in reflective narratives (critical incidents). If, however, the would-be-reflector does not develop their own questions appropriate to their own situation and issues, but instead responds with answers in turn to all the given questions, then they might lose authority over their own process. And authority over our own lives and work is key to reflective practice.

Reflective practice appears in many contexts, such as programmes using e-learning and e-portfolios, video, portfolios, action learning. Reflective practice is also the basis for (or an element of) other forms of professional development such as supervision, mentoring, co-peer mentoring. All these are described in this chapter.

Theories, Frameworks, Models of Reflection: Explanations

Many models, frameworks or theories describe reflective and reflexive processes. A danger is in thinking of them as 'recipes or instructions for making a thing' (Rowland, 2000, p. 51, Boud, 1999; for an example of 'recipe following', see Scaife, 2010, pp. 28–30). Learning is a dynamic process which varies every time and for every person; it is not a thing, like a cake.

Different theories give accurate reflections of reflective practice from different angles, and with different uses. Studying them is like standing in a hall of mirrors. I read about and learned from many and used what was useful to me, and which accorded with my ethical values and pedagogical principles. And you, my reader, can do the same.

Altering Critical Perception

Critically reflective practice for Stephen Brookfield involves examining descriptions of specific events or experiences. He defines '*critical reflection* as the deliberate attempt to uncover, and then investigate, the paradigmatic, prescriptive, and causal assumptions that inform how we practice' (2009, pp. 125–6). Paradigmatic assumptions are our 'worldviews'; prescriptive ones concern what best practice is and how we should behave; causal are about day-to-day what causes what.

Brookfield said critical reflection also specifically focuses on uncovering and challenging power dynamics that form practice. And searching out how we are hegemonically controlled: Brookfield gives the current western work ideology as an example of hegemony. He was hospitalised three times for something of which he was proud: extreme exhaustion due to overwork. Realising and altering this assumption was life-changing. Hegemony is colluding in our own oppression by acting in ways we assume to be in our best interests because they are part of the dominant culture, but are in fact harmful.

We need to go assumption hunting. When people think critically they question their fundamental assumptions. Nearly every action is based on assumptions. In critical thinking we attempt to work out what these are, because they are often counter to what we think we believe. So our actions often give indications opposite to how we intended them to be understood (Brookfield, 2012).

Assumptions from dominant ideologies are reinforced everywhere, and so are the hardest to look at in ourselves. His assumption that only women were prey to clinical depression, that a man could not stoop to take medication, horrified Stephen Brookfield, but uncovering it led to allowing himself to be helped. Gender, race, sexuality and politics all give us assumptions which unwittingly underlie our understanding of life. These are the hardest to question and among the most significant to counteract. A good way to recognise our own assumptions is to view as far as possible from other perspectives (Brookfield, 2012) (see Chapter 5).

This process creates emotional demands, because 'critical reflection is a reflexive habit… second nature' (2009, p. 127). There's no shutting the reflective journal and having done with reflection for the week.

Brookfield suggests we perceive through 4 'critical lenses':

1. The practitioner who is reflecting autobiographically
2. The students or client/patient/parishioner etc.
3. Colleagues
4. Theoretical, philosophical research and professional theory

Each lens gives a different perspective; together they challenge us to rethink our practice and assumptions.

1. Our autobiographies enable us to face emotions and perceive that issues are not private and personal but the same as others'.
2. Perceiving through students' (clients' etc.) eyes dispels assumptions that our actions and speech are interpreted in the ways we intend; service-users or patients often read us very differently from how we hope they do.
3. Gaining critical perspective from colleagues, or finding out how they perceive us, gives invaluable insight.
4. Critical research and professional literature enhance understanding and insight.

All this involves no less than 'calling the foundations and imperatives of the system itself into question, assessing their morality, and considering alternatives… Its focus is always on analysing commonly held ideas and practices for the extent to which they perpetuate economic inequity, deny compassion, foster a culture of silence, and prevent people from realising a sense of common connectedness' (Brookfield, 2009, p. 126).

David Purcell (2013) has found using Brookfield's lenses to write regularly extremely effective for developing his practice as a university sociology teacher. Like Brookfield he fruitfully shares some reflections with students. The use of the fourth lens has significantly also developed his practice as a sociologist as well as a teacher.

Single and Double Loops

Argyris and Schön (1974) divided practice development into *single loop* (reflection) and *double loop* (reflection and reflexivity) (see also Brockbank and McGill, 2004). Examining a challenging incident and seeking more effective strategies is *single loop* learning (for example, those that ask *What?*, *So What?*, *Now What?*, returning to *What?* again without asking critical questions at any stage) (Rolfe et al., 2001). Single loop learning develops awareness and more appropriate actions, while leaving underlying professional structures (theories-in-use) taken-for-granted and unquestioned.

Why? is a double loop question. Repeatedly asking *why* can face us with unquestioned assumptions, both our own and those of our organisation. We can then critically question these.

Practitioners finding the confidence and courage to enter double loop critical worlds of reflexivity question their own and their organisation's values, norms, policies, principles, theories-in-use, and work towards developing them. They dig below their questions and find new ones (Hawkins and Shohet, 2013). The metaphor of *double loop* is rather like walking along a Möbius strip (Figure 3.1): we travel inwards and outwards, gaining critical perspective of both planes. Walking a *single loop*, we will only explore one side.

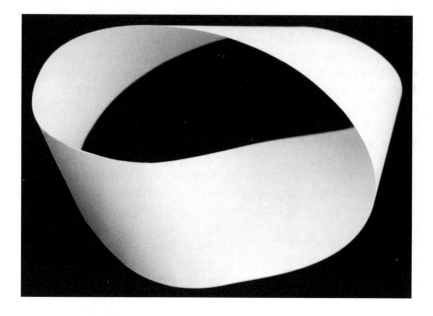

Figure 3.1   A Möbius strip

Reflective practice does not face us with *either-or* decisions such as 'do I walk the single or double loop?'. The distinction is useful, however, because it teaches us that there is something more we can do than just examine what happened and how it could have been better.

Critical reflective practice, and even more reflexivity, leads to un-simple changes. It is inconvenient, messy, takes time, provokes students and practitioners to complain 'I have more questions than when I started' (Hedberg, 2009, p. 30).

Cycles and Spirals

Kolb and Fry (1975) suggested learning from experience is cyclical (or spiral), going through: (1) concrete experience; (2) observation and experience; (3) forming abstract concepts; (4) testing in new situations. The last returns to practice (1). They suggested some people are practical doers, some thoughtful reflectors etc., leading to their learning styles theories (see below). Kolb (1984) thought the process begins by examining beliefs and theories, in keeping with Schön's examination of theories-in-use: a critical and practical process. The practitioner focuses upon their experience, observing like a hovering hawk (Schön's reflection-in-action). After the event, they undertake active questioning, seeking to understand how theories apply to their observed patterns of behaviour, and how the relationships function (or dysfunction): reflection-on-action. In the final stage they try out practically, experiment actively with, different strategies of practice which have been developed from the abstract concept forming stage via observation of their own practice.

The cycle itself is so simple, it's more of an outline description of how we learn from experience than a model. Whether it takes the practitioner on a single or a double loop journey depends entirely on whether they examine and test their theories-in-use (by asking *why* perhaps), and develop new and more appropriate ones as a result. If practitioners go round the cycle examining an incident and working out how they might act better in future, this is single loop learning. Further problems are that learning rarely occurs within such a simplistic cycle; different things will be happening at any one time and learning will need to be transferred from one context to another. Desmond (2012) and Creese (2008) found experiential learning a more fluid and co-constructed, relational and holistic process, than Kolb allowed for.

Gibbs (1988) inserted more stages with specific directions, such as about examining feelings. The model is prescriptive, and focuses closely upon a single event: what was thought and felt, what sense can be made, and what developmental action can be taken. Taken at this level it will also be single loop learning as it does not critically challenge assumptions (either individual or those of the organisation) or engage perception from a range of perspectives. Following the cycle can facilitate beginner-reflectors in the process. Listen to a first year mental health student's first reflective assignment, taking her a long way.

Description: I noticed Lisa seemed under stress. I watched my preceptor speak to her calmly and kindly. As Lisa stepped onto the rainy step I very gently placed my hand on her back as a sign that I was there for support. She said 'You hit me on my back. Why would you do that to me?' In private my preceptor explained that Lisa suffers from schizoaffective disorder and that I was not to worry.

Feelings: Defensiveness was quickly followed by anger. I have never hit anyone and how dare this woman accuse me, publicly. I also felt helpless, and lacking clinical experience. Unsure how to respond, I felt immature, naive and foolish. Finally, fear and sadness enveloped me: fearful my preceptor might believe these horrendous accusations. The thoughts of failing at the very beginning of something I want to do so desperately really upset me. I had an overwhelming sense of relief after speaking to my preceptor. I did, however, still feel inadequate that I'd never heard of schizoaffective disorder.

Evaluation: At first I could not see any good elements. However, I would have handled the situation differently if I had been familiar with Lisa's illness. After I spoke to my preceptor I knew I did nothing wrong but I couldn't control my emotions.

(Continued)

(Continued)

Analysis: This brief encounter also conjured up doubt about aspects of my communication skills. Putting my hand on her back may have crossed some boundaries.

Conclusion: I feel the approach I took was not very effective, although saying nothing was better than saying the wrong thing. Finding Lisa and I got on quite well later alleviated my reservations about my ability. I now know how I would approach the situation differently. My preceptor and the registered nurse show empathy towards every client. I found myself adopting this method, and saw vast improvements in clients' reactions towards me.

Action Plan: I will research and read as often as I can and become proficient in my understanding of each client's world. My reflection skills have developed substantially. I believe I am growing in confidence. I found I shouldn't be afraid to ask questions.

Eimear Allen

Learning Styles

These approaches are sometimes foundational to courses in a way not envisaged by Kolb (1984), who first theorised that people are feeling doers, feeling watchers, thinking doers, or thinking watchers. This has been developed to describe restricted ways people learn, with questionnaires purporting to tell people what 'type' of learner they are (e.g. Honey and Mumford, 1992), for example, 'Oh I can't do that, I'm not the reflective type'. The fixed learning style theory suggests people approach learning independent of context; yet learning is never context-free. The approach is based on a muddled assumption that the theory, or model, represents a reality above and beyond practice and life. Reynolds (1997) points out that use of such *learning styles* decontextualises diversity and encourages stereotypical thinking, perpetuating social inequality.

Structured Questions

Several models use structured sets of questions. Johns (2009) devised and developed a set of 'cues' for student practitioners to follow. Similar to Gibbs's model, the practitioner examines a single event, its consequences, and possible development. Aesthetic (description), personal (feelings), empirical (knowledge or theory) and ethical (values) issues are examined, other events are compared, alternative possibilities for action considered. This can give beginning reflectors an indication of valuable areas to pay attention to, if worked on according to the values and principles outlined in Chapter 2. A potential danger, however, is that reflectors will hand over responsibility to the question and answer form, if they merely respond to the given questions without developing their own narrative.

Hierarchical and Transformative Models

Dewey created a five-step model of reflective problem-solving: suggesting solutions, posing questions, hypothesising, reasoning and testing (1933a), and described essential reflective qualities: open-mindedness, wholeheartedness, responsibility (see Chapter 2). Van Manen developed this (1991, 1995). Jack Mezirow said that adult learners can transform their lives by critically questioning deeply held assumptions and beliefs (of others as well as the self), based on prior experience (2009). He suggested examination of these foundations can lead to perspective transformation when a significant change, disorienting dilemma, or epochal change disrupts life. Mezirow also developed a hierarchy of transformational learning (1981).

Such stages or levels are specific ways of perceiving experience, designed to aid insightful perspective into specific elements of experience. Such methods give an angle on the picture, but can never represent reality, and therefore will not work as recipes.

Theories, Frameworks, and Models of Reflection: Application

Many models point trainees towards essential critical questions to ask, suggest facilitative methods to use, and help them to understand the way experiential learning can happen. HOW such models are used is more significant than the individual elements of any one. Many involve the essential critical processes of uncomfortably challenging assumptions and theories-in-use, and working out not only what might be better, but what would be more in line with espoused theories, principles and values. Many require us to attempt to stand outside ourselves and our culture in order to critique it. Critical reflexivity demands that we focus on our own beliefs, feelings and emotions, and our taken-for-granted principles, values, assumptions, in short our theories-in-use. None of this is easy, and none of it can be done by responding to a set of questions about an incident without delving to this depth; all of it is risky in various ways. Non-examination of and unwillingness to query and develop theories-in-use leads to resistance to change in professional and organisational behaviour (Senge, 2006). Prescriptive guided methods, if not used critically, can constrain.

> The formal model is a substitute for practical mastery, much as a map serves the outsider who lacks the first-hand knowledge of the native. … Formal models can close off deep understanding rather than open it, thus providing a false sense of certainty and control rather than ambiguity and vulnerable involvement… The reductionism of formal models can… simplify and order, but… can [also] obscure and exclude important dimensions of the situation.
>
> (Gordon, 2001, pp. 228, 234)

People can only *take* power, give it to themselves; they cannot be 'empowered' or 'given a voice' by a more powerful other (tutor, for example). Tutors are not more 'enlightened' than the practitioner who is being guided; tutors are no more able to stand outside an oppressive regime than the professionals they hope to guide (Rolfe and Gardner, 2006). Usher adds the weight of his voice to this argument:

> We become active knowing subjects but now we subjectify ourselves rather than being subjected by others. We think we have mastered the power that imposes itself from 'outside' only to find that it is now 'inside'. We have the power, indeed the obligation, to exercise our 'freedom' but we are not thereby empowered to affect our social and political environment. (Usher et al., 1997, p. 87)

Practitioners can control themselves to work according to the wants and needs of the system. If their reflection leads them to improve their everyday practice by monitoring events when something has gone wrong and working out how to do it better another time, then they will become better workers, better employees. Reflective practice would thus be commodified, turned into an education product (Brookfield, 2009), which each employee has to have. Such management systems would never promote critical reflective practice, because they would not want their workforce to question the working of the organisation. Power is a slippery, omnipresent thing, and does not necessarily do what it *appears* to do. Professionals, tutors and curriculum designers have to be sensitive to undercurrents and meta-levels in education: the most dangerous forms of power are those which are not perceived as such, but as enabling or 'em-powering' (Usher et al., 1997, p. 190). Bleakley calls these 'governance of self by self through self-surveillance' (2000a, p. 406).

Critical reflective practice is risky, leading to unsettling development of one's own practices, and to a demand for change in the employing organisation. Many organisations actually want neither, although they do want more efficient and effective staff. An alternative to accepting Bleakley's 'governance of self' is to take all supervision, reflection and reflexivity out of the workplace and into professionals' own personal time (Scaife, 2010).

Critical reflective practice leading to significant change involves not only attempting to stand outside habitual day-to-day situations, but also engagement at levels beyond the cognitive, beyond thoughtful responses to questions. Some methods assume appropriate and useful material is cognitively accessible, to be selected by practitioners.

A danger is practitioners perceiving such didactic structures as ends in themselves. These models are constructs: neither things (such as bricks or cakes), nor reflections of reality. For example, a leadership student (Cunliffe, 2002, p. 55) felt he could not move up Maslow's hierarchy of needs in groupwork (1954), and blamed group and tutor. His tutor was able to encourage him to explore the nature of theories in general and his ready assumption that they represent reality.

Bulman and Schutz tell us that formalised structure can take the place of experienced knowledgeable facilitation of beginners (2013). However, using off-the-peg
strategies from a handout or book chapter is no substitute for skilful facilitation and
critical interaction with students by an experienced empathetic tutor.

Critical reflective practitioners take authority over their own learning. Clutching
the nursery leading-reins of structured methods can disable them from taking that
authority. Macfarlane and Gourlay (2009) liken structured reflection to television
reality shows. People are organised to expose themselves and their actions, show
their remorse and how they have developed as a result, with as little educational
impact as reality shows. Such methods, especially when associated with assessment,
can lead to reflection being reduced to 'little more than a mantra rather than a
model of practice' (Kuit et al., 2001, p. 129).

Most of the theories and models outlined above can lead to critical reflective
practice if supported by tutors who see themselves on the risky journey alongside
(rather than leading from above), staying with the vulnerable effort to perceive from
other perspectives, and the uncertainty and insecurity associated with questioning
theories-in-use. The problem has not been faulty models, but with the ways they
have been implemented by courses and organisations. Practitioners, who feel they
are cogs in a system which requires reflective competence yet blocks dynamic
change (or probably change of any kind), are disabled from critical reflective practice because their facilitators take authority, and because they fear to expose possible incompetence.

'To ask… what it means to educate, there are two essentially different starting
points… We can start by developing a theory of education and then let our
actions be informed by this theory. Or… we can start with life itself and let our
reflections… help us to better understand pedagogical life. Much educational
theory follows the first route. Here we have tried as much as possible to start with
life itself (Van Manen, 1991, pp. 213–4)'. Practitioners, as they gain experience
beyond the initial student stage, will find the most valuable critical reflection
comes from developing their own strategies and critical questions, working out
their own ways of writing their stories, critically examining and discussing them
with trusted confidential others, and challenging their own and their organisations' theories-in-use.

Contexts of Reflective Practice

Reflective practice takes place in a wide range of contexts, such as e-learning. Based
upon principles and values such as outlined in Chapter 2, these approaches can be
very effective. There are also many educational approaches with reflective elements,
such as co-teaching allied with reflective conversation (Crow and Smith, 2005). This
section suggests some, and is inevitably by no means exhaustive.

E-learning

Students taking fluid responsibility for their learning is replacing classroom, teacher-focused education. Web 2.0 tools such as e-portfolio and blogs can enable students to: 'answer each other's questions, take threads of each other's arguments... reflection in practice, reflection on action in action and it's going on all the time' (Hughes, 2012, p. 61). Electronic reflective work can use a range of digital tools, selected by the learner: writing, video, audio, images, are more readily available, communicable and collaborative than non-digital. These can enable immediacy of sharing developing ideas and feedback, in relationships that can be fruitfully informal with students as well as for human resource development (Nakamura and Yorks, 2011).

E-portfolios are learner-created products containing digitally created ranges of materials which can explore and express experiences and learning. Such 'Trojan mice' methods (Sharpe and Oliver, 2007, p. 49) require teachers to 'rethink... all of what they do', negotiate and make explicit the purpose of the course, 'prompt[ing] reflection, negotiation and adaption to what has, traditionally, been a private and tacit area of work' (ibid). In a process of which Barnett observed: 'out of the giving comes more giving, out of the daring comes more daring' (2007, p. 133). Hughes et al. (2010) found it an aid in inclusivity, specifically with dyslexic students. Hughes uses virtual learning Web 2.0 tools such as e-portfolios and blogs in teacher education for post-compulsory education.

Virtual groups, described by students as teaching and learning like a multi-reflective disco ball, receive overwhelmingly positive responses. E-portfolio allows for multiple asynchronous conversations. As e-mentor you are 'differently' available in the dialogue, deconstructing the once-a-semester tutor-student contact. The past five years have convinced me of e-portfolio technologies' potential for powerful transformational learning if the conditions are created for ownership, reciprocity, dialogic and narrative reflection.

E-portfolios emphasise dialogue and reflexive patchwork writing (Winter, 2003), offering unlimited peer and tutor 'talkback' (Lillis, 2001) instead of institutional summative 'spaces for telling'. E-portfolio dialogue's discoursal features are forward-looking and exploratory, concerned with the process-making nature of academic texts and literacies. My students have said:

'The eportfolio blog tool allowed us the safe space to share thoughts, feelings, anxieties, laughter and tears... The ongoing dialogue with my peers and tutor was fundamental in my development as a reflective writer and new teacher. It was a creative collaborative learning space, a lifeline on what could sometimes be a bumpy road' (Emma).

'...but shared I did, making a dreadfully painful experience into something which changed me and maybe others. My shared reflective journal was such a rewarding experience for me personally, I grew in confidence and as a practitioner' (Mark).

'Sharing my journals in an electronic format has facilitated my ease at sharing feelings with peers that I probably would not do face-to-face. The thoughts and comments from others also aid my evaluation and analysis of situations, importantly helping me to draw upon the incident and find the best way to move forward' (Jane).

Julie Hughes

Blogging is used by others to facilitate reflective communication (Mori et al., 2008; Chretien et al., 2008; Bruster and Peterson, 2013). Gardner et al. (2012) report an international web platform for dentistry reflection, students learning to communicate professionally with kindness and warmth and collaborate on assessment.

Ongoing dialogue with peers and tutors clearly has huge benefits, but without sensitive and skilful facilitation it can become surveillance (Ross, 2011): practitioners and students then don't choose to share the experiences which most need reflection. 'Calling a reflective learning journal a "blog" does not in some magical way make it any more or less significant than its paper-based cousin' (Hargreaves and Page 2013). Confidentiality can be an issue with social media: clients or others potentially being exposed. Each profession probably has guidelines relating to these issues (Howatson-Jones, 2013). Students could keep a private journal (handwritten or typed) to re-read carefully to decide which parts could safely be copied and pasted to the blog.

All e-communication requires careful facilitation and care from everyone involved, in my experience. Reflective practice makes people vulnerable. And the lack of physical and voice clues puts weight on each word; readers frequently understand text differently from how writers intended. Inducting all participants carefully with such advice as to check every communication draft before it is sent can prevent rushed messages leading to misunderstandings and damage.

Experience of, and potential for, other online work is tremendous; it has transformed distance learning. I have run online postgraduate continuing professional development courses for medical practitioners, each of whom compiled a portfolio of reflective writings, reflections upon the writings, responses from other participants and evidence of discussions with colleagues (such as team members), and research. Closed email communication enabled participants to write, comment, and make research suggestions. This mode of communication is particularly appropriate for busy, reasonably articulate professionals, especially those living in a remote region. A participant reflected: it 'enables you to *meet* colleagues you would probably never meet otherwise'.

Video

Video can be used to great effect (Copping, 2010; Lofthouse and Birmingham, 2010; West, 2012; Levin and Halter, 2013), and mobile devices can be used similarly to video (Thomas and Goldberg, 2007). See Miriam's experience below.

Jane, a nursery worker, brought tiny selected video excerpts of herself and 4-year-old Jimmy, whom she described as 'difficult, unresponsive', to a small group. Contrary to her memory, Jane noticed that Jimmy sometimes paid attention to her and did seem to enjoy their time together: video 'evidence' that reinforced a new and different narrative.

Sarah, the group guider (facilitator), received and amplified this back to her, pointing out Jane's agency. By repeatedly watching the video clips, Jane could see herself following Jimmy's lead, interpreting and following his cues, and responding sensitively to his verbally or non-verbally expressed needs. Jane began to see she had authority over improving her relationship with this child. Using the video clips as a retrospective mirror, Jane realised she already had the skills she needed to bring about positive change.

Sarah (a *Video Interaction Guidance* trainee) brought the video of her group facilitation to professional supervision with me. Following the same key concepts that she had used with Jane, I asked Sarah what she had seen, and how she had helped Jane to learn from the video clips. In her reflective journal Sarah wrote: 'I can see how effective it is to learn from my strengths, and not to be negatively self-critical. Can I carry this lesson through to the families I work with?'

When my supervision helps my trainees reflect successfully, I realise I am following their initiatives, responding sensitively to their needs, and asking myself how I can improve things further. Video enhanced reflective practice is therefore a nested construction, with reflection deepening at every level: my own, the trainee guider's, and the practitioner's.

One of my trainees said that even when the camera wasn't there, 'it was like... while I was doing things I could watch myself doing them and think how to do better'. That sounded to me like a reflective practitioner experiencing reflection-in-action (Schön, 1983).

Miriam Landor (see also 2015)

Action Learning or Research

In *action research*, practitioners study their own social situation (e.g. classroom) to improve the quality of action within it. Many go through four stages: plan, act, observe and reflect. Planning involves identifying the problem, formulating a hypothesis, identifying the theory in use and planning action. This is acted upon, observed, and data collected. All this is reflected upon: meanings, the relationship of espoused to practice theories and values, and how to develop practice. This process is reiterated, often with group support, attempting to bring theory and practice into greater congruence. Practitioners' writing critiques practice, principles and ethical values.

Action learning sets use Socratic non-analytic dialogue (Brockbank and McGill, 2004; Dehler and Edmonds 2006; Saran and Neisser 2004; see also Angela Mohtashemi, p. 193). Socratic dialogue helps develop clarity, insight and therefore understanding of appropriate courses of action. *Paradigm shift*, *double loop learning* or *peak experience* (*epiphany*: see Joyce, 1944) are key. Exposing experience to critical scrutiny in *action learning sets* can enable individuals to perceive and potentially alter previously taken-for-granted assumptions.

Kuit et al. (2001) report a successful *action learning set* reflective journal group for academic staff. A fictional 'Socratic dialogue', written by researchers Turnbull and Mullins (2007) was based upon *The Screwtape Letters*, a religious tract by C.S. Lewis (1961), in which Wormwood and Screwtape are apprentice and master in the art of wickedness. The authors adopted 'alternative persona' in reflexive writing dialogue to surface innate wisdom.

Personal Development Plans and Portfolios (PDP)

These 'offer a framework for reflection' (Hinett, 2002, p. 31). The UK Quality Assurance Agency defined PDPs as 'a structured and supported process undertaken by an individual to reflect upon their own learning, performance, and/or achievement and to plan for their personal, educational and career development' (2001, p. 1). Professional development plans and portfolios can be reflective and reflexive if students are facilitated towards critical attitudes and expected to write reflexively, drawing upon private writings for portfolios.

Methods from the Arts and Other Media

Innovative creative methods for reflection are reported, such as using drama (Boggs et al., 2007), conversation involving reflective interrogation (Ghaye, 2011), dance (Cancienne and Snowber, 2003), photography (Lemon, 2007), film (Brett-MacLean et al., 2010), letter writing (Yang and Bautista, 2008), metaphor (Scaife, 2010), storytelling, reflexive conversations and metaphors, repertory grids and concept mapping (Gray, 2007), creative approaches, the paper being written in the form of a play (Chambers et al., 2007), sculpting using course members (Scaife, 2010), stories, memory box, metaphor and drawing, and creative writing (Schwind et al., 2013). Cartoons offer a 'playfully ironic dimension for intensifying the process of critical reflexivity' (Cavallaro-Johnson 2004, p. 423). 'Creative self-expression allows tacit knowing to emerge. Students found creative activities enabled them to recall situations and glean deeper understanding and meaning from these events' (Schwind, personal communication, 2013). Cook-Sather (2008) describes student 'pedagogical consultants' (p. 473) offering feedback to tutors, 'both of which not only enrich the professors' capacity to reflect on their own practice, but also prompt students to reflect on theirs'.

Olwen Summerscales ran a course of reflective writing sessions with a multicultural group of inner-city social workers as action research (2006). The whole group were involved in the research in partnership, rather than subjects. This element strengthened the learning from reflective writing. The work could develop learning organisations (Senge, 2006).

Developmental Processes Involving Reflective Practice: Supervision

Supervision has been called a 'signature pedagogy', 'a primary instructional strategy' (Goodyear, 2007; Scaife, 2009, p. ix), and a form of experiential learning that supports reflective examination of practice, planning of development, and welfare of clients (Milne, 2009; Scaife, 2009). It is formative (educative), restorative (supportive), and normative (within the norms and standards of the profession and society – ethics, values, principles etc.) (Scaife, 2009). Unlike reflective practice, supervision is 'an intensive interpersonally focused one-to-one relationship in which one person is designed to facilitate the development of... the other' (Loganbill et al., 1982, p. 4), and develop greater work confidence (Hawkins and Shohet, 2013).

> Supervisees open up their work and their committed behaviours, performance, practice, writing, thinking and feelings, to scrutiny by another. Judgements will be made, usually by a person with greater experience and often in the context of a formal power relationship. The supervisor is handling supervisees' education and development, but also their vulnerability, needs and defensiveness. Supervisees will bring (explicitly or not) their varying degrees of distress... and joys... Supervision is... a process which encourages learning, development, growth and maturation.
>
> (Scaife, 2009, p. x)

Supervisees need to feel safe enough so they can begin to face, and use constructively, strong feelings engendered by work. Supervisees and supervisors need both/all to take responsibility for their work together and its outcomes (Scaife, 2009). Practice or clinical supervision will control and direct if it is conflated with managerial supervision. Scaife's book title, *Supervising the Reflective Practitioner* (2010), confirms the relationship of supervision and reflective practice. Reflective writing is used to prepare for and debrief from supervision (Scaife, 2009).

I use writing in my supervision: I require the supervisee to write down from memory a verbatim account of one session, but include their own feelings, ideas, and bodily sensations in the process (counter-transference). I receive it by email before the session, so I have a chance to mull it over. They agree producing this written account is hard work but very rewarding in itself. What I haven't yet done is to review these process recordings to track the progress of a particular patient. (Nathan Field)

Reflective practice is not always an integral element of all forms of clinical supervision.

Mentoring

The first mentor was the goddess Pallas Athene who took human form to help Telemachus, son of Odysseus: '"For you, I have some good advice, if only you will accept it"… "Oh stranger", heedful Telemachus replied, "indeed I will. You've counselled me with so much kindness now, like a father a son. I won't forget a word"' (Homer, 1996, pp. 86–7). Once Odysseus reached home, Athene took the form of a swallow with an excellent perspective on events from the rafters, and could advise from this wider viewpoint. Sometimes it's as if the swallow perches on the shoulder of another to perceive from their perspective; Scaife uses my image of the reflection-in-action observant hawk in the mind 'perched on the shoulder of another player in the scene' (2010, p. 145).

No mentor since then has been a god, although 'mentors are creations of our imagination, designed to fill a psychic space somewhere between lover and parent' (Daloz, 1999, p. 18). Mentoring usually involves an experienced professional supporting a less experienced colleague, ranging from formally organised (similar to supervision), to the offer of a supportive hand. Coaching is similar to mentoring (David et al., 2013; Garvey et al., 2014).

Critical reflective writing within mentoring can inform meetings, reflect upon them afterwards, or as email, letter or other e-communicative dialogue between meetings. 'Learning journals can be valuable between coach and client, developing and deepening the relationship, acting 'as a "window" into the client's feelings and experiences' (Gray, 2007, p. 509). Mentor or coach can, for example, agree personal objectives with the mentee, who then develops them in a learning journal discussed at sessions (Gray, 2007). Mentoring or coaching using writing could be similar to group processes described in other chapters, with one participant and one facilitator.

Mentors help mentees step 'outside the box of his or her job and personal circumstances, so they can look in at it together. It is like standing in front of the mirror with someone else, who can help you see things about you that have become too familiar for you to notice' (Clutterbuck and Megginson, 1999, p. 17). Mentors ask questions one does not, or cannot, ask oneself.

Mentors can act as role model, enabler, teacher, encourager, counsellor, befriender, facilitator, coach, confidante and supporter in 'unlearning' negative habits or attitudes (such as sense of lack of self-worth, or negative attitudes to diversity). These roles inevitably overlap, but research into helping-to-learn relationships shows that clarity of role expectations makes for greater effectiveness (Clutterbuck, 1998). The pair need to be aware of whose interests are pursued: mentors or supervisors, who are also professional superiors, can be experienced by mentees as controlling, thus destroying their own authority. They need also to realise when a matter is beyond their relationship, and help required from elsewhere. Reverse mentoring is gaining in popularity: junior employees act as mentor, senior employee as protégé (Garvey et al., 2014).

Mentoring deals with the whole person of the mentee: the professional base making this different from counselling. Mentors offer empathy and non-judgemental critique, helping reflection upon emotional, intellectual and behavioural content of issues. Mentors challenge: behaviour not people, assumptions not intellect, perceptions not judgement, values not value (Clutterbuck and Megginson, 1999). Garvey et al. recommend not setting goals: 'mentors and their clients can engage in the busyness of goal-setting at the expense of digging a bit deeper into difficult issues' (2014, p. 181).

Mentoring enables sharing of vital, often confidential, issues: uncertainties, hopes and fears, anxieties and angsts, shame or guilt, wants and aversions, the influence of intense emotions (positive or negative), tentative suggestions for action, lack of or partial understandings, questions of role, personal or career ladder issues, repeated errors or inadequacies, and stories of success, failure or conflict. 'Mentoring for me is about personal investment, and I wouldn't/couldn't do it if I didn't give a bit of myself to all of them: equally I expect to see them investing in their students and each other' (Julie Hughes, post-compulsory education). Everyone needs support, reassurance and challenge, even (or perhaps particularly) those at the very top:

> It's no disgrace for a man, even a wise man,
>
> to learn many things and not be too rigid.
>
> You've seen trees by a raging winter torrent,
>
> how many sway with the flood and salvage every twig,
>
> but not the stubborn – they're ripped out roots and all.
>
> Bend or break…
>
> it's best to learn from those with good advice. (Sophocles, 1982, pp. 95–6)

Co-peer Mentoring

Reflection and reflexivity can be supported by co-mentoring pairs of peers with no problem of payment, control or god(dess) worship. Two professionals might agree to co-mentor, or pairs from a group might work together independently between group meetings. They read and comment on each other's journals and discuss matters which might or might not be brought to the whole group, tentatively sharing issues with one trusted other. It enables the sharing of issues inappropriate to the group, but suitable for the privacy of paired work. Confidential pairs can cover more ground than a group, so each participant receives intensive feedback, journal and portfolio. My Master's student pairs supported each other through course and portfolio challenges, each pair creating their own working contract. The student group also met without tutors: group co-peer mentoring. Co-peer mentoring effectively enables professional students to learn from, and with, each other. Prior paired work can enhance confidence in group discussion (Carson and Fisher, 2006). Finnish teacher trainees are fruitfully paired with 'narrative friends' for portfolio development (Groom and Maunonen-Eskelinen, 2006). Sorting out boundaries and how to work together, although taking time, is also a significant learning process.

> My art therapy students use artwork and writing for reflective practice in their own time, sharing experiences fortnightly with peers. Initially many found the sharing burdensome, feeling they had to be careful about doubts, confusions etc. because of assessment and the difficult transition to the university from the safe private space of placement. Also many clinical institutions are beginning to claim students' material, even private process notes, as their property. Once they became more confident the peer-mentoring reflective practice was private and confidential, they used the process fully. (David McLaggan)

Elaine Trevitt and Carol Wood (both health practitioners) co-mentored, although from different professions, stages of career, and living 60 miles apart.

Elaine Trevitt:

We meet roughly three monthly, having swapped some writing, so we have something to 'work on'. We have lunch, then discuss writing and work, and then debrief and 'think forwards'. Once we met for nearly 24 hours and worked pretty well non-stop (apart from sleeping). We use emails and telephone, keeping our contact 'businesslike' and within our boundaries. We stress we are neither *friend nor teacher* to each other. This has involved a building of trust that we shall each be given and give time and attention when and where it is needed. At the original peer-mentoring workshop Gillie asked us to think of 'binary pairings' (Chapter 6, 109) and to consider how peer-partnerships might work. Mine was 'chip and pin': when the connections are made, the wealth (writing) spews from the hole in the wall. We are like chip and pin for each other. What has it done for me? It has been encouraging

(Continued)

(Continued)

(courage making) and given me a sense of authenticity. And it has moved me on. As I write I realise more than I ever acknowledged before.

Carol Wood writes:

It has left me standing on more solid ground in relation to my practice. We have worked on being truly congruent and fully present (Rogers, 1969) within work contexts through exploring and developing a strong sense of self as practitioner. A helpful vehicle has been metaphor (Chapter 6). Working in an increasingly time-pressured environment, I have valued immensely being given the space to 'stand back' and reflect confidentially in greater depth than I might otherwise, even when time constraints or sensitive material have made this difficult. For safe-practice, it is essential for me to do this. It sits outside any formal employment arrangement, allowing me to explore my 'stuff' without the potential filter of vested interests. This ensures I ask myself difficult questions I might otherwise shy away from. Finding out about our differences can bring new perspectives; there is also a lot of laughter within our sessions.

Elaine Trevitt and Carol Wood

Paying Attention

When the Spanish originally arrived in South America and were seen riding on horseback, indigenous people thought horse and man were godlike single beings, like centaurs. They sadly learned differently. Yet horse riders strive to be as close as possible to being at one with their animal. When achieved, this *throughness* means horse and rider have a circuit of energy between them, both soft, relaxed and supple, both in tune with each other.

We can think of ourselves as having a horse-self, a self we seek to make contact with, to be in tune with in reflection and reflexivity. Plato takes this further, likening us to a charioteer driving two horses, one white and biddable, one dark and wild (Plato, 1993, pp.67–8). The charioteer has to achieve *throughness* with both.

Reflective practice is a form of intense listening. We pay deep attention to the horse(s), and we pay deep attention to what the horses are paying attention to, because it'll be different from what we notice and find significant. We listen for nuances which will help us understand and make this communicative contact of *throughness*.

This chapter described the main theories and models of reflective practice, advising on how to use them to best advantage. It touched upon the diversity of methods used for reflective practice across many disciplines. Significant factors are: the principles of the course being consonant throughout, and the quality of the learning environment. Now we begin to move from what reflective practice is and should or could be, to how to undertake it. We start with the fundamental way humans grasp and make sense of their experience: narrative.

 Read to Learn

Brookfield, S.D. (2005) *The Power of Critical Theory for Adult Learning and Teaching.* Maidenhead: Open University Press.
Explanations and discussions of critical theory can be almost impenetrable. Brookfield makes it comprehensible and brings it to life with enlightening examples.

Garvey, B., Stokes, P. and Megginson, D. (2014) *Coaching and Mentoring: Theory and Practice.* 2nd Edition. London: Sage.
This book goes beyond popular prescriptions and seeks to explain and understand coaching and mentoring as forms of reflective practice. Case studies and questions provoke thinking about the place of coaching and mentoring in continuing professional development and creating sacred space.

Hughes, J. (2010) 'But it's not just developing like a learner, it's developing as a person.' Reflections on e-portfolio-based learning, in Sharpe, R., Beetham, H. and de Freitas, S. (eds) *Rethinking Learning for a Digital Age.* New York: Routledge.
This chapter is an excellent introduction to e-portfolio-based learning. The rest of the book is also valuable.

Johnson, R.S., Mims-Cox, J. and Doyle-Nichols, A.R. (2010) *Developing Portfolios in Education: A Guide to Reflection, Enquiry and Assessment.* Thousand Oaks, CA: Sage.
A very useful introduction to using portfolios, especially in association with Action Research.

Roffey-Barentsen, J. and Malthouse, R. (2013) *Reflective Practice in Education and Training.* London: Sage.
Focused on education, this book offers a useful chapter detailing 'How to undertake action research', and 'peer learning'.

Zwozdiak-Myers, P. (2012) *The Teacher's Reflective Practice Handbook: Becoming an Extended Professional through Capturing Evidence-informed Practice.* Abingdon: Routledge.
The section on action research (Chapter 2) is useful, as is that on mentoring (Chapter 5).

Write to Learn

For *How To* do this writing, please see *Write to Learn,* Chapter 1 (Chapter 8 for fuller advice). Do a *six-minute-write* about anything to limber up, before starting on the exercises below. Writings can be shared fruitfully afterwards with a group or confidential trusted other, if this seems appropriate once the writer has read and reflected on it first.

3.1. Brookfield's 'critical lenses'

1. Write an account of a work event from your own perspective.
2. Write about the same occasion from the viewpoint of the client (service-user, etc.).
3. Write again as if a colleague.
4. Now reflect upon the situation, bearing professional theory in mind.

3.2 Positive and negative

1. Write three sentences describing the sort of person you are (no-one else need see this).
2. What characteristics do you think you excluded? Be honest.
3. How many 'nots' are there (for example, I'm not good at numbers), compared to positives?
4. Rewrite these negatives as positives.

3.3 I value

1. Make a list of abstract (rather than concrete) elements (e.g. 'trust' or 'faithfulness').
2. Now decide which of these you value, put 'I value' before these, e.g. 'I value friendship'.
3. Write reflectively about each.

3.4 Wild solutions

1. Describe a work problem, occasion, or person which puzzles you.
2. List your hunches about it: go on, be wild.
3. Reread and choose one to write more about, thinking: *What if* ....

3.5 Pay attention to language

1. Write a list of proverbs or clichés (any, for example, 'a stitch in time saves nine', 'locking the stable door after the horse has bolted', 'moving the goalposts').
2. Take each in turn and write what you feel: is it useful, helpful or infuriating when said to you?
3. If possible list the person you associate each one with (e.g. my mother always said that!)
4. Can you invent a useful new proverb?

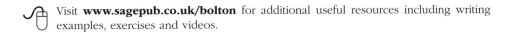 Visit **www.sagepub.co.uk/bolton** for additional useful resources including writing examples, exercises and videos.

CHAPTER 4

THE POWER OF NARRATIVE

Narrative is the form humans use to make sense of events and relationships. This chapter explains narrative, how we construct it, and describes its foundational value to reflective practice. How to develop narratives, and why, is shown, as well as how to develop them to enable the critical questions to be asked: these significantly develop practice.

Wherever we walk we put our feet on story. (Cicero)

A man is always a teller of tales, he lives surrounded by his stories and the stories of others. (Sartre, [1938] 1963, p. 61)

We do not 'store' experience as data, like a computer: we 'story' it. (Winter, 1988, p. 235)

Things come out because the story lets them out. (A reflective practice writer)

Narrative is an account which describes or explains an event, narrated afterwards, bringing together different elements, making a whole, and therefore sense, out of them. An incident is an event in life-as-lived, not a narrative: an incident is experienced, a narrative is telling about an incident. A story is a particular kind of narrative: generally with characters, in specific place(s), over a period of time, and with plot development of something causing something else. The classic story plot structure has beginning, middle and end, moving from a beginning situation, through action and change in the middle, towards another situation at the end. For our purposes in this book the words narrative and story can be taken to mean much the same thing.

Narratives, or stories, have themes which can inform reader or listener about the culture and society, about underlying values, principles, assumptions about role etc., about the theories-in-use of the characters, particularly the protagonist (main character). The theme is brought to life by the plot, the way the situation and characters move from their position at the beginning, through some significant experience, to a position at the end, different from where they started. The something which happens generally disrupts the protagonist's perceived security; the rest of the action is how they learn and develop through seeking understanding and regaining security by moving on in some way (Yorke, 2013). Stories often have more than one plot (main and sub-), and these generally fizz with ethical dilemmas, one of the reasons we are fascinated by them.

In a reflective practice story (narrated incident reflected upon critically), the movement from middle to end develops the protagonist. Take Eimear's story in Chapter 1: at the end she begins to grasp what it is to be a boundaried empathetic professional; the significant middle event is the encounter with the disabled patient; the ethical dilemmas are clear. As readers we are involved in Eimear's and her patient's experience: reader learning vicariously alongside the writer. Had she merely recounted an unplotted (non-developmental) list of events: I did this, I did that, and then I did…, then the account would develop no meaning, contain no ethical dilemmas, and so she (and we) would be unable to learn from it. Storytelling is 'a form of everyday theorising that enables the teller to bring experience into language' (Van Manen, 1991, p. 204).

Reflective practice is based on narratives of experience, often stories about specific incidents. These incidents could be from any part of practitioners' experience; the story might narrate one or a series of linked incidents. What makes these incidents critical is what we do with them. We focus a critical lens on them, we ask critical questions. The narration of the incident itself is the beginning of the process; the critical enquiry is where reflection and reflexivity takes place: 'the critical analysis makes the incident "critical"' (Dymoke, 2013, p. 37).

In life-as-lived we are generally unaware of our daily theories-in-use, or the values-in-use which underpin them, we work on implicitly known, tacit knowledge (see Chapter 2). Our personal values and theories are always embedded in any story we narrate about any incident in our experience. Reflexivity is focusing a critical lens upon the story to discover our values- and theories-in-use, what we want to do about them, and what feels possible to do about them. The role of trusted, confidential supportive others is significant, whether peers or mentors/supervisors: others look through different lenses and helpfully perceive different elements.

Reflective Practice Narratives

Reflection is rather like film direction. We become film-makers and authors of our own lives, standing back for a critical view, 'a discussion with myself' (Wright, 2005,

p. 514). Paula (2003) described critical reflexive writing 'as being like self-supervision, like watching the self on video' (p. 28).

Our film starts with a wide-angle lens: a hawk's eye city view. From this height cars and buildings look like toys, and streets and fields make a pattern: pretty but with little human meaning. People are too small to be seen.

The camera zooms: into focus comes one particular street; people walking and talking. Closer and closer, up to one building; we pass through one window into a big secondary school staffroom. The atmosphere is stiff and almost silent; only one, head of maths, is humming to himself; the rest look anxious and jumpy. The head-teacher enters and the quiet deepens; she invites the hummer to her room. He follows her; the tension shifts but does not lessen. This tension has been building for months: since the biology teacher began to suspect the head of maths of sexual relations with a pupil.

The camera pans out, circles at hawk level again, zooms. This time it focuses on a terraced house, its front door straight onto the street. A distraught mother thrusts her dead baby into the health visitor's arms. The tiny body is cold: so cold. The little girl wants to play with 'dolly', thinking the nurse might be kind and let her; Mummy would not. The health visitor is in anguish, knowing the baby has had an autopsy: a horrifying sight unclothed.

The camera takes us now to a high-rise block of flats with walkways, lifts which work sporadically and jerkily, and flat numbers assigned by a dyslexic infant. A grey-haired social worker confusedly studies number after number as the wind whistles, blowing crisp packets to reveal hypodermic needles. Her heart misses a beat at heavy footsteps and a dark-looking shape.

What do our characters do with the distress, guilt, anxiety, horror, anger, humiliation, which they cannot, or do not, express at work? How do they prevent these powerful feelings from draining energy, disabling effective practice? How do they learn from their own feelings, turn those negative energies into positive? How do they learn from each other's mistakes and successes, each other's ideas, experience and wisdom? How do they learn to empathise with another through experiences which they will never know?

Our films zoomed in from the distant and impersonal to the close and intensely human. Reflective practice can focus on the 'rag and bone shop of the heart' (Yeats, 1962, p. 201). We move from the grand ideals of practice, to precise stories of individuals who cry and laugh, shout and tremble, and are involved with clients at the thresholds of life and death, at periods of intense change and development. Our professional heroes come to terms with powerful emotions, learn from mistakes and successes, and develop their role and values as well as empathy with colleagues and clients. And they question and seek to change seemingly unchangeable situations.

All these stories were written about, reflected upon and discussed by practitioners. The departmental head's affair with a pupil greatly distressed the Master's in Education student. He was deeply entwined in the drama, but could discuss it with no-one. A confidential reflective group was an ideal forum. The story was written in the genre of romantic love (see Chapter 5), providing confidentiality and distance to enable reflection. Discussions and group support were so valued, the group continued as a special study module the following semester.

The health visitor did keep the toddler from the dead baby; but was distressed she had not been sufficiently sensitive. The group helped her see it through the eyes of the child. The black man courteously asked if he could help the social worker find her way. The group supported her out of shame at her assumptions, and to develop fresh strategies; 'rich narrative practices promote tolerance towards difference' (Horsdal, 2012, p6).

We ask searching questions, opening up fascinating avenues. Few definite answers arise, however much we seek a clear answer to 'What should I have done?'. Instead more questions arise, such as: 'Why did the maths teacher not hide his relationship with the pupil?' The walkway story was capped by a colleague's, who turned to face a threatening young gang and asked them to tell her the way (although she knew it): they immediately became normal kids who communicated with her as a person. This supported the social worker to reassess her attitudes.

In the 1966 film *Blow-up*, a character notices figures in park undergrowth, in a photograph. These indistinct, previously unnoticed details, blown-up in size by photographic chemical methods, prove to be a body and a gunman. In reflective practice no detail is too trivial or insignificant to write, think and talk about. Life-changing details go unnoticed, unless they are *blown-up* and focused upon.

Film-makers use devices to help viewers perceive from other perspectives, such as holding the camera at child height (see also Mark Purvis in Chapter 2, pp. 39–41). Practitioners experiment with seeing through the eyes of another, student/client perhaps. The funny thing is that one *can* re-experience (or re-create) an event. Listen to Jean Cocteau holding his own camera at child height:

> I thought of going along the street from the Rue Blanche to number 45, closing my eyes and letting my right hand trail along the houses and the lamp-posts as I always used to do when I came back from school. The experience did not yield very much and I realised that at that time I was small and that now my hand was placed higher and no longer encountered the same shapes. I began the manoeuvre again.

> Thanks to a mere difference of level, and through a phenomenon similar to that whereby a needle rubs against the grooves of a gramophone record, I obtained the music of memory and I discovered everything again: my cape, my leather satchel, the name of the friend who accompanied me, and the name of our teacher, some precise phrases I had said, the marbled cover of my note-book, the timbre of my grand-father's voice, the smell of his beard and the material of the dresses worn by my sister and mother, who were At Home on Tuesdays. (Cocteau, [1930] 1968, p. 137)

The film camera zooms upon a drained doctor at the end of a long week. She takes something out of her lowest desk drawer which will enable her to cope, to continue to see her profession as growing and worthwhile. It is not a bottle, hypodermic syringe, or pills, but a pad of yellow paper and a pen. She starts to write…

Reflective practice and reflexivity can take its non-judgemental camera down to any aspect of practice, with patients, colleagues, administrative and other staff, the interface of home and work, and the impact of experiences in the past on present actions. No feeling, thought or action is too small or too big for this zoom or wide-angle lens.

Narratives of Practice

Practitioners focus upon detailed stories of practice: actions, thoughts, feelings, assumptions, prejudices and engagement with others' point of view. Seen as inter-locking plots, the problems, anguishes, and joys of practice become comprehensi-ble: to be taken seriously, creatively and developmentally. The use of the aesthetic imagination provides a screen as wide as life itself, drawing upon all faculties, much more than reflecting only upon 'what actually happened', following with rational questions such as 'how might I have done it better?'. Antonia Byatt (2004, p. 4) warns that we need to take the power of stories seriously.

Practice, and its attendant education and research, primarily concerns individual people. Each life is made up of stories of inextricably linked psychological, emo-tional, spiritual and physical elements, and impinged upon by cultural and social forces. Gaining access to all this via narrative can make sense of seemingly unman-ageable complexity.

What we want and need to explore is not just stored, but held in our minds as story (Winter, 1988). Humans do not make rational logical decisions based on infor-mation input, instead they compare stories from their own or collective experience. 'Our stories impose a structure, a compelling reality on what we experience' (Bruner, 2002, p. 89), and offer access to and articulate what we know, think, believe, feel and remember.

Who we are, what we stand for and why, are integrated with how we act: near impossible to perceive since we are right inside ourselves and our lives and can-not get outside ourselves to gain an objective view. So we tell and write stories to take some of these incidents outside of ourselves, to understand our actions, deep-seated beliefs, ethics, ethical values, emotions, sense of professional identity, and the way we relate to colleagues, our political, social and cultural world and it to us. 'Not only are we able to go beyond the present, remember what hap-pened, imagine what is going to happen, and tell a story about it, we are also able to identify with the experience of other people through their stories' (Horsdal, 2012, p. 4). 2008).

Stories are educative partly because they penetrate our understanding more deeply than our intellect, they engage all our faculties, including emotions.

> Many hold their failures inside, allowing them to smoulder and decay; others step into self-destructive habits; others tell [and write] stories. (Borkan et al., 1999, p. 11)

We are embedded and enmeshed within the stories and story structures we have created, and which have been created around us: some we are aware of, some very much not. Dr Mark Purvis was unaware how deeply his life and work were affected by his brother's death when he was nine, until he wrote a reflective story-poem about it (see Chapter 2, pp. 39–41).

Confidence and ability with narrative can be developed (Brett-MacLean et al., 2010). Laurel Richardson, a pioneer of writing as a method of enquiry, said 'Writing stories and personal narratives have increasingly become the structures through which I make sense of my world, locating my particular biographical experiences in larger historical and sociological contexts' (Richardson and Adams St Pierre, 2005, p. 966). And Attard (2008) systematically wrote narratives, and compared them to films, because he realised this was the best reflective tool to interpret his lived experience.

We can develop awareness of narrative structure (plot, characterisation, chronology, environment), sensitivity to perspective (from whose point of view is the story told?), and the function of metaphor, simile, metonymy, alliteration, assonance, and so on. Interpretive abilities can be developed: the narrator's role (omniscient? reliable?), the value of multiple perspectives (viewing the same situation from the point of view of doctor and patient, teacher and student), and inherent ethical and value structures depicted.

Autobiographical Reflective Stories

The term autobiography was invented in the early nineteenth century (Heehs, 2013). Most reflective stories are based on direct experience, exploring and making sense of identity, memories, understandings and feelings. They have enabled critical reflection on racial and cultural differences in Australia (Hollinsworth, 2013), and writing narrative significantly helps people find themselves in career learning (Lengelle et al., 2013).

'Affording students and residents (medical registrars) an opportunity to describe and share their illness experiences may counteract the traditional distancing of physicians' minds from their bodies and lead to more empathic and self-aware practice... one means toward recognizing, acknowledging, and incorporating the physician's self-story into their clinical practice' (DasGupta and Charon 2004, pp. 351, 355; Charon, 2006). The skills and sensitivity necessary to story writing helps enable medical students and physicians (Manning, 2008) to enter patients' worlds, and empathise (Langer, 2012; Baruch, 2013). Memoirs from experienced practitioners can also be invaluable teaching material, as well as insightful reading (Helman, 2006). Read the following from a midwife professor:

I have successfully cared for women through long home labours. After a long period with no apparent problems, I had to leave the room because of nausea, occasionally actually vomiting. After my return, on each occasion the labouring woman then started to push.

My first reaction was the traditional female response of blaming myself. I concluded that I am getting old, tired and possibly past coping well with long labours. I arranged better back-up against my own exhaustion and need to leave women at a crucial time.

Then I heard Susie Orbach describe physical experiences of counter-transference in therapy. This, and subsequent discussion with her, led me to realise that my nausea occurred at the same point in each labour.

My next labour my stomach somehow picked up that the woman was approaching second stage well before I could see or hear any signs. Because I learned this through my stomach, rather than my intellect, I had to leave the room, later returning with fresh energy that was picked up by the tired woman and her tired supporters.

This experience led me to ponder a midwife's ways of gaining knowledge, which are discounted because they do not appear in textbooks and are not congruent with measurable medical knowledge. A colleague is aware of changes in the smell of women as they progress in labour.

The rhetoric of reflective practice takes place within the accepted sphere of authoritative knowledge. Therefore it does not seem to have had much impact upon what we accept as knowledge or our recognition of patterns in our own experience. As women caring for others, we tend not to see our own feelings as important enough to reflect upon.

Reflecting on bodily knowledge has made me aware of the wisdom of my own perceptions and of the ways in which I can learn that are not intellectual. It has also made me aware that I am trained in ways of knowing that prevent me from acknowledging my own wisdom. (Adapted from Kirkham, 1999, p. 15)

For me the whole 'business' of my writing and the vignettes I use [as a psychotherapist with Southeast Asian refugees] is an attempt to find out what I am thinking/experiencing – which I don't know except as I begin to reflect and to 'talk' in written form about what is moving around inside me. It doesn't take full shape and meaning until I begin the writing process, which creates the meanings out of what has been inside me, unbirthed in thought or language. ...

> Writing... enabled me to make a bit of sense out of what was inside me that I hadn't been able to do in any other way. Certainly not by talking. [Writing] helped me express my despairs and longings and hopes. For me the writing was discovering something that felt real and true about me at a time when I felt on the verge of losing myself. (Gerber, 1996)

A person's (or autobiographical character's) identity is not static or fixed, however. 'We all talk about "me". How do we know that there is such a person as "me"?' (Chuang Tsu, 1974, p. 136). In life-as-lived, identities change and develop; telling and writing stories celebrates this, and enables dynamic understanding. 'Who I am' does not and cannot remain stable:

> It is important to view the self as an emergent and changing 'project' not a stable and fixed entity. Over time our view of our self changes, and so, therefore, do the stories we tell about ourselves. In this sense, it is useful to view self-definition as an ongoing narrative project. (Goodson, 1998, p. 11)

Reflective practice and reflexivity help us perceive *the character who is myself* as dynamically evolving, just as the life-stories this character finds itself within are neither stable nor definite, but 'ongoing narrative projects'. This fluidity is contained within the expression human *being*. Words ending with -ing involve movement and change, as in *doing* and *playing*.

We narrate a range of stories about ourselves (as parent, doctor, teacher, patient perhaps, or from different points of view); each aspect of our situation constructs a slightly different story, a slightly different self, which also change over time. People could therefore be said to be made up of multiple changing selves, rather than a unitary *true self*. In constructing and re-constructing stories about lives and work, people could be said to narrate themselves in writing. This narration and re-narration can be critical reflexive processes: actions, perceptions, assumptions, values, taken-for-granted roles and point of view are all open to question and rewriting.

This reflexive focus upon the self as 'something to write about... is one of the most ancient Western traditions' (Foucault, 1997, p. 233), beginning with the philosopher Montaigne who explored his doubt, uncertainty and ignorance. Virginia Woolf said Montaigne's rule was to 'observe, observe perpetually' (1969, p.78).

Autoethnography is a form of research with similar aims and processes, a blend of ethnography and autobiography. 'Making the personal political' (Holman Jones, 2005), it involves critically examining and rewriting personal narratives, and challenging accepted surrounding stories (Denzin 2014; Etherington 2004).

Our Storied Nature

Humans store and share information as narrative (Lyotard, 1984). We do not go to a particular section within a file within a drawer within a cabinet in our memories, we go to a particular place in a narrative, an event, some characters and voices, place, scents, foods, and sense of touch. Perceiving, recording and discussing life as narrative is a natural human mode, more than understanding of abstract theorised social, cultural and psychological forms and structures.

Lives are made sense of and ordered by the stories with which they are told and retold daily through actions, memories, thoughts, dreams, habits, beliefs, speech and behaviour patterns. We story and re-story ourselves, contributing to wider social stories around us, as naturally as we eat and breathe. 'We are all, in our actions and practices, storytelling animals, and storytelling plays a major role in educating us in the classic virtues' (MacIntyre 1985, p. 8); 'narrative is international, transhistorical, transcultural: it is simply there like life itself' (Barthes, 1987, p. 79).

Since the Enlightenment we have suffered under mechanical metaphors that bodies and minds are machines. We are not. Our feeling, cognitive, physical, spiritual selves are intermixed; they condition and are conditioned by political and cultural contexts. All are experienced, understood and expressed as narrative. Narratives express the values of the narrator; they also develop and create values in the telling.

We are brought up surrounded by stories: they flow through us and ratify us from birth, telling us who we are and where we belong, what is right and what is wrong. Our culture is transmitted through, for example, folk tales, political history and literature. Lévi-Strauss, social anthropologist and philosopher (1978), tells us our myths classify and order our society.

Stories tell us how to perceive our place in society, and how we see it moulded around us, what to expect of each other and ourselves. 'Storytelling is therefore an important management skill' (Gray, 2007, p. 499). They shape and make sense of our world by reiterating the social and political order. Soap opera, Verdi opera, strip cartoons and Shakespeare tell us what is good and what bad, what likely to succeed and what fail. Tales where wicked wolves receive come-uppance explain that bosses can act unethically, but that good will conquer over evil (Bettelheim, 1976), if we take action based upon reflection rather than being passive.

Meanings are usually implicit, as in Aesop's *Fables*. New Testament parables are perhaps the closest to didactic storytelling, with explicit meanings. Had Jesus and Aesop omitted the story, the lessons would not have been remembered for millennia. We remember to sow corn on good fertile ground rather than among stones; that it is more comfortable to assume the unattainable bunch of grapes is probably sour; and that killing your father and marrying your mother is not a good idea (Sophocles' *Oedipus*).

This world and our lives within it are complex, seemingly governed by forces not only beyond our control, but beyond our understanding. Telling and retelling episodes both minor and major to colleagues, loved ones, therapists and priests, strangers on the train, a wedding guest (Coleridge, [1834] 1978), prevents us feeling like pawns.

If our lives were not constantly told and retold, storying each new experience, we would have no coherent notion of who we are, where we are going, what we believe, what we want, where we belong and how to be. Just as my skin holds my organs and body fluids in a form which is recognisably me, my psychosocial self-hood relies upon my grasp of my narratives of relationship, chronology and place.

These stories form a complex volatile system. Complex, because my apparently coherent life is constituted out of a range of interrelated plotlines, characters, and situations. Volatile, because it constantly changes with every individual action or event: mine and those around me.

Stories offer the fictive comfort of structure (beginning, middle and end), and give sufficient closure for us to grasp experiences and their implications. Yet reflecting upon stories never offers complete closure: our lives and practice are too dynamic for that. Humans are involved in an endless search for something lost: Eden, Lacan's Imaginary, Freud's pre-Oedipal stage, Sartre's 'Being-in-itself', a unity with the mother's body, a sought-after haven where the signified has a direct innate correlation with the signifier:

> Something must be lost or absent in any narrative for it to unfold: if everything stayed in one place there'd be no story to tell. This loss is distressing but exciting as well: desire is stimulated by what we cannot quite possess. (Eagleton, 1983, p. 185)

We relate to loss or lack in every story because we want good characters to gain their hearts' desires, the bad to founder. We experience joys and tragedies vicariously. Stories reinforce assumptions about what we might desire and what fear, affirming values and principles. We follow Odysseus past the Sirens holding our breath, and when a fair wind brings him back to Penelope, we will him to shoot his arrow straight to prove he really is her husband; we help Dorothy find her way back to Kansas, and are breathlessly involved in *Star Trek* battles in space.

People vary a great deal in awareness of their story structure. Some, like Hamlet, struggle with it daily: questioning and reformulating their understanding of their own agency and control. Some, such as Celia in George Eliot's *Middlemarch*, live in blissful unawareness. Strawson took this further and postulated a non-storying type (2004). But everyone else, at the very least, retells aspects of their day for re-creation: listening and re-storying collaboratively (*re-creation* is used advisedly here). They make further sense of their lives by relating to the cultural, social, political and spiritual narratives in which their lives are embedded: all those relating to work, as well as mediated news or drama, in newspapers, magazines and literature. Booker (2004) maintains that our stories 'emerge from some place in the human mind that functions autonomously, independent of any storyteller's conscious control' (p. 24).

Small children are clear about story structure, requiring any story to be told to the very end. This is partly because stories can also be a 'source of consolation' (Eagleton, 1983, p. 185), of comfort. Children's imaginative play is often continuous story, and first writings have a good grasp of structure. Ask a small child about their drawing or painting and they will tell its story, rather than describe the images. We too live our lives by telling stories about them.

And the story has to be communicated: told, or read to gain its power. A.A. Milne expressed this with perfect simplicity through his wise characters:

> 'Is that the end of the story?' asked Christopher Robin.
>
> 'That's the end of that one. There are others... Don't you remember?' ...
>
> 'I do remember,' he said, 'only Pooh doesn't very well, so that's why he likes having it told to him again. Because then it's a real story and not just a remembering.' (Milne, [1928] 1958, p. 31)

This is a mature acceptance of how we are, rather than a naive assumption that only children need stories (Gherardi and Turner, 2002). 'It is in restorying ourselves that it is possible to remake experience' (Clandinin and Connelly, 1990, p. 31). Connolly and Clandinin's three-dimensional space of narrative enquiry looks at a dense weave of multi-perspectival, multi-chronological, and multi-located set of stories (Connolly and Clandinin, 2000). Phillion and Connelly (2004) use this three-dimensional space of narrative enquiry to help educate people to work in complex situations of diversity.

Dr Lucy Henshall wrote whatever came into her mind. It concerned a boy presenting with listlessness and stomach pain. By attending carefully to what child and mother expressed, she gave him the confidence to confess his deepening anxiety about his mother's new boyfriend.

> His mother, quieter than I had ever seen her, reached over, took his hand and squeezed it.
>
> 'It's going to be fine' she whispered, 'We'll work it out together, Bill'.
>
> Bill didn't look quite as small as he went out, and his Mum didn't seem quite so tall and loud either. It was almost as if, while we had been talking, he had grown taller and she had grown smaller so became much closer than before. (Lucy Henshall)

Reflecting later, Lucy felt proud of having valued listening, rather than maintaining professional distance, being open to be trusted with the sensitive kernel of the problem. The story enabled her to re-experience and re-evaluate the event, and clarify her implicit values.

The Relationship Between Life-as-lived and Narrative

Stories might be what we live by. But life-as-lived lacks the confident story structure recognised from infancy, with a beginning, middle and end, clearly defined characters and sense of place. These stories are constructs. Life as it is lived is not structured like an adventure; adventures only happen in stories (Sartre, [1938] 1963).

Trying to *live* our lives as *adventure* or *story* could only lead to depression or mental instability: 'I wanted the moments of my life to follow one another in an orderly fashion like those of a life remembered. You might as well try to catch time by the tail… You have to choose: to live or to recount' (Sartre, [1938] 1963, pp. 63, 61). 'The past is beautiful because one never realises an emotion at the time. It expands later, and thus we don't have complete emotions about the present, only about the past' (Virginia Woolf, quoted in Holly, 1989, p. 26).

In life 'we always begin in the middle' (Lyotard, 1992, p. 116), and 'we are always in the middle' (fourth-century BC philosopher, Chuang Tsu). Here is the hero of *Nausea*, in the process of realising that those essential aspects of adventure – beginnings and endings – are only in stories, in the recounting of a life, rather than in life-as-lived:

> First of all beginnings would have had to be real beginnings. Real beginnings, appearing like a fanfare of trumpets, like the first notes of a jazz tune, abruptly cutting boredom short… Something begins in order to end: an adventure doesn't let itself be extended; it achieves significance only through its death…

> When you are living nothing happens. The settings change, people come in and go out, that's all. There are never any beginnings. Days are tacked onto days without rhyme or reason, it's an endless monotonous addition. (Sartre, [1938] 1963, pp. 59, 61)

When life events or incidents are recounted, they are re-created with the story form, giving them a spurious, satisfying, recountable, and memorable sense of shape. Once it is expressed in such form, we can learn from it. It is almost impossible to grasp the themes and events of the muddle of life as lived. 'Narrative seeks to redeem life and pain from chaos by creating sequence… In narrative form, one event seems to belong before and after others – not to happen randomly but to make sense exactly there' (Frank, 2004, p. 213). Hélène Cixous asserts that only masculine stories have beginnings and endings. 'A feminine textual body is recognised by the fact that it is always endless, without ending… at a certain point the volume comes to an end but the writing continues and for the reader this means being thrust into the void.' And 'a feminine text starts on all sides at once, starts twenty times, thirty times over' (1995, p. 175).

From Uncritical Storymaking to Critical Reflective Narratives

Critical reflective practice and reflexivity meet the paradoxical need both to tell and retell our stories in order for us to feel secure enough, and yet recognise responsibility for our own life stories, and bring critical enquiry to bear on the organisational, social and political structures and ideologies in which we are enmeshed, and our actions within those structures. We can then create strategies for actions over which we have authority. We also learn critically from the stories of others. Frank (1995, 2004) describes dynamic involvement with narrative or story as working *with* stories, rather than *about* them: 'what counts about any story is what those who hear it [and who tell or write it] choose to do with it' (2004, p. 209).

Constant repeating and refashioning of life stories in everyday communication can be uncritical, merely tucking ourselves under a security blanket patchworked out of safe and self-affirming accounts. The stories about our lives we tell each other every day frequently do not approach difficult or sensitive issues, but express what we feel (or would like to feel) comfortable with; or, even worse, are 'cover stories' (Sharkey, 2004), self-censoring tools. These reflections might ask: 'How could I have done it better?' or 'Do you think Mrs S thought it was OK?' The answers, whether in solitary reflection or conversation, are unlikely to be challenging. I've heard practitioners say 'Oh I reflect in the car on my way home', or 'we talk about it over a pint in The Bull'. Seeking strategies for development cannot be done when driving or over beer. The car would certainly crash, and drinking colleagues become bewildered or angry.

An extreme example was the sexually harassed secretary who complained to her friends, lost sleep and self-confidence, but continued to be unaware of how she tacitly invited sexual advances. A professor and departmental head with a severe alcohol problem created all sorts of explanations for the situation, none of which touched on the central problem, despite sincere efforts of his staff. Colleagues found ways to prevent the situations boiling over; the secretary and professor were themselves stuck, however, unable to change and develop their stories.

Such story structures, even while shifting and changing all the time, often seem inevitable, how things are, based on inviolable assumptions. But each one of us is responsible for the creation of many of them and aspects of others, for connivance at, and even uncritical acceptance of, wider social narratives or 'norms'.

Supporting and facilitating such critical enquiry 'requires a moral and political culture characterised by openness to diverse perspectives and ideologies, and a respectful acknowledgement of the importance of each person's contribution' (Brookfield, 1995, p. 140).

A constant barrier I face is learners not being able and or willing to peel back the layers and challenge themselves to accept or at least question that there may well be other ways to look at situations, behaviour and thoughts. Helping students is hard to achieve without them taking offence and experiencing it as some form of negative critique, particularly in their first years of trying to think critically and write reflectively. I wrote a reflective poem, in the voice of the student, to express my frustration:

Mmm I get what you are trying to say but that's not me
I'm doing fine; you don't need to think about me

I don't see the things that you see
It's my position and thanks but no thanks
Again I don't do that, it's not possibly me
All of the others don't get it so let me just be me.

I consistently challenge myself to burst the bubble of one-dimensional reality: sometimes quite a long process. Key factors for me in achieving this within small group tutorials include: creating an open supportive and questioning group culture; demonstrating fallibility and that 'mistakes', learning and personal/professional growth go hand in hand; and finally that methods and presentation of reflective thought are fluid, diverse and supportive of learner needs/styles.

I find that if this is created and accepted by learners I get rid of the 'monkey' on their shoulder blocking their ears, eyes and mouth!

Mark Jones

Critical reflection questions and challenges the assumptions held in the narratives and metaphors by which we structure our lives. Many of our life stories can be altered or struggled against: they are not inevitable or given. We are free to choose how we act and influence others. It does take courage; some students can fear the challenge of critical questioning.

We take full responsibility, and can experiment with alternative perceptions of our environment, ourselves and colleagues; fresh angles from which to grasp our roles as protagonists of our life plots. We might lose well-worn assumptions: the baddy might have previously unperceived good qualities, the good adviser might be lining his own nest, the impossible workplace might have a magically transformable space, the terrible blunder might have good consequences. And, of course, the opposite.

Questioning our everyday stories is an adventure. No-one adventures securely in their backyard. We face the uncertainty of what is round the corner, our destination, how we will travel, when we'll meet dragons or angels, and who our comrades are, and even why we are going. A student commented: 'What a relief it is to know that this uncertainty is essential; knowing that makes me feel less uncertain of being uncertain. Now uncertainty is my mantra' (see Chapter 2).

Our success rests on our ability to juggle this complexity, and our flexibility in response to the volatility and constant change created by our own behaviour, that of others, and of our social, political and professional surroundings. The acquisition of skills and experience in relating to, and handling, the narratives of professional life develops the comprehension of complexity. Harnessing the power of story-making in reflecting critically upon the joyous but utterly messy and uncertain complexity of professional life can help us to hear the story without missing the plot.

Chapter 5 focuses upon the perspectival nature of narrative, and how the ability to reflect from different perspectives is essential to critical reflective practice.

Read to Learn

Engel, J.D., Zarconi, J., Pethtel, L.L. and Missimi, S.A. (2008) *Narrative in Health Care: Healing Patients, Practitioners, Profession and Community*. Abingdon: Radcliffe.
Engel et al. give a clear, straightforward account of the value of professionals writing narratives of their experience.

Helman, C. (2006) *Surburban Shaman: Tales from Medicine's Front Line*. London: Hammersmith.
Helman's memoir is an excellent example of how writing stories about our professional experience elucidates both for writer and reader.

Horsdal, M. (2012) *Telling Lives, Exploring Dimensions of Narrative*. Abingdon: Routledge.
The first three (particularly the first) chapters give a good introduction to narrative.

Sartre, J.P. ([1938] 1963) *Nausea*. Harmondsworth: Penguin.
Sartre embedded his philosophy in his fiction. In *Nausea* he offers a clear grasp of his theory of narrative and story. Understanding existentialism, which Sartre explored and expounded, is valuable for reflective practice. I recommend at least Chapter 1 of this fascinating novel.

Write to Learn

For *How To* do this writing, please see *Write to Learn,* Chapter 1 (Chapter 8 for fuller advice). Do a *six-minute-write* about anything to limber up, before starting on the exercises below. Writings can be shared fruitfully afterwards with a group or confidential trusted other, if this seems appropriate once writers have read and reflected on them, and made any alterations they wish, first.

4.1 The film of your life

1. Write the title of the film of your life (or work).
2. Create advertising blurb.
3. List the cast.
4. Choose one 'character', write their name and fill a page about them.
5. Choose another 'character' (or more) to write about.
6. Which actor would you choose to play 'you'?
7. Where will be the shoot location (anywhere)?

8. Write a detailed story of one of the scenes.
9. Write the ending of the film (optional).

4.2 Who was I being?

1. Write the story of an incident including all details.
2. We respond to different situations in different ways:

a. leading   b. involved   c. active participant   d. just carried along
e. protesting angrily against   f. angry, but stuck

(Roffey-Barentsen and Malthouse, 2013, p. 104).

3. Work out which of these you were at different stages.

4.3 Stepping stones

1. Create a list of life/work stepping stones (significant moments).
2. Choose one from your list. Write a story...

4.4 Heroes and villains

1. Write an account of a time you experienced someone as 'heroic', or 'villainous'.
2. Now reread, being particularly alert to assumptions made. Reflect on these (see Brookfield, 2005).
3. Reflect again: do any of these people remind you of someone in your past?

 Visit **www.sagepub.co.uk/bolton** for additional useful resources including writing examples, exercises and videos.

CHAPTER 5

PERSPECTIVE

Everything in life and practice is viewed from a perspective, a viewpoint. Critical reflective practice is based upon attempting, as far as possible, to perceive from perspectives other than our own. This chapter explains perspective and how to handle some of its constituent elements, such as who the narrator is in reflective accounts (practitioner or client; myself now or me-in-the-past, for example), and the significant insight this can enable. Confidentiality of narratives is discussed, as well as how to write in different genres to enable perspectival insight.

I'm not sure I can tell the truth... I can only tell what I know. (Cree hunter, in Clifford, 1986, p. 8)

Imagining the other is... a major moral imperative. (Oz, 2005, p. 4)

Central to the reflective process is this attempt to see things from a variety of viewpoints (Brookfield, 1995, p. 7).

Perspective and Reflective Practice

In critical reflective practice we create and re-create narratives of our lives from different perspectives, taking us beyond our narrow point of view, to perceive fresh possibilities. A significant value of this book is the way it offers strategies for creating this hall of mirrors (Schön, 1987).

A different narrator, especially from another culture, might write a different account, based on different values and assumptions. Postulating what others might have thought and felt in a particular incident by writing fictionally, empathising with them and the situation, as well as imaginatively reconstructing, offers understandings and insights as no other process can.

Sam, a midwife, wrote about a 'stupid, hostile upper-middle-class cow who felt she had the right to boss me around'. The birth had been exhausting and unhappy for both mother and midwife: Sam still felt bitter 25 years later. The Master's reflective practice group offered insight and comparative cases, and suggested Sam wrote from the mother's perspective (the mother being 'I' in the new account).

The following week, Sam said: 'That mother wasn't a bossy cow; she was upset and confused. I made assumptions about her, and never listened properly. I'll see demanding mothers differently in future'. Sam didn't *know* the mother's feelings, thoughts, experiences, but learnt to understand imaginatively by writing a fictional account from her perspective.

Writing from other perspectives fictionally is also valuable for describing emotionally loaded events at a safer-feeling distance (Douglas and Carless, 2009). Significant details can be changed, or it can be written in the third person (practitioner-writer becoming 'he' or 'she'), rather than a straight personally-charged autobiographical account. Further writings can then explore other points of view, etc. (see Chapter 5).

Here is a family doctor's awareness of patients viewing themselves centre stage, and the way she handles that; significantly the patient does not become 'I' (first person singular), but 'you' (second person singular):

Performance

This is your stage.

Sit down, compose your face.

Lines rehearsed in the waiting room.

Family can't hear you –

'Leave mum she has a headache.'

Headache.

Muscle ache.

Spirit ache.

Tired all the time.

Tired of the time.

Too much time.

Let me perform for you.

Let me touch you,

measure your blood pressure,

measure your worth.

You are worth my time.

When you get home, they'll ask what I said.

Rehearse the lines. (Jo Cannon)

Alice, in Lewis Carroll's *Through the Looking Glass* ([1865] 1954 pp. 132–6), learned significantly from familiar things and situations becoming so different the other side of the mirror, ensuring she could take nothing for granted. She wanted to reach a hill, but bumped into the house every time. She had to learn to walk *away* from anything she wanted to reach, trusting looking-glass methods to get her there.

Reflection and reflexivity critique anything taken-for-granted. To gain perspective we need to gain distance, walk away from things. Why? how? what? who? where? when?, and then why? again all need to be asked of everything, constantly. Alice, a reflective, reflexive stubborn character, did not take 'no', or 'I don't know' for an answer. She asked significant questions because nothing worked as she expected; professionals have to push themselves into this state of critical enquiry.

Stories attempt to order a chaotic world. But for our experiences to develop us – socially, psychologically and spiritually – our everyday world must be made to appear strange and different, and at the same time the extraordinary seem ordinary. 'Stories render the unexpected less surprising, less uncanny: they domesticate unexpectedness, give it an… ordinariness' (Bruner, 2002, pp. 31, 90). We, and our students, must be encouraged to examine our story making processes critically: to create and recreate fresh accounts of our lives from different perspectives, different points of view, and to elicit and listen to the responses of peers. Attending to the stories of those peers also enables learning from their experience. It is exploration of experience, knowledge, values, identity that matters, rather than any attempt to arrive at a 'true' account.

Reflecting critically from another's (e.g. client) perspective, or of everyone at key points, is a skill to be learned, to gain insight and release of emotion. Medical students write from the point of view of patients, gaining insight (Engel et al., 2008). An allied approach is to collect accounts written by other people in an incident, as midwifery professor Mavis Kirkham (1997) has with a series of births (mother, midwife, doctor, and so on), to give a 360-degree-view.

Telling the same story through different characters' eyes is common in fiction. Jane Rogers's *Mr Wroe's Virgins* (1991), about an eighteenth-century religious fanatic, is multi-voiced, giving insight achievable in no other way. Frankenstein (Shelley, [1820] 1994) and Dracula (Stoker, [1897] 1994) are both also written with 'I' taken in turn by different characters.

A range of reflective stories and writings are possible around a core story. One doctor wrote from the perspective of the sofa on which his patients sat day in and day out: it had quite a story to tell. A butterfly's eye is a myriad of tiny eyes, each recording an image from a different angle. Bodies of reflective writings offer similar width of view.

The Narrator

Every fiction, biography, autobiography, case study, history is presented from the narrator's point of view. But who is the narrator? According to Janet Malcolm, 'This "I" is a character, just like the other characters. It's not the person who you are. There's a bit of you in it. But it's a creation. The distinction between the I of the writing and the I of your life is like Superman and Clark Kent' (2011, p. 12). Narratives told by narrators other than the autobiographical 'I' offer further distance on experience, as we have discussed above. A fictional narrator gives a different point of view from my own, therefore widening my perspective on the situation, character, or place.

The *narrator* has a critical role in stories; awareness of what narrator is being used, and when, gives power to the storyteller/writer. Each narrator projects a different (sometimes surprisingly divergent) perception of the self, society, and culture, and can help clarify the ethics of a situation (Bolton, 2009). This can give greater authority over our narrations and therefore greater responsibility for our life and work.

Fictional narrators can enable exploration of a wider range of perspectives than the seemingly given autobiographical 'I': a strategy for gaining contact with previously unperceived understanding. These alternative narrators (angry parent, child self, dying patient) all derive from writers' experience; they don't pretend to give the perspective of the individual-in-life. They enable significant observation and insight.

Dr Antonio Munno experimented with narrators to clarify his understanding of patients' perspectives, developing his professional perception and therefore his professional conduct.

> The family asked to meet me. Their daughter had recovered from meningococcal septicaemia, and they wanted to know why I hadn't diagnosed it… My stomach wrenched with anger and frustration. Can't they see?… There was nothing that morning to indicate meningitis or septicaemia… As the date for our meeting drew closer, that black churning bitterness was still there, and I realised I had to do something… I decided to write the story of the family's complaint from the point of view of the parents. The first line came easily: 'She nearly died you know. Our daughter nearly died.' At that point my perspective on the complaint changed. I felt the parents' fear, and I understood their terror… The complaint wasn't about diagnostic skills or statistical probabilities but about a family trying to make sense of the horror of nearly being ripped apart forever. By thinking about the complaint from the family's point of view, I understood that my role in the meeting wasn't to defend but to listen. (Munno, 2006, p.1092)

The parents (the model for Munno's narrator) gave him clarity; he didn't know what they *really* thought and felt, but writing this account gave him insight to act empathetically and professionally (without anger). This gave insight about the impact of actions, and of cultural or social forces. Mark Purvis's (Chapter 2, pp. 39–41) narrator was his own child self. Dr Cecil Helman reinforces this approach:

The art of medicine is a literary art. It requires of the practitioner the ability to listen in a particular way, to empathise and also to imagine: to try to feel what it must be like to be that other person lying in the sickbed, or sitting across the desk from you; to understand the storyteller, as well as the story. (Helman, 2006, p.1)

Omniscient, Reliable and Unreliable Narrators

Many fictions, such as Eliot's *Middlemarch,* are 'told' by omniscient narrators who speak from outside of the story and know everything: every character's motives, inspirations, thoughts and feelings, social and cultural forces, what happened before and what will happen after. The omniscient narrator takes readers into characters' hearts and minds, future outcomes, the impact of the past. Readers follow plots fizzing with ethical dilemmas, their interest held by the amount of inside knowledge divulged at key points.

Autobiographical life stories cannot have omniscient narrators; only fiction can have these godlike authorities. There can be no outside authority to take readers by the hand through the maze of writers' own ethical dilemmas.

Narrators are reliable or unreliable. Ann Kelley's unreliable heroine Gussie (2007) tells of living heroically with heart disease; it resembles Victorian moral tales of unfaltering bravery in the face of suffering, with no existential pain, terror, physical pain, distress.

In autobiographical writing, my narrator-self is likely to be more or less reliable or unreliable as in life, and certainly not omniscient. We cannot stand outside ourselves objectively and know omnisciently, or know others' thoughts. It is possible, however, to choose the way the story is told, for example as close to reliable as possible, or as close to unreliable.

Dr Mark Purvis, unaware how deeply his life and work was affected by his little brother's death, wrote a story-poem with a pretty reliable narrator: his child self (Chapter 2, p. 39). He learned that he could allow writing to choose his narrator for him. A child is often a wise or illuminative narrator (see Chapter 5):

> Every society needs a barefoot Socrates to ask childishly simple (and childishly difficult!) questions, to force its members to re-examine what they have been thoughtlessly taking for granted.
>
> (Matthews, 1980, p. 95)

A medical student wrote from the perspective of an angry child in a consultation, helping her see how she might talk to him in a way he could understand. A manager wrote what a dominating senior colleague might have been thinking (as 'thought bubbles') at key moments in a meeting: some were surprisingly unconfident, giving the manager future coping strategies. Writers can choose their narrators, and can therefore take greater authority and control.

Ghosts and Shadows from the Past

Oil paint on old pictures can thin with age, becoming so transparent that underlying figures show through. Perhaps the artist changed their mind, or was re-using an expensive canvas. This *pentimento* can cause confusion: we can see flying ghostly figures; the woman with six arms, like an Indian goddess.

This is like past situations over-influencing present actions. A woman professional, who was once a pretty girl, still simpered. She didn't realise her present mature self needed to be painted strongly over the coy child. Normally there is no way to recognise how *pentimento* behaviour is inappropriate later. We are unaware how our pasts affect us. This professional, confused at colleagues' negative responses, developed only unhelpful defensive strategies. Her colleagues couldn't confront her with the problem. Writing an account narrated as if by a particularly negative colleague, she came face to face with it. It was well worth changing a habit she'd had for so long, although not easy.

Reflective writing can help us stand back to perceive *pentimento* in the painting which is the self. It can lead writers into uncomfortable but valuably reflexive liminal spaces (part way between the present picture and the past one). Discovering strategies for painting appropriately and strongly over the out-of-date image is complex. We do not easily step out of our frame and view ourselves critically. Reflexively constructing the narrator can help perceive the *pentimento* and find out how to cover it over permanently. Then the painting might develop appropriate depth and intensity, a lovely patina of age.

Perspective and Truth; Fact and Fiction

Narrated from the perspective of its narrator, a narrative cannot tell the whole truth. The truth in a story, as in ethnography (Clifford, 1986) and other forms of writing, can only ever be partial. Told from the narrator's perspective, it contains the details noticed and remembered, interwoven and shot through reflexively with memories, dreams, reflections. We can experiment with a range of narrators, glorying in the shift and change of perspectives, and therefore understanding, which emerges (or flashes).

> The factual can never give us the kind of illumination, the ecstatic flash, from which truth emerges.
>
> (Werner Herzog, 2011, p. 18)

> It's under the mask of fiction that you can tell the truth.
>
> (Xingjian Gao, 2009, p. 11)

Fictional narrators can also be illuminative, such as when I retell the story of an experience from the point of view, say, of someone else who was there, my patient for example if I am a doctor. I cannot know how she perceives the situation, so such an account is fictional. Recreating the account in this way will inevitably enhance my understanding. This is a critical use of fiction under whose 'mask' I can begin to 'tell the truth' (Gao, 2009, p. 11), and can hope sometimes to perceive the 'flash from which truth emerges' (Herzog, 2011, p. 18) (see also Munno, p. 85).

To be objective is to be 'not influenced by personal feelings or opinions in considering or representing facts; impartial, detached' (*Oxford English Dictionary*). Humans, however open about themselves and their practice, however empathic and professional, cannot decide to be uninfluenced by personal feelings. 'We don't see things as they are, we see them as we are' (Nin, quoted in Epstein, 1999, p. 834).

There are strategies for attempting to look in through a mirror from outside of ourselves. Writing fiction removes the straitjacket of *what really happened*. Writers are therefore free to draw deeply upon their imagination and aesthetic sense, and upon their intuitive knowledge of social and human areas such as relationships, motives, perspective, cause and effect, ethical issues and values.

Realising that accounts of practice do not need to stick to life-as-lived can offer confidence. Fiction can omit slow episodes or effectively combine events which took place at different times and with different people. Writing fictionally from deep professional experience can be more dramatic, leap over the boring bits, tackle issues head on; convey multiple viewpoints; sidestep problems of confidentiality, fear of exposure, and some of the inevitable anxiety which accompanies the exploration of painful events.

Fiction can be a vehicle for conveying the ambiguities, complexities and ironic relationships that inevitably exist between multiple viewpoints. It can offer an intelligible research summary of the huge body of data that qualitative research tends to provide. The creation of a fiction, with the awareness that it is a creation, can enable the writer to head straight for the heart of the matter. 'Thinking up a plot and a range of characters in a certain context is analogous to formulating a theory of that context' (Winter, 1988, p. 241).

Use of the critical imagination is not inventing out of nothing. Memories of complex unresolved, unsorted-out experiences which have touched people deeply are drawn upon (Tóibín, 2009). These memories, by their very nature are a muddle of half-remembered inconsistencies with no clear beginning or middle, let alone ending. Creating fictional narratives experiments with storying experiences in different ways: less or more realistically, less or more close to the actual events. All illuminative.

Fictional characters and situations take on a life of their own. If writers try to discipline them to do what they want, the writing will be flat, lifeless and dull; Munno (p. 85) and Purvis (Chapter 2, p. 39), for example, both allowed their writing hand to dictate what they wrote (Chapter 8). Each character is an aspect of the author, and needs full expression via the creative process. This allows expression to the non-logical, non-rational parts of the writer's mind, allowing contact with previously unperceived internal elements and themes. Fiction gave Gully (2004) insight into his work with sexually abusive adults. Stories can be performed like plays (Alexander, 2005; Holman Jones, 2005). Experiment found that the value of writing about a fictional trauma is as effective therapeutically as writing about a memory (Pennebaker, 2000).

Case studies, also, cannot be true, detached or impartial depictions, although they concern real people and events (Clark, 2002). They can have only 'indirect or partial correspondence with reality... despite their apparent verisimilitude' (Pattison et al., 1999a, p. 43). They include biases of inclusion and exclusion, prejudices and values, and are generally written from the perspective of and by professionals, not service-users. Bleakley (2005) says 'case studies are autistic in their futile attempt to be true, detached and impartial' (p536). Even a video only records what comes within its field: no smell, taste, sense of touch, or sight and sound beyond its range. Everyone has selective perception:

Selective hearing syndrome: female

He: You are the most beautiful, fascinating, intelligent, witty, sexy, well balanced, creative woman I have ever met, even if you are a bit moody sometimes.

She: Me? Moody?

Selective hearing syndrome: male

She: You never take the children to the park, or read them a story; you never even cook an egg, and have never made the bed.

He: Bed? Now?

Reflective practitioners often need to examine a particular incident, exploring motives, feelings and thoughts, their actions and those of others, narrating it as accurately and as widely as possible from their own memory, and possibly also consulting others' perceptions. And at times fictional scenarios are appropriate: what might have happened, what others might have thought, and so on. And on occasion genre gives the best exploration (Chapter 5). None can be objectively *true*. Yet within some social work training there is an assumption that 'the aim of the narrative is to persuade the listener or reader that the story is true and that the author is to be believed' (Knott and Scragg, 2013, p. 28).

Critics have been dissatisfied with forms of research or reflection which make overt use of fiction. Just as tourists are unsatisfied with the copy of Michaelangelo's *David* in a Florentine piazza free of charge, with no queues: they need to see the very lump of marble from which Michaelangelo himself 'released' David. Stories, however, are not *objects* like *David*: they are constructions mediated through writers or narrators. There is no *real account* in literature, like the *real statue of David*: we need to lose an obsession with seeking objectivity, and enable authentic scientific experimentation and exploration. The distinction between fiction and fact is often not helpful.

Charon (2000) has reflected upon medical patients' charts as if novels: 'literary critics who write about the novel provide useful frameworks for doctors who reflect on their practice' (2000, p. 63). Helman's (2006) medical memoir, written like a novel, gives invaluable insight.

Hargreaves discusses how nursing students are forced by the system to present reflections within a professionally acceptable frame, or to fictionalise. At the same time they have to sign to say that their work is a true, faithful reflection of their actual practice. 'Exploring the value of fictional narratives may reveal a powerful medium for the development and understanding of professional practice' (Hargreaves, 2004, p. 199).

Clients' Confidentiality and Privacy

Fiction can explore and express practitioners' understanding and perception, bringing this to critical reflection. A collection of stories around an incident can get as close as possible to what the different people felt and experienced. Professional accuracy of perception is not jeopardised, nor are interpretations about patients (students, clients, members of the public) distorted (Garro and Mattingly, 2000) by the use of fiction.

We cannot intrude into another's thinking and feeling, and ethically would not want to. Fiction removes this practical and ethical barrier. Fictional characters have no privacy: they live and act and think and feel with no social cloaks between them and their readers.

> If privacy is life's most precious possession, it is fiction's least considered one. A fictional character… stands before the reader with his 'real, most interesting life' nakedly exposed. [In life] there is a veil between ourselves and even our closest intimates, blurring us to each other. We feel no discomfort in our voyeurism. We consider it our due as readers.
>
> (Malcolm, 2003, p. 4)

Reflective writing with a patient (client, student, colleague) as model for the narrator, might seem to cross a privacy boundary. Yet these people will never know. If Munno's patient's parents knew, and they'd probably have felt profoundly grateful as it enabled him to approach them ethically and empathetically and with his espoused values consonant with his values-in-practice (Bolton, 2009). It is not themselves as people who are 'exposed' thus 'nakedly', it is significantly the writer's own understanding and perception of them, and this is always done carefully and respectfully. Reflective writing work is undertaken privately, and discussed only with carefully chosen confidential peers or tutors.

Using Genre to Develop Perspective

The range of fictional forms (genres) which can enable perspectival exploration – fairy story, romantic fiction, detective, fantasy, fable, whodunit, social realism, sci-fi, comedy, Aga-saga, thriller – tend to have archetypal characters, place and type of plot, setting practitioners free from having to depict realistic characters, chronology, events and environments. 'Writing "works" because it enables us to come to know ourselves through the multiple voices our experience takes, to describe our contexts and histories as they shape the many minds and selves who define us and others' (Holly, 1989, p. 15). Writing in genre can help us perceive facets of the self and of experience, the 'webs of significance' (Geertz, [1973] 1993, p. 5) we spin around ourselves. Critical understanding follows from a grasp of genre and the way the content is moulded by the form. 'Realis[ing] the hospital chart is a genre with its own strict rules of composition, unlock[s] a powerful method of studying the text itself as well as the actions it tries to represent' (Charon, 2006, p. 155). Mercedes Kemp asked students to write in genre, to '*create* self' (2001, p. 353).

Different forms of writing can take writers by surprise, confronting them with issues forgotten, or previously assumed to be negligible. 'I try… to reintroduce people to the previously unconsidered. It's a passionate, almost religious belief of mine that it is in the negligible that the considerable is to be found' (Miller, 2009, p. 12).

People unwittingly live in genre, just as they think through metaphor. As soon as I suggest the use of genre to a group, several will set off instantly and unthinkingly towards *romance* or *detective* or *fairy story*: a particular genre will grab each (see the teacher's use of romantic story, Chapter 5 pp. 94–95). A nurse tried to write a *doctor–nurse romance*, swapping the roles to male nurse and woman doctor. She could not make it work: the genre relies on a power structure of habitual male dominance. We all laughed, but learned a great deal about medical-nursing relations, and the way they are seen by 'the public'.

All this writing is artistic, developing the artistry of practice (Schön). The culturally refined Nazis have forever disabused us of the idea that the aesthetic necessarily makes us act morally. Rather if we can allow ourselves to go beyond the stage curtain (see Chapter 1) in critical reflection and reflexivity and enter a state of *mindfulness* (see Chapter 2), *negative capability* (Keats, 1818), *willing suspension of disbelief* (Coleridge, [1798] 1969), then our moral and ethical faculties will necessarily be brought to the creative process. The Nazis called this *degenerate*, and denigrated, expatriated or murdered those who used it.

Fantasy, Folk Tale, Fable, Myth

Cultural, professional, political and familial forms all seem to be in flux. Organisations constantly upgrade, update, innovate, modernise, and no one expects to be long in a particular post. Fantasy deals with people not knowing in what dimension they live, what kind of being they will meet, what kind of communication is appropriate. The main characters remain reassuringly constant, as in *Star Trek*: strong and moral, or obstructive and wicked; events either turn out very right or very wrong. Enjoying fantasy is part of our relentless attempt to create moral order in a chaotic world. Confronting elements in our everyday world by exploring fantastic ones has been called 'structured fabulation' (Gough, 1998). Huxley's *Brave New World* ([1932] 1994), Orwell's *1984* ([1949] 1987), Shelley's *Frankenstein* ([1820] 1994), and Pullman's *His Dark Materials* (1995) are examples of fantasy which both create and critique our own world.

> Now that we have no eternal truth we realise that our life is entirely made up of stories... truth is made of stories. So we can rehabilitate myth... myths are the stories people live by, the stories that shape people's perception of life. (Don Cupitt, 1991)

Myths, folk tales and fables, as Don Cupitt tells us, help us to know how to live our lives. Folk tales and fables consist of oppositions and contradictions which are mediated and resolved as the story progresses (Bradley Smith, 2008). 'Mythical thought always progresses from the awareness of oppositions toward their resolution' (Lévi–Strauss, 1963, p. 224), making such stories effective, if surprising, vehicles for reflective practice. They traditionally involve character archetypes such as wicked witch, good godmother, hen-pecked ineffectual husband and father. Like ancient Greek plays, they help us make sense of perplexing lives and fate. Just as people tend to tell their lives according to a particular genre, so they relate to particular archetypal characters. Are you, or a colleague, wily beautiful Scheherazade, Baba Yaga the witch, Anansi the tricksy spiderman, the boy who knew the king was wearing no clothes and was not afraid to say so, or perhaps 'Mudjekeewis, /ruler of the winds of heaven' (Longfellow, 1960, p. 37)?

   John Goodwin, higher education tutor for adult learners, uses fiction writing for reflection alongside his teaching team, to share professional issues. This was written in a half-hour session, using folk tale to distance and yet focus the writing: especially useful when staffing had become a tense matter.

She sat in a small dark room. Scared. Bored. Miserable. Alone. The woodman had left for his day's work in the forest bolting the door. Clunk went the bolt. Clack went the lock.

   She waited for the hours to pass. Heavy long hours. Darkness began to fall in the forest. Birds made wing in the thickness. Clack went the lock. Clunk went the bolt. The door of the room was flung open wide. She peered out. No woodman.

'Hello,' she called. No voice answered.

'Anybody there?' she called again.

Still nobody answered. She got to her feet and went timidly to the door. Nothing but blackness. Her foot hesitated. Dare she step out? He had forbidden her to do so yet forward went her foot and touched pine needles on the cold earth. An owl shrieked.

Earth shrank. Pine needles vanished. There was no forest now only a clear path onward which she began to step slowly along. Cautiously. Nervously. Then there were others walking along the path each like herself stepping nervously and holding themselves back a little. At both sides of the path plans sprang up. Each was in gold writing on rolls of parchment. Each had a big red wax seal on it stamped with a coat of arms.

Then the plans began to speak. Excitedly. Enthusiastically. Happily. They sounded like her. Yet it was a strange and mysterious language. A language she'd never known in all her life. How she wanted the language to go on and on. Never stop. All the others along the path were speaking in the strange new language and now her lips moved too just like the rest.

The pathway was pulling her on. So on she moved. Quicker. Easier. All the others were moving too with the same ease and comfort. The pathway climbed skywards. It twisted and turned and the going was harder. Some fell off and were not seen again.

She had climbed long and hard and when now she looked back at the way she had come all she could see was a mirror. On the mirror was a bold and clear image of herself. Oh how she had changed. There was no way back now to the forest. The lock and bolt were broken beyond repair.

John Goodwin

Writing for Children

Writing for, or as, a child can open up straightforward, lucid understandings and insight, 'a child's wise incomprehension for defensiveness and disdain' (Rilke, [1934] 1993, p. 46). (See Mark Purvis in Chapter 2, pp. 39–41.) Jonathan, a physician, speaks to his *writing self*, a child:

My head is full of stories and poems. I told my friends about the stories and poems that you've written, and some I've listened to. I wonder – would you write me some more? And will you read them to me?

And can I read my stories to you? Can we learn together about writing stories and poems? Can we? Can we? (Jonathan Knight)

Dear Sarah and Jenny

I know you have been puzzled about my job as a doctor, especially because I always tell you that your illnesses will get better on their own. But that's the truth; people come to me all the time with things they perceive as illnesses which are not illnesses at all, or, if they are, will get better on their own. There is very little use of the skills and scientific knowledge I struggled so hard with. A lot of my work involves creating a pleasant place for people when they feel they need help. What we do barely matters very often, but making the place welcoming and relaxing goes a long way to helping people feel better, and helping people feel better is the main part of my work.

Nowadays we put everything in terms of illness and disease, and pills or operations to 'cure' people, but they don't cure people really. People and problems are much more complex and we really only ever scratch the surface.

I like to be genuine and honest with people, without having to sell them something which, for the main part, I don't believe in: sometimes I feel like a dodgy car dealer, which is a bit of a funny thought, isn't it?!

Mairi Wilson

Parody

Parody helps us understand (or deride) an everyday matter. Like fantasy, parody often uses archetypes to which we all relate.

A simple, amazingly effective device once helped me resolve a problem. I took the *Winnie the Pooh* (Milne, 1928) format, style and characters (Tigger and Eeyore etc.) to represent the various people and their relationships in my own psychodrama. The extraordinary thing was, I started writing it as a means of venting my spite against those who had hurt me. But I found the very act of writing (and I suppose using that particular model) induced a feeling of generosity in me which spilled over not only in the little story (now lost!) but into the real-life relationships as well.

This actually did have a permanent effect on my working life, because it awoke me to an effect of creative writing I'd only intellectualised about before. I determined to introduce this form of writing into my English Literature students' experience, and from that small beginning a whole undergraduate degree course in writing has now sprung. (Susanna Gladwin)

A good-looking patient: that's a change. And smart: so why is he living round here? New patient card – always a frisson of expectation, so easy to impress on first acquaintance by a charming manner and efficient style.

He's just off to the Far East tonight, 'just needs some antimalarials'. Exotic lifestyle then: and wonderful scent. His shirt is white, bit creased, touchingly ruffled. Does he smoke? No. Keep fit? Yes. Drink? A smile – eye contact – 'now and again, how about you?'

He's flirting! But I don't mind. Married? No. Lives alone? Mostly. Will he be in Sheffield long? No, 'fraid not, just passing through.

I take a chance and suggest he might like a blood pressure check 'since he's obviously a busy man and probably doesn't get much chance to look after himself'. An excuse really. I see a masculine forearm, and some rather stylish leather braces, but not much flesh. Oh well. He leaves, thanking me, shaking my hand: the firm dry grip of all romantic heroes. I notice the name: Bond, J: patient I.D. number 11 – 007.

Amanda Howe

Poetry

Poetry is an exploration of our deepest and most intimate experiences, thoughts, feelings and insights: distilled, pared to succinctness, and made music to the ear by lyricism, gaining insight from image, particularly metaphor and metonymy. The writers Adrienne Rich, Jean Cocteau, and Seamus Heaney, knowing its power from their personal experience, sought to encourage others to experience it.

Every poem breaks a silence that had to be overcome. (Rich, 1995, p. 84)

The inexplicable importance of poetry. (Cocteau, [1930] 1968, p. 128)

Each poem is an experiment. The poem carries you beyond where you could have reasonably expected to go. The image I have is from the old cartoons: Donald Duck or Mickey Mouse coming hell for leather to the edge of a cliff, skidding to a stop but unable to halt, and shooting out over the edge. A good poem is the same, it goes that bit further and leaves you walking on air. (Heaney, 2008, p. 3)

For some, poetry is the only way to explore and express vital things, directly diving for the heart of the issue, with no messing around with sentence structure or grammatical sense: a way of saying exactly what we want to say, and finding out what we need to say (Abse, 1998). Even Shakespeare's sonnets were a 'way of working out what he's thinking, not as a means of reporting what he thought' (Paterson, 2010, p. 3). Ted Hughes felt poetry is a vital form of expression:

Maybe all poetry… is a revealing of something that the writer doesn't actually want to say, but desperately needs to communicate, to be delivered of. Perhaps it's the need to keep it hidden that makes it… poetry. The writer daren't actually put it into words, so it leaks out obliquely, smuggled through analogies [metaphors]. We think we're writing something to amuse, but we're actually saying something we desperately need to share. (Hughes, 1995)

Poetry can enable exploration and expression of 'things we don't actually want to say', but 'desperately need to share', because meanings are released slowly and kindly. Image, such as metaphor or simile, can succinctly express vital experiences. It can clearly describe and explain something, both for reader and writer.

Ted Hughes thought poetry should be an uncivilising force (Middlebrook, 2003). Poetry strips away cloaking veneers, lays bare thoughts, ideas, feelings, values, dilemmas about identity, through image, metaphor and other poetic devices. These devices allow insight subtly, graciously and acceptably. Take another look at the poetry of Jo Cannon (Chapter 5, p. 83), Mark Purvis (Chapter 2, p. 39), Maggie Eisner (p. 97). Each employs lightness, humour, gentleness, and image to communicate vital messages succinctly, subtly, yet surely.

Sir Philip Sidney was desperate to 'faine in verse my love to show', yet could not find a poem good enough: '"Foole," said my Muse to me, "look in thy heart and write"' (Sidney, 1965, p. 165): he had to write it himself. The right words can be used in the right place, and only them; and these right words might be ones no prose writer could possibly put together.

The poetic mind knows with a different wisdom from the cognitive: 'I like poetry because I can't make it do what I want it to do, it will only do what *it* wants. I didn't want to write that poem: I wanted to write a nice glowing poem about being a mother' (a medical reflective writing course member).

Strict form, such as sonnet or villanelle (controlled rhyme, rhythm, syllables or repetition), is often preferred for expression of deepest experiences. Such control seemed to contain the otherwise uncontrollable unlimitedness of grief for a friend's death from AIDS (Doty, 1996; Hamberger, 1995), the work of a busy clinician (Campo, 1997), or unrequited love (Shakespeare's sonnets). Yet 'Poetry should be… unobtrusive, a thing which enters into one's soul, and does not startle or amaze it with itself, but with its subject… if poetry comes not as naturally as the leaves of a tree it had better not come at all' (Keats, 1818).

Poetry-writing, utterly absorbing and rewarding, offering immense surprises, tends to be self-affirming, as well as challenging and demanding. It draws upon deeply held memories, knowledge and values. Initial drafts can be intuitive, intensely absorbing, hypnagogic even, the hand writing without conscious direction: 'That willing suspension of disbelief for the moment, which constitutes poetic faith' (Coleridge, [1817] 1992). Winnie-the-Pooh, who expressed wisdom with simplicity, said: '"It is the best way to write poetry, letting things come"' (Milne, [1928] 1958, p. 268). Wordsworth took this a stage further: 'Poetry is the spontaneous overflow of powerful feelings; it takes its origin from emotion recollected in tranquillity; the emotion is contemplated till by a species of reaction the tranquillity gradually disappears' ([1802] 1992, p. 82).

Laurel Richardson (1992) 'breached sociological writing expectations by writing sociology as poetry. This breach has had unexpected consequences for my sense of Self'. Her carefully crafted poem was the expression of a research interview. She found it 'one way of decentering the unreflexive "self"… In writing the Other, we can (re)write the Self' (p. 136). Writing about another in poetry, particularly in the first person singular ('I') is writing about the self as well as the other (see Chapter 6). Her research poetry-writing was a deeply reflexive experience. The following examples are accompanied by explanations by their writers on how the poems came to be written and how useful they are to their writers.

I write to make sense of organisational life and couldn't imagine living without hearing my voice and practising being me. Here I explore selecting people for redundancy with an apparent 'option' to go.

> We targeted them. Singled them out
> Because they were old or simple
> Didn't have the required milk
> Dried up cash cows.
> We asked them. It was voluntary.
> When they wondered what would happen if…
> We talked of subtle pressures. And no cash.
> Best go now we said.
> They were severed. We couldn't wait
> To get them out. Gave them boxes
> To collect their bits. Stains on the carpet
> Affect morale.
> And now they are gone.
> Those who remain
> Speak in whispers.

Angela Mohtashemi

Maggie Eisner's villanelle

On a muggy Saturday afternoon after a busy week at the Health Centre, I sat down with two hours to do my homework for the next day's meeting of the Reflective Writing Group. It's one of my very favourite things – I wonder why I always leave the writing till the last minute. I felt exhausted, uncreative and devoid of ideas. Six minutes' *free writing*, recommended as a kind of warm-up, produced a long moan about how tired I was. Then I remembered reading how to write a *villanelle*:

(Continued)

(Continued)

I'm spending too much time on work, I know,
The pressure's putting lines upon my face.
I'd like to sit and watch the flowers grow.

Sometimes I feel the tears begin to flow:
I'm leaden tired, I'm desperate for some space,
I'm spending too much time on work. I know!

Do they want blood? Why don't they bloody go?
I'll crack if I continue at this pace.
I need to sit and watch the flowers grow.

Those piles of paperwork oppress me so,
They never seem to shrink, it's a disgrace.
I'm spending too much time on work, I know.

If I could take my time and take it slow,
If life could be a pleasure, not a race,
Perhaps I'd sit and watch the flowers grow.

If I got bored, there's places I could go,
I'd stretch my limbs, write poetry, find grace.
Must get to spend less time on work – although
I might do more than just watch flowers grow.

When I'd finished it, I felt rejuvenated and alive. It's always good to express my feelings in writing, but I was surprised to feel so dramatically better. Possibly the villanelle, or the challenge of writing in a tight poetic form, had a specific chemical effect on my brain (maybe serotonin reuptake inhibition like Prozac, or dopamine release like cocaine). (Eisner, 2000, p. 56)

Writing *Evacuees*

Add these to all the other voices:
Rima says *We're here, but our souls are in Lebanon.*

The night we took them to the rough bed and breakfast
Bassima said *I am proud. I will walk the streets with my children.*
Minu says *When a door slams*

we hear the bombs again.

Nouha says *I won't look ahead. In Lebanon we say*

....

you can only eat a bunch of grapes one grape at a time.

Six years old, handing me a George the Fifth penny
Zacharia said *I found this in the grass.*

Yahia says *It aches along my jaw,*
round my ear. I grit my teeth in my sleep.

Salma says *Lebanon is full of rivers.*
When it's over we'll take you there.

Leaving to try his luck in London
Hilal said *In Lebanon we kiss three times.* (Hamberger, 2007, p. 27)

As a Team Manager for Adult Services, in July 2006 I wrote in my journal: 'I've had a week working with 36 Lebanese evacuees, now in a Loughborough hotel. It's been painful, exhilarating, exhausting, and I worry about what's coming next for them, feel responsible for them, being ripped from the land they love to here, safety but uncertainty. I'm responsible for treating them as humanely as I can, wanting it right for them, but admitting at the end of this week, really making it right for them remains outside my power. So to continue to do the best I can remains the task, the challenge. To remain human I suppose. To respond, be equal, to their humanity.'

I felt driven to write a poem about them, but struggled with whether I was misappropriating their privacy by attempting to turn the unsayable into poetry. I found out more about 'ghazals' (see www.poets.org/viewmedia.php/prm-MID/5781), a Persian form of poetry using couplets and repetition. I realized each couplet might give voice to the people I'd met, letting them speak for themselves: a sense of people talking to me, trying to express how they felt about the war, their homeland, being evacuated.

In giving them a voice I hoped to unloose their phrases from my head, to set them free onto the page. Writing their words meant I no longer needed to carry them, although it was a burden I'd been changed by, far outside my usual scope. I could tell their stories in the poem and, by doing so, both honour them and give myself some relief from an inspiring, disorientating, absorbing experience that I was only beginning to understand.

Robert Hamberger

I like this idea of writing. I wrote poems in my youth, like we all. Then, writing for what? But now it feels like a silent friend. (Rita)

Narrative and the perspective from which it is viewed are cornerstones of reflective practice. Metaphor also significantly underpins our understanding of our lives and practice, even if we aren't aware of it. The next chapter explodes the myth that metaphor is only for poetry, and demonstrates its centrality to reflection and reflexivity.

 Read to Learn

Brookfield, S.D. (1995) *Becoming a Critically Reflective Teacher.* San Francisco, CA: Jossey-Bass.
Stephen Brookfield explains and exemplifies how to critically and reflexively examine professional practice from four different viewpoints or *Critical Lenses.* The whole book is recommended, but at least please read chapters 1–5.

Charon, R. (2006) *Narrative Medicine: Honouring the Stories of Sickness.* New York: Oxford University Press.
Rita Charon shows in depth how to create and reflexively and reflectively examine professional stories of experience.

Munno, A. (2006) A complaint which changed my practice, *British Medical Journal,* **332**, 1092.
Munno's 'critical incident' is an insightful account of a reflexive exploration of a professional event.

Rowland, S. (2000) *The Enquiring University Teacher.* Milton Keynes: Open University Press.
This text offers two forms of writing used to explore the emotional dimensions of teachers' work. One is a fictional story based closely on the author's experience of providing consultative support for a teaching and learning project for the newly qualified, and identifies what he learned from writing it. The subject of these writings is teachers and their work. Any practitioner from any profession, needing to explore the human dimensions of their work, would do well to attend to Rowland's experience, and have a go at exploring different forms of writing.

 Write to learn

For *How To* do this writing, please see *Write to Learn,* Chapter 1 (Chapter 8 for fuller advice). Do a *six-minute-write* about anything to limber up, before starting on the exercises below. Writings can be shared fruitfully afterwards with a group or confidential trusted other, if this seems appropriate once the writer has read and reflected on it first.

5.1 Points of view

1. Write a narrative of an event which puzzles you, in as much detail as you can remember, calling yourself 'I'.
2. Write about the same occasion, this time from the perspective of a significant other person who was there; this person now calls themselves 'I'.
3. Write about the same occasion, this time from the perspective of an omniscient narrator: in this version there is no 'I', you and the significant person become 'she' and/or 'he'.
4. Now write a final piece, reflecting on the significance of these three stories.

5.2 Who are you? What is your work?

1. Think of a story significant to you (*Cinderella*; *Pride and Prejudice*; the Sherlock Holmes stories).
2. Rewrite it, setting it in the present, in your work.
3. What is different between the story and your work? What similar?
4. Who is 'you' in this story (Cinderella/Handsome Prince/Father/Prince's servant 'Buttons'?)
5. Are you this character consistently, or sometimes Cinderella and sometimes Buttons?
6. How do your colleagues fit into the other character roles?
7. Reflect on what insight this brings.
8. Write another story, set in your work, beginning 'Once upon a time...'.

5.3 The story of your work

1. If your work were a book, film, play or radio programme what would it be? A romantic, detective or fantasy novel, diary, roadmap or atlas, telephone directory, DIY manual, *Desert Island Discs*, reality television show, *Strictly Come Dancing* (*Dancing with the Stars*)? ...
2. Describe it.

5.4 The essence of your work

1. Write a letter you won't send to a young child, telling them about your job.
2. Reread, remembering the age of your interlocutor, keep it simple.
3. I hope you find you have got to the heart of your feeling about your work.

(Continued)

(Continued)

5.5 A senses poem

1. Do a *six-minute-write* (see Chapter 6).
2. Write a line for each of these:

   (a) something you saw which struck you yesterday
   (b) a memory of a smell from a long time ago
   (c) a sound from yesterday
   (d) a taste for tomorrow
   (e) a touch last week
   (f) a feeling about the future.

3. Write more about one or more of these, to develop the poem.
4. If this is done in a group, the poems can be read to the whole group with no comment. If the group is very large, each person reads only one line. This can feel like a group poem.

 Visit **www.sagepub.co.uk/bolton** for additional useful resources including writing examples, exercises and videos.

CHAPTER 6

THE POWER OF METAPHOR

Metaphor is the strategy humans use to make sense of anything and every-thing which is otherwise difficult to grasp or communicate, particularly abstractions. This chapter explains that expressing metaphor as foundational to reflective practice is itself metaphorical because reflection is an abstract noun, not bricks and mortar, and therefore otherwise difficult to grasp. Metaphor is explained, and how and why to examine and use it consciously for developmental reflection and reflexivity, is described.

Our ordinary conceptual system, in terms of which we both think and act, is funda-mentally metaphorical in nature… human thought processes are largely metaphorical. (Lakoff and Johnson, [1980] 2003, p. 6)

Metaphor is the birth of meaning. (Hogler et al., 2008, p. 400)

The greatest thing by far is to have a command of metaphor. (Aristotle, *Poetics* 1459 a19)

Metaphor is the frame through which we perceive and feel; our thinking and understanding is 'fundamentally metaphorical' (Lakoff and Johnson, [1980] 2003, p. 6). A form of cultural interpretation, foundational to communication, values, ethical beliefs and practices, we use an astonishing six metaphors a minute (Geary, 2011). Every utterance and every perception is imbued or informed metaphorically, some perceiving it 'as the highest form of cognitive activity' (Hogler et al., 2008, pp. 400, 408). Playing with metaphor can illuminate, because we focus upon the metaphorical object, which can be far less personally emotive than what it stands for. Metaphors encourage us to be daring, to think freely with novelty (Deshler, 1990).

Three therapists interviewed by Collins used metaphors to describe reflective practice: (1) a 'tool to aid practice' (Collins, 2013, p. 61); (2) 'reflecting on the bigger picture' (p. 64); (3) 'a personal journey' (p. 65). Each indicates a different relationship from reflection and its role in their lives: (1) a solid, stable technical reliable implement; (2) a way of perceiving the social and cultural implications of their work; (3) an individual developmental process.

Each metaphor, consciously used or created, gives authority, and extends and vivifies that which it describes. Metaphors used unwittingly, however, can restrict perception and understanding because one thing is never exactly like another (e.g. Roche, 2012).

Once we grasp the metaphorical nature of conceptual systems and communication, and experiment with fresh metaphors, our perception of culture, society and work is irrevocably altered. This chapter offers a route to greater awareness of, and responsibility for, our metaphors, and therefore our lives and work.

Metaphors are culturally powerful, forming understanding and attitudes, certain elements being foregrounded, others ignored. Reflexive awareness and conscious use of metaphors and metaphorical systems gives authority. We cannot change the way we understand an issue without changing the metaphorical systems which express it. We can become critically aware of hitherto uncritically assumed views, values and principles (Steger, 2007); the conceptual frameworks constructive of our values, understanding, and feelings and therefore actions can become apparent to us. Take the image of the body as machine: it leads to patients assuming doctors can mend bodies with spare parts or oil, and physiology can be logged as in car owners' handbooks. The economy as marketplace: in the current economic climate I do not need to enumerate the problems this simplistic assumption has led to.

We can take responsibility for the moral and social consequences of our metaphors; 'metaphors can kill' (Lakoff, 1991). 'Evocative language can take on pernicious and evil power if wrong metaphors are chosen – we are liable to be captives of our own phrases and must be careful how we speak' (Osborn, 1993, p. 306). George W. Bush responded to the attack on New York's Twin Towers with a '*Crusade* against Terror'. Metaphorically likening American forces to medieval Crusaders was an expression of animosity against Islam. The belief that hearing voices indicates incurable psychosis, like aliens arising from untameable and unknowable unconscious realms, might lead hearers to kill themselves or others. If these voices are perceived as part of the self, they can be talked to, reasoned with and controlled to some extent: a life project (Smith, 2009; www.hearing-voices.org). Struggling to conceptualise an issue is often a search for appropriate metaphors.

> My client is a locked filing cabinet; no, a surprise chest of drawers: every time she opens a drawer there's something different. To some people's buttonhole she's the button; to some buttons, she's the buttonhole.

We are mostly unaware of professional, political and social metaphors and metaphorical systems they live and work with. I asked a group of medical undergraduates if one could give an example of metaphor. They looked blank and rather scared (I could see them thinking 'we're scientists…'). One responded, 'I can't think of any, my mind's a blank sheet', comically unaware she'd used a brilliant metaphor: empty mind = blank sheet. Science uses metaphor constantly to elucidate the otherwise unexplainable. The physicist Feynman described a drop of water magnified 2,000 times as a teeming football match, and the operation of electromagnetic fields as two corks floating in water (1995). Roche and Commins, in the introduction to their cognitive neuroscience book, pile on the metaphors, for example 'constant chatter of neurons' (2009, p1).

Susan Sontag wrote a polemic (1991, p. 91) against metaphors used in medicine and healthcare, such as battlefields for diseases such as cancer, which 'doesn't knock before it enters … a ruthless secret invasion' (1991, p. 5).

To enlighten groups, I often initiate discussion about prevalent professional metaphors. It only takes one participant to shout one out for the whole group to contribute excitedly, discovering a dominating force they can tackle. The ensuing task is to see if they can rewrite any habitual and unnoticed metaphors into new and dynamic ones. For example *hit the ground running* could become *take wings and fly*.

What is Metaphor?

Metaphor, a major way of making sense of the world (alongside narrative), is something otherwise unrelated or logically inconsistent standing in place of another: 'my work is the baby thrown out with the bathwater'. 'Giving the thing a name that belongs to something else' (Aristotle, 1995, p. 105); 'the essence of metaphor is understanding and experiencing one kind of thing in terms of another' (Lakoff and Johnson, [1980] 2003, p. 5). 'Th[ey] pervade how we understand the world' (Elkind, 1998, p. 1715); metaphors *prescribe* even how our world and work *ought* to be viewed and evaluated (Gray, 2007).

Metaphor makes the abstract concrete, grasps the ungraspable, makes visible or audible the normally invisible or inaudible. The human mind thinks concretely: feeling, emotion and spiritual experiences are tangible when touched, heard, smelled or seen. What *is* love, anxiety, guilt? Love is a beautiful, scented flower, anxiety a beast gnawing at your guts, guilt the heavy bird you should never have shot, strung inescapably around your neck (Coleridge, [1798] 1969). For our purposes, metaphor (my love *is* a red red rose) is the same as simile ('My love is *like* a red red rose': Robert Burns [emphasis mine]). A simile is a metaphor with linking words *like* or *as*.

Metaphoric images from the five elements are culturally common: my body was leaden, their heads were lumps of rock, our legs turned to water, he talked hot air, she breathed fire. And the body as container: I'm full to bursting with pride. John Dewey used countless metaphors for the essence of teaching, including artist, lover, wise mother, navigator, gardener, servant, composer, physician, builder (Simpson et al., 2005). Metaphors enable verbal painting, creation of symphonies, banquets, perfumes, silk; the use of all five senses to enable 'cognitive, affective and somatic ways of knowing' (Shafer, 1995, p. 1331).

Our dominant cultural metaphors are static. Fluid and active elements are often expressed as commodities. Nursing and teaching are relationship based. Yet teaching *plugs a knowledge or skills gap, a module*; nursing *delivers packages of care*. We have *human resource management*, rather than *personnel*, as if people were bricks. Everyone has a metaphorical way of understanding their lives: some with a half-empty glass and others half-full, metaphorical expressions of native optimism or pessimism.

'The metaphorical *is* at once signifies both *is not* and *is like*. If this is really so we are allowed to speak of metaphorical truth' (Ricoeur, 1978, p. 7). 'Metaphorical truth' is an essential aspect of our mental and physical understanding, the 'open sesame' to memories and understanding. 'Metaphor is the "aha!" process itself ' (Shafer, 1995, p. 1332).

Metaphor at Work

A team using the same metaphor/image system for what they are doing will be harnessed in harmony, especially if it is congruent with their principles and values and with their project or activity. An organisation wishing to implement change needs images consistent with that change. A senior manager who found his colleagues difficult, consistently used war metaphors. Once he moved from perceiving work as war, to playing in an orchestra, he began to seek harmony rather than discord (Geary, 2011).

Alison Duffy's research into metaphor in organisations (2013) found that metaphor in meetings breaks tedium, relieves tension and lifts energy, and clarifies, summarises and reinforces points or concepts (metaphor *'nails it'*). Carefully constructed metaphors were even reported as 'completely re-wiring people's minds'. When leaders were stuck in daily task overload, the metaphor 'you're too busy fighting the alligators to remember to drain the swamp' became a 'memorable mantra'. Whereas the dead metaphor or cliché 'not seeing the wood for the trees' would have gone unnoticed.

Metaphor in Business

Eighty bemused professionals think 'pipecleaners at a strategy session?' This is an invitation to play, but with purpose: to take business facts and figures and productively rearrange them. Today we craft 80 visions of the company's future into compelling three-dimensional visual 'landscapes'.

Metaphors are like zip files, compressing big information into small packets: excellent for expressing business truths. Humans are natural metaphor-makers, hardwired to solve problems metaphorically. We 'surf' the 'web', 'reach out' to customers, and spend money 'like water'.

How to start? By paying close attention to kernels of metaphor within ordinary business conversations. We divide into groups. The company is a 'hive of activity'. What kind of hive? One in which every bee knows its purpose, but is free to cross-pollinate ideas. A moment's pause; then the metaphor becomes contagious. The hive is constructed from chairs wrapped in paper, then populated with a swarm of balloon bees. Another group creates a large prism that refracts the company's mission into seven strands that are 'always clear to everyone, even when it's cloudy'. A third group constructs a fortress that safeguards the strategy: its high walls 'let innovation in but keep competitors out'.

Important themes emerge. The need for an organisational structure to promote collaborative working shows up in every landscape. Perhaps most eloquently, one group's archipelago of 'project islands' remain linked even when 'high tides flood them with work'.

Metaphor landscapes express what is otherwise difficult to say. Long-standing tensions are addressed by the fortress having a tower for each team, but a shared feasting hall.

The landscapes provided a language. Six months later, a dozen newly appointed 'purpose bees' are tasked with making 'project islands' a working reality.

Margaret Meyer

Examining metaphorical structures is a reflexive process. Schwind (2008) (Schwind et al., 2011), using herself as an example, describes nurses reflecting upon their own illnesses through metaphor significantly enhancing patient understanding. Leslie Boydell describes her leadership programme as:

A team of horses of different sizes and colours pulling a heavily laden wagon at different speeds. One is going full tilt with the bit between its teeth, another is taking it easy, a third wants to eat grass, while another is grumpy and nipping the others. Every so often we pull together and fly. I am inconspicuous, without a whip or loud voice, yet constantly keep my eyes on the road to steer around dangers. Others ride with me for a while and use their greater strength to control the horses. (Leslie Boydell, in Denyer et al. 2003, p. 19)

Audrey Shafer argues that 'anaesthesia is much more complex than commonly used metaphors seem to suggest' (1995, p. 1339). *Under* anaesthetic is simplistic and negative: *down* is normally bad, perhaps related to the devil and hell (*bottom of the heap, under the weather*). Mercedes Kemp asked students to describe a well-loved landscape, then their classrooms as if they were landscapes, then their imaginary classrooms, then to write about events in these classrooms. 'We ask [participants] to describe education as a pudding, then to write up their luxury version. Much of this activity is light-hearted... but nevertheless, startling, surreal images abound, aesthetically subverting the humdrum world of everyday practice' (Kemp, 2001, p. 350).

My evolving sense of vocation as a pastoral theologian

I have worked through my own understanding of the relationship between theory and practice as it affects my teaching and practice of ministry. My academic world implicitly continues to value the conceptual, abstract, or ideal over the concrete, particular and embodied. I reflected upon *abstraction* and *risk* and *vulnerability* in the ministry of leadership, free-associating metaphors, following where they took me, then described the thing, then what it does, using a verb.

If **abstraction** were a:

- bird, a graceful yet fierce eagle, it would fly high, seeing a broad landscape
- plant, a venus flytrap, it would capture and devour
- musical instrument, a piano, it would have great range and possible variations, depending on the pianist's skill
- piece of furniture, an art deco sideboard, it would be sleek and elegant, combining form and function
- sea creature, an eel, it would be slippery and hard to handle, or a puffer fish which inflates when it senses danger, can be dangerous if consumed
- means of transportation, a motorcycle would take you places fast, but needs steady hands, and is dangerous if you underestimate its power.

Together these are evocative for movement, sound, and functionality. What do they tell me about my attitude toward abstraction?

Danger: eagles, venus flytraps, puffer fish and motorcycles all pose a risk to the unsuspecting; all call for attention to issues of power and the possibility of seduction. Yet there is beauty and elegance as well as empowerment: of getting where one needs to go, seeing more than one could otherwise, and the opening up of multiple possibilities rather than a closed and limited world. Several point to the utilitarian aspect of abstractions; they are a means to an end and whether they work for good or ill depends on the person riding the cycle, filleting the fish or playing the piano.

Kathleen Russell

Using Metaphor to Develop Reflection and Reflexivity

Metaphors can express abstractions, memories, ideas, thoughts and feelings, and explore constructive contact with painful or difficult areas of experience and memory. Effective metaphors can appear to *come from nowhere*. Facilitators help images bubble up, presenting themselves on the page; it seems they appear from nowhere because we are used to the Cartesian 'I think, therefore I am': they do not arise through cognitive processes. Such powerful images occur once we have the courage to be 'absent-minded', or to pay attention to absent-mindedness (as Freud suggested about parapraxes). If reflective practitioners are encouraged to experiment *playfully* with words – *doodle* with metaphors, they can 'absent-mindedly' enter areas of experience and even locked categories of memory (Modell, 1997).

The psychiatrist Modell (1997) said metaphors enable us to grasp feelings, a vital element of reflective practice. Traumatic memories lose connectedness with the rest of the memory, hindering living in the present and looking to the future. Metaphor is the only way to make contact with this material (1997). And writing is an enjoyable process to use, overcoming trauma survivors' isolation.

Metaphor reveals because it sidles up sideways, giving non-traumatic images for traumatic events. We often don't understand our metaphors initially (as with dreams); when we do, the illumination can be astonishing. Articulating our own new-minted metaphors can have a powerful effect; patients feel better understood, for example, when expressing their own metaphors for symptoms, rather than using pre-existing ones (Geary, 2011).

There are many ways of encouraging awareness of habitual metaphors, and wielding metaphor's perceptive power. Practitioners also create powerful new metaphors, like Boydell, Wilde and Forrestal above. Julie Hughes's education students gave in-depth explanations why teaching was disco ball, river, road network, and mountaineering (Chapter 3).

I ask professionals to write lists of binary pairs, then assign one of the pair to client or student, and one to themselves. A therapist wrote this:

silk & sand	I put the smooth on her rough
light & dark	she's in the light and I'm in the wings
Hansel & Gretel	I'm a boy and she's a girl and we're searching our way
mountains & streams	she flows round me and I stay fixed
horse & cart	she takes the lead and I follow on
grass & green	she's growing while I reflect her colour
sad & happy	I carry her tears as she learns to smile (Charles Becker)

Here is a family doctor: I am the sunshine. My depressed patient is the showers. I try to brighten his life to help him pull through the storm. Maybe I am too light-hearted and minimise his sufferings. When the rain is fine the sun makes a rainbow. As the shower becomes heavy it clouds out the sun. Are my football stories irritating and patronising? He now chooses to see my colleague.

> I found it useful putting my feelings down on paper, by sharing it I was able to put it into perspective. The patient concerned is now causing my colleague some anxiety also. Maybe it is transference. (Kate Milne)

Carol Wood and Elaine Trevitt are peer-mentors who played fruitfully with metaphor, even calling their joint educative process 'chip and pin' (Chapter 3, p. 61). Metaphor enabled Carol constructively to perceive her *inner mentor*, whom she metaphorically personified as *Crow*:

> Over time, in exploration with Elaine, I realised *Crow* was, perhaps, my inner mentor. Realising *Crow* can rise above the tortuous winding road full of dark and dangerous pitfalls, and fly, was an epiphany. Realising I did not have to settle for compromise and a 'quiet life', that sometimes a discordant voice is vital to achieve best practice, I began to notice subtle changes in my practice and interpersonal relationships. Significantly, *Crow* enabled me to recognise and deal with suppressed anger at perceived injustice. (Carol Wood)

Playing with metaphors can help practitioners and students move to a wider overview than everyday practical concerns. In pre-service teacher training, metaphors help students confront attitudes to diversity and disability. Students write educational life histories developing their metaphors for *teacher* (gardener, rainforest tree, weather forecaster), and present student-led seminars throughout the module, for 20 per cent of assessment marks (Graham and Paterson, 2010). A teacher said: 'I thought that all teachers were the same, [but] when I heard what some of the other metaphors were, I thought, "this is so different from what I've been doing or what I've been experiencing", and I liked that' (Bullough, 1991, p. 49). And metaphor examination and creation significantly informs organisational theory (Cunliffe, 2008).

> Metaphors contribute to theory construction, help to structure beliefs and guide behaviour in organizations, express abstract ideas, convey vivid images that orient our perceptions and conceptualizations, transfer information, legitimate actions, set goals, and structure coherent systems. Because metaphors are enacted and surface through everyday language use, they can… illuminate organizational practices, including capturing perceptions and reactions to ambiguity with organizational goals; norms, motives, and meaning in studying organizational culture; the nature of struggles between competing ideologies; and covert practices that mask power relationships by highlighting certain features while suppressing others. (Hogler et al., 2008, p. 396)

Metaphors are used in educational leadership (Pellicer, 2008). Cherry and Spiegel's (2006) leadership students focused upon beliefs, values and ethics, using three themes: (1) touchstone, standard bearer; (2) advocate for a cause beyond oneself; (3) parent. School principalship trainees (Linn et al., 2007, pp. 163, 166, 168) responded to: 'The principalship is like… because…' with four 'themes: (a) protection and nurturing; (b) skill, adventure or problem solving; (c) challenge, risk and threat; (d) chance and luck. They generally depicted it as uncontrollable and unpredictable, yet each expressed determination and resolve to remain steadfast'.

Practitioners use metaphors unwittingly (see Turner, Preface, p. 19). A doctor wrote a precise account of his drive to work: tricky roundabout, blind corner, frustrating traffic. Such metaphors take writers by surprise. Here is a searching self-portrait by a palliative medicine consultant:

Jug by Sam Kyeremateng

A terracotta jug sits on a stone floor, in a dark space. The Jug surveys the gloominess of its surroundings. Why am I here? Who am I? What am I? The unspoken questions are unanswered.

The Jug was crafted with care. Someone had lovingly sculpted its form. Taking great care moulding its short spout and stout handle. Despite this the questions remain unanswered. It understood it was a jug. It knew jugs could hold all manner of things. But it could not hold all things at once, and it could not decide what it should hold. It was not enough to be simply a jug, was it? It did not think it wished to be an empty vessel, and it did feel so very empty.

If it held water it could be used to sustain people or to hold beautiful things like flowers. If it held wine it could bring life to a party, solace to the lonely and joy to the sad. If it held oil it could fuel a fire, or ease the workings of some great machine. If it held marbles it could be an ornament to be admired and adored. As the thoughts danced through its imagination the Jug realised that in the darkness of this room it could see no water or oil or wine or even stones let alone marbles and even if it could, it could not decide how to choose between them all. The Jug sat empty.

In the distance footfalls tapping the flagstones pierced the darkness. The Jug pondered a new thought. Perhaps someone would find it and fill it up with something that would make it something worth being. Delighted by the prospect it sat thinking soon it would find the answer to all its questions. As the steps drew closer the Jug's excitement changed to anxiety. What if the person chose the wrong thing? Once filled with wine it could no longer hold water for fear of tainting the taste and vice versa. Would oily marbles have the same appeal? Panicked by the new dilemma the Jug remained frozen in the spotlight. The steps stopped. The Jug sensed the gaze of the unseen figure. After a moment the silence that had nurtured its thought became unbearable. The steps clacked back into life then faded.

The terracotta jug sat on a stone floor. In the silence it decided it was better just to be and not ask too many questions. To be an empty jug was enough for now.

(Continued)

(Continued)

Sam's afterword

I wrote this at a time of uncertainty, primarily about career paths. There was also, though, uncertainty about my place in society. As a black Scotsman (or Scotsman of African origin to be pc) I often wonder about my place in the world and what my attitudes should be. Being young, male and black all have their own associated dilemmas. Whilst I am undeniably Scottish, I have a deep love of my African roots. All this is further complicated by the media concept of *blackness* which is very different from that which has been passed to me by my parents. In my experience there are very few role models for the young, black Scotsman even in today's multicultural world. Even now the only one I can think of is the guy who was in *Porridge* with Ronnie Barker and I'm sure he doesn't count.

The story was never meant to be a self-portrait. I think I was just trying to capture certain emotions. It was certainly never meant to be published. Only now reading it again do I realise how embarrassingly personal (and at times sad) it is. Despite the blushes I am happy for it to be published as it surprises me by capturing my thoughts at a certain moment in time. I guess I hope that someone else might gain some comfort knowing that they are not the only ones to have similar uncertainty (Kyeremateng, 2003, pp. 101–2).

Image and Reflection

The reflection in Van Eyck's convex mirror in *The Arnolfini Portrait* (National Gallery, London) allows a view of the couple from both sides. Our night sky would be denuded without the power of reflection: the moon and planets are only visible because they reflect the sun's light. 'The Lady of Shalott', cursed to live her life indirectly through mirror images, wove them into tapestry. When handsome Sir Lancelot appears in her glass she can stand it no longer: The mirror cracked from side to side / 'The curse is come upon me!' cried / The lady of Shalott (Tennyson, [1886] 1932, p. 82). She dies because she challenged her curse to perceive life only reflected.

Reflective practitioners look at life fully, and perceive right through the mirror rather than merely musing upon reflections. The route is a critical rendering and re-rendering of life's narratives, and critical re-viewing of habitual metaphors. This chapter has opened our eyes to the power of metaphor and how to use it. Now we examine the key to reflective practice: writing.

Read to Learn

Geary, J. (2011) *I is Another: The Secret Life of Metaphor and How it Shapes the Way we See the World*. New York: Harper Collins.
An approachable introduction to metaphor, and how to reflect upon it, to develop practice.

Graham, L.J. and Paterson, D.L. (2010) Using metaphors with pre-service teachers enrolled in a core special education unit, *Teacher Education and Special Education*. In press.
A fascinating and clear example of metaphor exploration for professional student education.

Scaife, J. (2010) *Supervising the Reflective Practitioner*. Hove: Routledge.
Scaife's writing is refreshingly readable, yet informative and theoretically significant. Chapter 6 (pp. 127–40) gives an insightful account of metaphor in reflective practice.

Write to learn

For *How To* do this writing, please see *Write to Learn*, Chapter 1 (Chapter 8 for fuller advice). Do a *six-minute-write* about anything to limber up, before starting on the exercises below. Writings can be shared fruitfully afterwards with group or confidential trusted other, if this seems appropriate once the writer has read and reflected on it first.

6.1 Empowering your work

1. Think of a picture, object of beauty (for example, a shell), or an element of nature (for example, a mountain, a tree) you particularly like.
2. Describe its qualities: those that make it inspiring, beautiful, restful...
3. Now replace the name of the thing with the name of your work.

Example: This ancient Greek jug has a firm base and large capacity, is graceful and elegant, yet also functional, containing liquid safely and pouring effectively.
  My work is graceful yet functional, with a large enough capacity and firm ethical and practical base. I can use it to carry wisdom to other people and pour it carefully, the amount they need.

(Continued)

(Continued)

6.2 Binary pairs (see example, p. 109)

1. List as many binary pairs as possible (e.g.: needle/thread, horse/cart, Adam/ Eve, knife/fork).
2. Picture yourself and one other work person: client, colleague, whomever.
3. Write who is which from your pairs (e.g.: I am needle, you thread); note which ones seem not obvious to assign.
4. Choose one, and write more (e.g.: I'm a big fat shiny darning needle, she a length of black wool darning a hole in an old sock).

6.3 If your work were a...

1. Respond to each of these with a phrase for each:

   (a) If my work were an animal what animal would it be?
   (b) If my work were a piece of furniture what would it be?
   (c) If it were a season or weather what would it be?
   (d) A food?
   (e) A drink?
   (f) A flower?
   (g) A form of transport?
   (h) And so on.

2. What does this tell you about your work?

 Visit **www.sagepub.co.uk/bolton** for additional useful resources including writing examples, exercises and videos.

CHAPTER 7

WRITING AS REFLECTION

Writing is itself the reflective and reflexive process. This chapter explains the power of reflective writing; that we write to learn about ourselves and our practice. It explains the discipline of writing, the finding of the writer's voice, the difference between writing about events, and abstract musing, how to increase perspective with perceptive questioning, and last but not least, how to undertake the dynamic but sensitive process of sharing writings with colleagues.

We write before knowing what to say and how to say it, and in order to find out, if possible. (Lyotard, 1992, p. 119)

We… write to become what and who we are. (Hwu, 1998, p. 37)

Alice was through the glass, and had jumped lightly down into the Looking-Glass room… Then she began looking around and noticed that what could be seen from the old room was quite common and uninteresting, but that all the rest was as different as possible. For instance, the pictures on the wall next the fire seemed to be all alive. (Carroll, [1865] 1954, pp. 122–3)

Reflective writing *is* the reflective process, rather than recording what has been thought. Its value is stressed by, amongst others, Kerr (2010) and Branch (2005). Writing can find out not only how and what we need to say (Lyotard, 1992), but also significantly WHY. Reflective writing captures events, individuals, thoughts, feelings and values; it can structure and illuminate them. Reflective practitioners write for self-illumination and exploration, not to create a product. Teachers of young children say: *pay attention to what the child is paying attention to* because they notice and work on different things than we assume. In writing we pay deep attention to parts of ourselves we do not listen to often enough. We can get beyond our assumptions and obedience to social, cultural, organisational rules, in order to pay attention properly, and learn. 'Roland Barthes... said a writer uses language as an end in itself, as something that in itself has justification' (Llosa, 1991, pp. 114–15). Reflective and reflexive writing can collate and make sense of the muddle of stuff in our minds, facilitating:

- wider view from a distance
- close acute observation: a vitally active, not passive, process
- perception from significant others, e.g. clients
- authority over practice
- a critical challenging attitude to assumptions
- fruitful relationships with professional and academic literature

It can do this when we have full authority over our own writing, rather than producing it in the *right* way for another authority (e.g. examiner). To author reflective writing, we take full authority over it.

> Writing is drawing the essence of what we know out of the shadows.
> (Karl Ove Knausgaard, 2013, p. 2)

In this writing everything can become 'as different as possible' (Carroll, [1865] 1954, pp. 122–3) and yet the same. And it can make the extraordinary more comprehensible and seem ordinary. Actions, interactions, professional episodes, memories from long ago, spirituality, thoughts, ideas and feelings become 'all alive'. Developmental change becomes possible.

Writing can enable us to *go through* the mirror and gain perspective, rather than merely reflect on back-to-front mirrored images of self. A creative adventure through to the other side of the silvering, it can give confidential and relatively safe access, using narrative, accurate observation, metaphor and critique; constraining structures can clarify, releasing power to take more responsibility for actions.

A valuable mode of expressing, sharing, assessing and developing professional experience, writing is excellent solo, and with colleagues (Rowland, 1993), and as a research tool. Students write to express themselves, store aide-mémoires, present arguments, demonstrate knowledge, explicate experience. A playwright, working in medical and healthcare, however, 'was shocked by how difficult [students] found reflective writing, and how worried they were about being honest about their feelings when they knew their work was going to be seen by tutors' (Hargreaves and Page, 2013, pp. 178–9). Tutors with first-hand knowledge and experience of the processes themselves will be able to help students and practitioners beyond this (Kuit et al., 2001). Here is a physician's personal, undrafted writing:

Six minutes' Writing

Now back at the round table with knights of the order of reflective writing. The sun sinks low through the picture window. There is the scratch of pens on paper, heads bowed and thoughts flying out from 20 different 4 acre compartments behind the 'red curtain' (see Chapter 1, p. 17). I feel excited to hear the writing from the other knights after tea and look forward to the feeling of closeness we all get from sharing what is hidden and yet so important in our lives.

Again it never ceases to amaze me as to what can be done and how good it feels to write for only 6 minutes! We always think of 5 minutes as a short time, not enough to start something new, but maybe this is how we can make the most of a very small pocket of time!

You could do it in the morning as part of your morning routine. You could do it at the end of surgery or even in the middle! All you need is a pen and paper and the mind-set that it is not only possible but immensely valuable and life affirming simply to get pen on paper and move the thoughts that seek to overcrowd onto a clean sheet of paper.

Maybe this could be given to patients as a prescription such as: 'Write for 6 minutes o.d (once daily) or 6 minutes o.n (once at night)' to start with to see if there are any unwanted side effects and to help with compliance. If there were no side effects and the patient felt better, the prescription dose could be increased to b.d (twice daily) tds (three times daily) qds (four times daily)!!

Jane Calne

Write to Learn

Reflective writing distances (puts out there, onto the paper), but also creates closer contact with emotions, thoughts and experiences. Writing is the vehicle for reflection and reflexivity: reflection *in* writing. Writing precedes thinking, not the other way round. Not only does writing enable the most appropriate reflection, but also: 'one of the values of writing is that you can freeze the film: reflect upon one frame or a short series, then run the film backwards and review a previous scene in the light of reflections upon a later one. This would be difficult to do in talking: it wouldn't make sense; impossible to do during action' (a reflective practitioner).

> I consider writing as a *method of inquiry*, a way of finding out about yourself and your topic… Writing is a way of 'knowing' – a method of discovery and analysis. By writing

in different ways, we discover new aspects of our topic and our relationship to it. Form and content are inseparable. (Richardson, 2001, pp. 34–5)

Writing *is* thinking, writing *is* analysis, writing is indeed a seductive and tangled *method* of discovery… I trust you will… use writing as a method of inquiry to move into your own impossibility, where anything might happen – and will (Adams St Pierre, 2005, pp. 967, 970, 973, emphasis in original).

To write is to measure the depth of things, as well as to come to a sense of one's own depth' (Van Manen, 1995, p. 127).

Writers' own feelings and ideas can be explored further by writing fictions in which events are altered in some specific way (such as switching genders). A multiplicity of themes can be perceived within a single incident. We know in so many different ways, yet constrain ourselves to a tiny portion of knowledge. Writing fictionally is one way of engaging with this complexity, of being aware of the embeddedness of our knowing in experience. Wider knowledge and opinion can be drawn upon through reading and discussion.

Explorative writing (with no plan about the content or form) was recommended as early as 1823 (Farber, 2005). This started Freud on a method to further his own understanding (Mahoney, 2002), saying he never started a single paragraph knowing where he would end up (Freud, 1985, p. 319). To illustrate this he repeated a current story about a Sunday rider: 'Where are you going?' 'Do I know? … Ask the horse.'

This requires concentration likened by one student to a long refreshing swim, another to a deeply dreaming sleep. Another student audibly whispered 'disgusting', scribbling hunched over her page: we had all disappeared from her consciousness. This concentration is highly focused, just as window-shoppers filter out unwanted reflections by restricting light sources, cupping their eyes against the glass.

Writers interact with and respond to drafts, subjecting them to interpretation and analysis, clarifying and extending understanding, deepening their critical involvement in the text: 'The only time I know that something is true is at the moment I discover it in the act of writing' (Jean Malaquais, quoted in Exley, 1991, p. 64). Reflective practitioners say: 'I didn't know I thought/knew/remembered that until I wrote it'; one said: 'it is an opportunity to inhabit the unknown'. Writing is reported as being used similarly, with students (Charon, 2006) and practitioners (Charon, 2006; Helman, 2006). Fiction writing can humanise medicine (Shem, 2002).

Elbasch-Lewis runs courses for teachers to enable enquiry, re-storying, appreciation of diversity of voices in education; one student said writing 'enables me to continually examine assumptions and patterns of living and to maintain a dynamic of ongoing change… to confront, understand and study ourselves, what we were, what we are now, how we got here… we didn't expect these to appear in such a significant and lucid way in our stories' (2002, pp. 425–6). 'Theology by heart' is a dialogic reflexive writing portfolio method used for theological reflection turning 'life into text' (Graham et al., 2005). 'We observed that doctors felt the process of writing and talking about the stories was both profound and helpful. The process stimulated clarification of personal values and priorities, created a context for peer support (which doctors often seem to resist), and fostered recognition of opportunities to make constructive changes in their professional lives… Amid so much discussion of what is wrong with medicine, the workshops seemed to help them remember what is right' (Horowitz, et al. 2003, p. 774; see also Svenberg et al., 2007).

To write is to open oneself up to chance, to free oneself from the compulsive linking up of 'meaning, concept, time and truth' that has dominated Western philosophic discourse (Flax, 1990).

The Discipline of Writing

The discipline of reflective and reflexive writing allows freedom of exploration and expression. A 'sort of emotional discipline' (Winter et al., 1999, p. 204), it needs a carefully boundaried space providing sufficient security to enable surrender to the process. Paradoxically it needs 'circumstances in which it is safe to be absent-minded (that is, for conscious logic and reason to be absent from one's mind)' (Freud, 1950, p. xiii) and 'safe' 'circumstances' of creative 'discipline'.

> Surrendering to creative discipline is neither simple nor straightforward. Insight engendered by expressive exploration can be dynamically unsettling: 'One leaves a piece of one's flesh in the inkpot each time one dips one's pen' (Tolstoy, quoted Exley, 1991, p. 25). And we need strategies to get us there: 'The progress of any writer is marked by those moments when he manages to outwit his own inner police system. Writers have invented all kinds of *games* to get past their own censorship' (Hughes, 1982, p. 7). Schiller called such 'police' 'the watch upon the gates of reason' (Freud, 1900, p. 103). The function of *games* is to bypass the everyday thinking mode, to enter a deeper wider mode of experience, 'loosening cognitive control' (Hunt, 2013, p.19). Methods, such as *six minutes' writing without thinking*, are *games* (Chapter 8, p. 136) designed to help practitioners develop their own discipline of writing; just as games are used to develop the discipline of teamwork or language learning. In her *six minutes' writing*, Chris Banks explored the discipline of her writing process: It's happening – that thing where I dismiss my own thoughts: *No, not that. You'll get stuck if you go with that. That's so dull, you'll bore yourself stupid. Not that, not that, not that*. It makes it so impossible to get started and follow through. It's the Thought Police, as Gillie said Ted Hughes said. I have a whole battalion of them – bobbies on the beat, sergeants in the office, sharp-eyed interrogating inspectors – loads of them. And then there's the Crown Persecution* Service complete with judge and jury and some hopeless, depressed woman from Victim Support as my only ally.
>
> Is it experience that tells me, Don't go there, it'll be dull? Not just dull – something more like, It won't get born. It'll be a messy miscarriage, a deformed foetus that'll die shortly after it slips into the world. Is it experience? In fact, experience tells me, Focus, write, give yourself over to it and whatever comes out will be healthy, with full lungs and kicking limbs.
>
> *This is what I actually wrote instead of *Prosecution*.
> (Chris Banks)

Many take a while to find their own rhythms and voice, their own discipline, or permission, in their own space and time, having been supported to write in a group where: 'everybody writes alone yet together'.

Penny wrote effectively in the group, where the discipline was organised for her; but struggled at home. I suggested she try somewhere else, or with carefully chosen materials, or at a different time. Penny then wrote two pieces, the first in a café, having bought a shocking pink folder, a new pad and a bright pink pen. Once she was outside her home, which had its own too strong set of disciplines, she could create her own writing rules.

Some find it hard even to begin to think of writing. One new participant looked startled, rummaging in her bag, saying: 'I've only got lipstick.' Many professionals find it difficult to find the time, though are very glad when they do:

> All of us lead busy lives, and a lot is done like naughty children's homework, at the last minute. I think this may be what gives some of our efforts an immediacy and seriousness which is occasionally beautiful, and always interesting. (Seth)

Many find writing on their own easier, finding discipline structured by a facilitator problematic. And there are those who cannot start at all until they have experienced others doing it:

> I know this small group now (after only a few hours) in a deeper way than I could ever have done in a whole course worth of sessions. You [a colleague] look different now. You have become a person for me. I'm so glad. I had been so nervous of writing when we started, feeling I can't write what comes into my head; I really can't. And Gillie said 'fine, we must all write in the way that suits us, you do whatever that is'. But having heard all your pieces I can now see how I can do it; I'm going to rewrite mine with all my feelings, thoughts, ideas and other things – some of them really personal. (Lee)

Finding the Writer's Voice

People are often nervous, not realising written expressive ability is as innate as speech. They gain confidence as they gain trust, faith in themselves (that they can do it), and a desire and determination to write. Positive encouragement is facilitative. Offered positive encouragement, beginners will progress from inexpressive, imitative or inauthentic writing.

This *voice* is found with 'willing suspension of disbelief for the moment, which constitutes poetic faith' (Coleridge, [1798] 1969)).

Seamus Heaney says 'Finding a voice means that you can get your own feeling into your own words and that your words have the feel of you about them... A voice... possess[es] a constant and unique signature that can, like a fingerprint, be recorded and employed for identification (1980a, p. 43). Ted Hughes likened it to silent, still night-watching for foxes: 'Till, with a sudden sharp hot stink of fox / It enters the dark hole of the head' (1967, pp. 19–20). Heaney also said: 'Between my finger and my thumb / The squat pen rests. / I'll dig with it.' (1980b, pp. 10–11). And:

> Usually you begin by dropping the bucket half way down the shaft and winding up a taking of air. You are missing the real thing until one day the chain draws unexpectedly tight and you have dipped into water that will continue to entice you back. You'll have broken the skin of the pool of yourself. (Heaney 1980a, p. 47)

Hélène Cixous becomes a jewellery thief: 'These pearls, these diamonds, these signifiers that flash with a thousand meanings, I admit it, I have often filched them from my unconscious. The jewellery box… Furtively, I arrive, a little break-in, just once, I rummage, ah! The secrets!' (1991, p. 46).

If we take this creative leap, then the professional arena can be opened up to observation and reflection through the lens of artistic scrutiny. Artistic processes such as writing can harness memories which we do not know we remember and give greater access into possible thoughts and experiences of others. These are *possible* thoughts, we are empathetically imagining from others' perspectives.

Details and subtle nuances of behaviour and situations become available in writing. A teacher- or clinician-writer observes details missed by good observant teachers or clinicians (Charon, 2006). Try it. Observe a student or client walking into your practice place. Capture on paper how they hold themselves, breathe, move their limbs, their characteristic gestures and sayings. What do they remind you of: a cat? A soft deep armchair? A locked filing cabinet?

Writers have the unparalleled privilege of entering empathetically into the imagined life of another, giving insight into another's feeling, thinking, perception and memories. This is writing beyond what we know, and on into the unknown. Try it. Take the person you have just described. Write the conversation they might have had on returning home that night. Remember they will never see this; let your hand write, free of normal controlling thought. If you add in something about how they got home, where they live or drink, your imagination is really taking you through the looking-glass. Writing taps into latent understandings about that person.

We bring what we understand, think and feel about this person into conscious thought through writing, and it is this that can take us towards critical reflection. It doesn't matter that this probably didn't actually happen. It is not quiddity we seek – the real nature or essence of a thing – but our experience of it. Reflecting on our experience is what can help us change our attitudes and behaviours. Medical students write patients' illness stories in the voice and vernacular of the patient, imaginatively and vicariously entering patients' contexts. They 'become the other' (Engel et al., 2002, p. 32, 2008).

Arriving for my first Reflective Writing experience I suddenly found myself properly empathising with my phobic/anxiety patients. I was terrified! What had possessed me to enrol?

It was incredibly reassuring to discover that you do not need any writing skills. By what seems to be simplicity itself, we are led into unlocking memories, thoughts, reactions, experiences by acting as a catalyst, sowing seeds, stimulating us to truly reflect on our day to day experience as family doctors – and how that affects us ourselves. Like all newbies I was haunted by the prospect of the blank page before me staying blank, but the almost mystical unlocking process created by those simple words 'Write anything that comes into your head for six minutes' was, and indeed remains, baffling. Hard to believe, but that acts as the key to access parts of our thinking that most of us seldom use. It's almost impossible to convey to the uninitiated.

Brendan Boyle

Writing about Events, or Abstract Musing

Writing narratives can grapple with everyday issues, shedding light on feelings (for example, a sense of alienation). Writing an abstract and generalised (non-narrative) piece about mistakes in general offers less access to meaning and understanding (Bos et al., 2013). Memorable literature all concerns specific events and people, their thoughts and actions: never only abstract philosophising. Wordsworth's magical poem about daffodils carries a significant message; we understand and remember it because of the illuminatory story in the first stanza: the philosophy, or theory, is embedded. Sartre's philosophy ([1938] 1963), is part of the story, making the theory memorable and comprehensible.

> We got so much further than I could have thought in one short session. We slipped between theory and story in the discussions about the writing. Somehow the stories seemed to open up the theory and clarify it. (Brian)

> Writing about an incident clarifies thought. Instead of a rambling account that moves back and forth in time (which I'm particularly prone to), writing makes me create a sequential story. Various particulars, or gaps stand out as I try to present a story that makes sense. (Jane)

William Carlos Williams said 'no ideas but in things' (1951, p. 231). These 'things' are objects, people, events, experiences which carry or infer 'ideas' and feelings, rather than abstractions. We '*show don't tell*': readers learn from characters, place and actions, rather than from the authorial voice. Don't *tell* me she is pregnant: *show* me her ungainly movements, swelling belly, hand to her back as she stops to get breath. We learn much more from 'things' than abstractions.

Abstract writing, however, is excellent for reflecting upon a story. This next piece was wonderfully useful to a group because it related *directly* to the writer's previous story about a specific thing (event).

> So at the end of this I know where I started, and that is being a good creative confident practitioner is about love not fear. It's about looking at what we do and others do with honesty and loving criticism and not with a big stick. It's about learning from the good and bad bits even if it's painful sometimes. It's about the excitement and satisfaction of doing the job a bit better.
>
> Behind a lot of bad practice is fear. Fear of getting it wrong, fear of patients' strong feelings, fear of our own strong feelings, fear of the demons inside us, of change, of saying 'I don't know', of our own inadequacies, of being out of control.
>
> In making more and more rules perhaps we are in danger of making the fears more powerful. We build rules, threats, edicts into huge castle walls to keep fears at bay. What if we took the walls down stone by stone and invited the fears in?
>
> For within our castle walls are the good fairies, the kind caring fairies living alongside the fears. If we dismantle the walls and let the fears in they wouldn't go away because they are real, and many of them are necessary but they might mingle a bit better with the good fairies. The fears might spice us up a bit and the good fairies – care, compassion, love and laughter – would maybe be able to stretch their wings and fly about a bit better.
>
> What if, in taking down our castle walls, we started with a piece of paper and a pen?
>
> (Lindsay Buckell)

Lindsay said: 'When I wrote it, it didn't feel like an abstract piece at all, more an expression of my passionate hatred of the current climate of fear and blame.' Hatred, fear and blame are all abstract, but here they have a strong affective meaning for Lindsay and her readers because instead of writing about them generally, they are grounded in the incident which brought them out so forcefully:

> It is a summer's day and I am looking after Simon. He lies, poor young thing, deeply unconscious, the machinery puffs and blows, whirrs and chugs. I love this young man, not sexually or romantically but from somewhere in my middle. I am not accepting that he is as ill as he is, nor denying it. I do not believe in a miracle cure, I am simply not engaging with it. I am concerned, at this moment, with looking after him and his machines.
>
> The ward sister asks if I would like help to turn him. It is a question, not an order, acknowledging that today Simon is my patient and she is simply offering to help me. She says 'wouldn't he have hated this'. She is right – he is a diffident and intensely private young man. His mother died of the same disease. He has that depth in people whom personal tragedy has robbed of that illusion we all carry that life is essentially benign. He is quiet and shy, but laughs and chats with the other patients who are all much older.
>
> Now he lies, totally dependent, his body exposed to anybody. As we turn him she is very careful with the body which is on loan to us, because he can't protect his dignity himself at present. We talk to him, not across him. This young man is still a person with right to care and dignity, whether he knows or not.

> In that moment I learned the truth of empathy; I received permission to have empathy with my patients, to believe in their rights as individuals, to allow myself to love them as a professional, not as a friend. She didn't talk about it, she didn't analyse it, she simply modelled it and all I'd heard about not getting involved which had never made sense inside me fell away. I understood something profound about the nature of being truly involved in a professional relationship with my patients. (Lindsay Buckell)

Lindsay's critical incident is undeniably a story. But is it fiction? Any narrative is inevitably fiction, in that events are reconstructed or recreated from a perspective. Ward sister or patient would tell it differently. Lindsay may, furthermore, have embroidered certain bits, and downplayed others, to make her point persuasively, interestingly and confidentially.

A story can re-create with powerful re-presentations of interpersonal relationships. A writer can draw unconsciously on deep professional and personal experience to convey nuances of gesture, speech, intention, memory, thought and feeling. Rereading such an account therefore offers insight to writer and reader. Readers then share insights with the writer, thus expanding the knowledge gained.

A clash of codes is embedded in Lindsay's sentence: '*We talk to him, not across him*'. Aha, thinks non-nurse me, some nurses would treat this nearly inanimate body as an object. Lindsay responded to my guesses:

> The bit that was so unusual and liberating for me was 'wouldn't he have hated this?' I had met many nurses who would treat unconscious patients well, in not talking across them, and so on. What was so unusual was this indication of her deep understanding of him as an individual, therefore of empathy, rather than seeing him as 'patient' in the sense of the collective noun: i.e. part of the institution and all alike to be worked round as if they were all identikit, and those who wouldn't co-operate being labelled difficult or manipulative. (Lindsay Buckell)

A student palliative care nurse wrote in her reflective journal: 'patients must be seen as real people not just patients. Patients need to see nurses as people… not mere nurses doing their job' (Durgahee, 1997, p. 141). Stories can tell how we might or ought to act, think and feel, in a way abstract writing never could.

Perception and Questioning

Writing creates questions, leading writer and readers to answer them, and frame new questions:

> The truest respect which you can pay to the reader's understanding is to… leave him something to imagine, in his turn, as well as yourself. (Sterne, [1760] 1980, p. 77)

Writing allows multi-dimensional exploration. Observing and describing insightful details can be like an inner eye opening. Our actions and emotions are observed as well as others. Awareness of detail, inculcated by writing and discussing, increasingly slips into daily practice, making it more aware and reflective. Reflective writers I have trained are amazed at vital details previously missed. For example, when a Children's Services social worker reread his writing, he noticed he'd described the expression on a child's face. This led to further writing, attempting to understand what the child was perhaps trying to communicate silently, enabling him to act positively in support of the child. Non-verbal communication varies culturally, however: we can readily misinterpret if we are not culturally aware, or at least open to variation of meaning (Hook et al., 2011).

> This course helped me, encouraging me to be more aware of each day, and making me more observant. (Brimacombe, 1996, p. 15)

Novelist Lesley Glaister told me her ideas come from her eyes, ears and gut feelings, that she stares, eavesdrops, never stops wondering. Such awareness inevitably benefits practice. Non-reflective professionals, rather than fully perceiving their students, clients, colleagues and environment, are only aware of what they themselves think, just as Virginia Woolf depicted Orlando:

> He opened his eyes, which had been wide open all the time, but had seen only thoughts. (Woolf, [1928] 1992, p. 101)

Carefully observed, detailed descriptions are reflective (Farrell, 2013): 'we theorise every time we look at the world' (Goethe, 1998). Picasso (n.d.) said 'we must not discriminate between things. Where things are concerned there are no class distinctions'. Awareness of details can enable insight, pushing away assumptions and habitual perspectives and modes of understanding. 'God is in the details' (Verghese, 2001, p. 1013). A closely observed event, however small, written about, reflected upon, discussed critically and re-explored through further writings, can stand metonymically for the whole of that reflective writer's practice, just as we saw with Lindsay's event described above.

Careful observation and description can create dynamic re-looking, re-observing and re-understanding in the writing. We take much for granted: yet when we observe reflective acuteness, we find there is a great deal of significance we have never noticed. 'Important art... invites your attention to the previously over-looked and negligible, and shows that the unconsidered is deeply considerable' (Jonathan Miller, 2009, p. 12). As a reflective practitioner discovered: 'We don't truly listen, but spend most time waiting for the moment to say what we think' (Tarrant, 2013, p. 69).

The vital questions *Why* and *How* naturally follow from, for example, the precise recollection of a child's expression. Take Mark Purvis's simple, but acutely observed re-rendering of his little brother's death (Chapter 2, p. 39). A forgotten memory until the poem was written without forethought; the writing and the subsequent discussions enabled a wealth and depth of insight and learning. This is working 'with stories' rather than 'about them' (Frank, 1995, p. 23).

Stories are fragmentary texts offering narrow experiential slices. Associated writings deepen the learning for both writers and readers. Lindsay, in her abstract reflective passages above, worked out what she meant, developing her own understanding and enabling readers to relate it to their own experience.

Through-the-mirror writing provides safe-enough environments for facing troubling issues, helping reduce anxiety and stress, and giving insight. Practitioners regularly cry when they write, and even more when they read out; they are comforted, supported to see events from different and enlightening perspectives, helped to find solutions to problems.

All stories are perspectival; no story has only one meaning. They are essentially ambiguous and resist singular interpretation. Critically tussling with narrative at every level is challenging because it forces a questioning of taken-for-granteds, reassessment of previous certainties and assumptions, and recognition of contrasting (possibly opposing) points of view. This can lead to greater responsibility and authority over role, relationships with professional organisation, culture and society (professional and personal), feelings, beliefs and ethical values.

> Important knowledge about reality always comes out of [writing]... through a... transformation of reality by imagination and the use of words... When you succeed in creating something different out of... experience, you also achieve the possibility of communicating something that was not evident before... But you cannot plan this transmission of knowledge. (Llosa, 1991, p. 79)

Reading and Sharing Writing

Reflective writing, although illuminative on its own, is only part of the reflective and reflexive process. Generally written at the gallop, writers then take space to read and listen to it. Once they have read it privately, sharing as much as possible with trusted, confidential other(s) is the significant next stage (Wiener, 2012; Hunt, 2013). There is full interplay of story, teller and audience, or text, interpretation and intentionality, without alienation (Tyler, 1986). 'Individuals are generally more willing to write about emotionally charged events than they are to tell such stories de novo... Sharing occurs even though the stories, reflecting the hidden curriculum, may be disturbing, embarrassing, or even shameful' (Branch, 2005, p. 1064).

> Dialogue becomes the medium for critical reflection to be put into action, where experience is reflected on, assumptions and beliefs are questioned, and habits of mind are ultimately transformed... trustful communication, often at times highly personal and self-disclosing... Research has revealed that dialogue helps identify the learner's 'edge of meaning', a transitional [liminal] zone of knowing and meaning making. (Taylor, 2009, pp. 9–10)

[In] this liminal space we can come to terms with the limitations of our knowing and thus begin to stretch those limits. (Berger, 2004, p. 338)

Listeners and readers hear from their own perspective, qualitatively different from (sometimes even opposing) that of the writer/teller. They offer their own viewpoint. A writer may perceive certain meanings clearly, and formulate specific questions. Different readers perceive other meanings from their individual perspective, and pose different questions. Questions and theories arising from a single text may conflict: stories are essentially ambiguous. Many insights into a story's implicit meanings will be new to the writer and other listeners, and widen their view. A story by its very nature resists singular interpretation. 'Story captures nuance, indeterminacy and interconnectedness in ways that defy formalistic expression and expand the possibilities for interpretation and understanding' (Doyle and Carter, 2003, p. 130). Our perceptions are enmeshed within the frame of our social, political and psychological perspective: we cannot know ourselves and our experience independently. So reflective readers' responses are vital.

When readers understand differently from writers, it is not misunderstanding. Mehri read a story about a difficult encounter with a service-user, feeling the story reflected compassion and care. Rainer, however, unwittingly opened a critical discussion by commenting 'you felt pretty hostile to him!' Words are not bricks given to interlocutors, with inherent meanings. Bricks are for building physical structures. Words are for building meaning. Speakers and writers create not a solid wall but a permeable evanescent web which looks different in different lights, whose meaning depends on the angle at which it is viewed.

Discussing reflective writings in depth enables hitherto unperceived assumptions to be questioned, and issues of hegemony (Brookfield, 2009) tackled. Outcomes of reflection can be taken back into practice, improving and developing (Kolb, 1984). Reflection reaches the stage when 'words can do no more… / Nothing remains but the act' (Aeschylus, 1999, p. 115). This gives a 'different way of being', or as another course participant said: 'It seems like a new country, one which we've all been peering into for a long time.' This insight facilitates developmental change.

The students look so confused. They have voices and wonderful stories to share but they produce 'polite' stories that always show them in the most positive light. We have yet to establish trust; most are still reluctant to share. We try to make eye contact. They look away… shrinking in their seats, trying to not be the first to respond.

(Continued)

(Continued)

The silences feel like dense fog that makes reaching a destination difficult.

The passageway

Is spottily illuminated

Pot holes, black ice

Forks and roundabouts.

They seem to fear being 'wrong', being judged. They fear vocalizing that a session might not have gone well. How can we increase the holding environment that will enable growth? Have we trained them to focus on attention to details without reflection on the larger picture?

We have been experimenting with how to teach reflection to build the therapeutic voice and to reduce the students' tendency to provide safe stories to their instructors. We wonder what combination of trust, good instructions and time to experiment with the reflection process is needed to learn to reflect.

Through the passageway

We had a breakthrough! Last week we asked them to read aloud to the group and then try to name or describe the issue without referring to themselves or the client/patient. What was it that didn't work in the relationship? What was the issue that needed to be resolved or addressed, if possible? What are the larger themes that can be addressed?

We forget each semester how important it is for them to read aloud and hear their own voices. This is such a powerful experience, risking the 'self' by sharing a story which did not have the desired outcome. We underestimate the courage required to read and discuss reflections. One student stated 'This is very personal and I can write it for myself, but reading this to others is difficult.' That was a turning point.

Faces were more animated, and there was a sense of relief from recognizing that others experience what we experience, and that our peers can provide mutual aid. They began to realize that their voices have value and that the themes were universal to clinical practice.

Meryl Marger Picard, Ruth Segal

Readers and discussants suggest incidents can be rewritten with the fresh insight, or from another point of view. And perhaps a colleague, also present at the encounter with the patient, might write an account. Listeners' roles are as important as writers', 'the joint effort of author and reader' (Sartre, [1948] 1950, pp. 29). And:

> so there is an art of listening… to every narration the listener makes a decisive contri-
> bution… The individual listener also shares responsibility for that… narration: you
> realise this when you tell something over the telephone,… you miss the visible reac-
> tions of the listener. (Levi, 1988, p. 35)

Reflective writers write for *embodied* readers, real people: peer group, supervisor or mentor. My practitioner students say how *re-storying* with colleagues is as essential as initial writing. Sharing reflective writings with patients deepens and clarifies understanding (Charon, 2006); some responded by writing also.

> Reading it is the final act of legitimacy. (Becky)

A colleague reported by email she had been badly treated, but failed to elicit my support because she communicated her self-centred world-view, and lack of professional team spirit. A piece of writing is the joint responsibility of writer and reader; writers cannot determine what readers might infer from their writing. Readers usually do not know, and generally do not need to know, exactly what a writer intended; they develop their own understanding. Another reader might have inferred differently from her email.

Writing can also be shared effectively online using Web 2.0 tools such as e-port-folio and blogging. This needs very experienced, careful facilitation (see Chapters 3 and 9).

Silence

Understandings and clarities do not necessarily emerge through argument or dis-course. Silence is powerful in any group, particularly an interactive confidential group discussing deeply held principles and vital experiences (see Rowland, 1993, pp. 87–107). Tutors who are fearful of it miss an invaluable resource. There are dif-ferent sorts of silence: reflective, anxious, embarrassed, puzzled, thoughtful, angry, or portentous. Silence feels supportive and reflexive if participants are responsible for their group, with authority over their own contribution; if not, silence can feel confronting and aggressive.

Handled wisely and carefully, silence facilitates deep reflection. If no-one has anything to say, then no-one need speak. A silence might be used, for example, to allow previous words to sink in, and an appropriate ensuing response sought.

When a participant has read their writing, a positive silence might well ensue, allowing listeners to marshal thoughts and feelings. A new anxious group needs support to say something positive quickly, having heard a piece, as new writers feel exposed on reading their work. I never break silence when someone has read their writing; the discussion belongs to the group. If I, as facilitator, break the silence, undue weight is placed on my words, and the group loses authority.

More can be said by silence than words: 'a long heavy silence promises danger, just as much as a lot of empty outcries' (Sophocles, 1982, l. 1382), and 'Long ago we learned to keep our mouths shut/Where silence is good health, speech can be fatal' (Aeschylus, 1999, p. 29).

> Silence is but a feeling silence. Someone has just finished reading their contribution – perhaps a difficult encounter with a patient or a partner or even memories of training and hospital days which still have the power to hurt. The group has lived through that moment with the speaker, shared the emotions, and for a few minutes there is nothing to say. We are amazed at the power of each other's writing. Certainly when we come down to discuss, with Gillie's help, there are ways that the writing could be made more telling, but the inspiration comes from the group. It is not afraid to face the feelings aroused daily in medical practice and is learning in the safety of the group to translate them into words. (Naomi)

Reflective Writing and Artistry

Donald Schön said we practise with artistry (see Chapter 1, pp. 4–7). Art has always questioned boundaries of existence. Artists, ethnographers and philosophers put themselves in situations in which conventional orderliness of everyday systems of thinking is suspended. Artists cross dangerous mental and social boundaries/barriers to create images that jolt or shock audiences into reassessment. Bertold Brecht, for example, set viewers questioning taken-for-granted structures.

The belief that only writers can write, that art is born not made, is erroneous. Poets do not lie around (either luxuriously or starving in garrets) waiting for the muse. Writing is 1 per cent inspiration and 99 per cent perspiration: 'I rewrote the ending of *Farewell to Arms* thirty-nine times before I was satisfied' (Ernest Hemingway, quoted in Exley, 1991, p. 13).

Reflective writing is ours to write just how we want and need to write (see Eagleton, 1983). Quiet, powerful internal voices clamour to be heard. Expressive and explorative writing develops confidence, co-operation and collaboration, enables challenging of assumptions about diversity, taken-for-granted unequal or unjust professional structures, encourages skills sharing, the development of team-building, and enhances ability to deal with conflict in an artistic, aesthetic process.

Writing: an Ancient Power

Writing is first known in the Near East in 3300 BC. A hieratic papyrus from Thebes from about 1850 BC, the teaching of Ptahhotep, says: 'It is good to speak to the future the future will listen.' And we can listen to what was written all those years ago. Writing belonged to the gods, because of this power to enshrine text. Thoth, the Egyptian god of writing, 'knows the mysteries and sets the gods' utterances firm… proclaims all that is forgotten'. Egyptian hieroglyphs were called 'gods' words', and were considered to have numinous power as amulets. Stelae were inscribed with magical texts for water to be poured over and drunk to ingest the magic of the texts. 'Damnatio memoriae' was attacking a dead enemy by damaging or erasing their written name: destroying a written name was to deprive its owner of identity and existence.

Reflective and reflexive writers gain power over their practice by naming it in writing. 'Theorising is a practice of writing. One writes about the meanings in practice and through writing creates the meanings of practice. Practice is itself always changing hence there are always new meanings to be written about. At the same time, through writing, the meaning of practice is re-created, always cast anew' (Usher, 1993, p. 100). 'Writing taps tacit knowledge; it brings into awareness that which we sensed but could not explain' (Holly, 1989, p. 78).

> I even enjoy the physical holding of the pen, the shaping of the words, and I like the way it unfolds before you, like thought unravelling. The rest of the book is blank; I wonder what the next chapter will be? (Jenny)

We have explored why writing is the reflective process itself. Now we turn to how to do it.

 Read to Learn

Elbow, P. (2012) *Vernacular Eloquence: What Speech can Bring to Writing*. New York: Oxford University Press.
Peter Elbow has been researching and writing persuasively about the magical value of personal writing for many years. Parts 1 and 2 are recommended.

Hunt, C. (2013) *Transformative Learning through Creative Life Writing*. Abingdon: Routledge.
Celia Hunt is a good, well articulated and reasoned guide to personal and professional writing for reflective practice and reflexivity.

Purcell, D. (2013) Sociology teaching and reflective practice: using writing to improve, *Teaching Sociology*, **41**(1), 5–19.
David Purcell uses an autoethnographic method for reflecting upon his teaching practice. He explains how he focuses through Brookfield's *critical lenses*.

Write to learn

For *How To* do this writing, please see *Write to Learn,* Chapter 1 (Chapter 8 for fuller advice). Do a *six-minute-write* about anything to limber up, before starting on the exercises below. Writings can be shared fruitfully afterwards with a group or confidential trusted other, if this seems appropriate once the writer has read and reflected on it first.

7.1 Truths, lies and fantasies

1. Write one truth about yourself, one wish, and one outright lie.
2. Read back to yourself, adding or altering positively.
3. Write in more depth about one or more.

7.2 What makes me tick?

1. List 20 (50 or 100, depending on time: repetition is allowed and usefully shows you which items are vital) words or phrases which make you:

    (i)   focused and productive, or
    (ii) furious, or
    (iii) happy, or
    (iv) serene, or
    (v)   lazy and unproductive, or
    (vi) uncooperative
    (vii) and so on.

2. Reread and order with the most important at the top.
3. Choose one to write about further.

7.3 Another point of view

1. Think of someone you really admire; you need not know them personally.
2. Describe them briefly.
3. Imagine they come and observe you at work: write their observations about your work.
4. List questions they might ask you about your work.
5. List questions you would like to ask them.
6. Write their replies to your questions.

7.4 Mentoring from a helpful observer

1. Think of a puzzling or unsatisfactory work event.
2. Choose an object generally in view in your consulting room/office/class-room/other, such as:

   (i) your work coffee mug
   (ii) work chair
   (iii) work mirror
   (iv) or similar...

3. Write a narrative from its perspective (the mug/mirror will be 'I') about the event.
4. Reread this to yourself.
5. Now write about the same event from *your* perspective, bearing in mind your object's observations.
6. Reread all your writing with attention; what has this told you about the event?

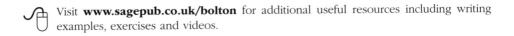 Visit **www.sagepub.co.uk/bolton** for additional useful resources including writing examples, exercises and videos.

CHAPTER 8

REFLECTIVE AND REFLEXIVE WRITING: HOW

This chapter is a practical guide to writing. The how of beginning to write, and how to develop it is given in five stages, as well as what reflective and reflexive writing is and can be, for whom, why, and where and when. What *writer's block* is, and how to approach it, is also examined.

The captain unlocked his word hoard. (*Beowulf and Grendel*, 1973, p. 12)

I learned the science of letters... and this opened before me a wide field for wonder and delight. (Shelley, [1820] 1994, p. 119)

[Writing] is a bit like looking at the world through a kaleidoscope. You can look at the same scene but find it different every time you turn the viewer. (Diski, 2005, p. 31)

Introduction to Writing *First Draft* Reflections

Trust the Writing Hand

Writing is an expressive and explorative method to be wondered at and delighted in itself, much more than a mere reporting instrument. The *content* is the only important element: not grammar form or any other rules. Writers are their own first reader; no one else will read it without their permission. No teacher, editor or examiner will draw blood with red correcting pens on this draft because they'll never see it. This allows for almost anything to be written uncensored: redrafting or editing can be done before anyone else sees it. Every piece of writing is right because it is an exploration of the writers' own work, knowledge, memories etc.: in fact right or wrong are not appropriate here.

Staying with this intuitive method will create reflective and reflexive material. If it is skipped, redrafting and editing focused upon too early, or awareness of a reader allowed, then writing is likely to be unreflective, and certainly unreflexive.

This draft, the heart of reflection and reflexivity, is written primarily for the self. The process matters, not the product. Exploratory and expressive, it is initially only intended to communicate to the writer, and possibly a few trusted confidential others, once it has been read by the writer. Undertaken often at speed, it is a dynamic, initially private process of discovery. Speed leaves no gaps for destructive internal critics to leap in, interrupting flow and destroying confidence. The pen/keyboard follows the writer's mind in any direction, and might put anything on the paper: insightful, illuminating, funny, mad, bad or even dangerous, occasionally dull, sometimes entirely irrelevant to reflective practice. This process can enable burdens to be put down, lightening the writer. Sometimes it comes like a flash of lightning out of nowhere. And it can be enlightening.

Suspend Your Disbelief

> Might we not say that every child at play behaves like a creative writer, in that he creates a world of his own, or, rather rearranges the things of his world in a new way which pleases him? (Freud, 1995, p. 54)

Freud reckoned the grown-up version of playing is fantasising. We gain a great deal from reading published fantasies. How much more powerful to write our own, however big or small?

The sound of pencils on paper, a page

Torn roughly from a notebook, or

Scrunched and discarded

Someone is frowning,

Another, smiling…

Everyone concentrating.

Time's up. (But this isn't an exam and doesn't feel like one)

There's a growing excitement – like that moment when someone is about to

open the present you've given them…

My gift to them, theirs to me – words on paper.

We're sharing very private thoughts…

Thoughtful silence and lots of laughter too.

It's a kind of communion. (Becky)

How to Start: the Five Stages

Stage 1: The Six-minute Write

Your writing is a gift to yourself. Choose a comfortable, uninterrupted place and time, and writing materials you like. Make sure you have everything else you need, for instance coffee and biscuits.

> Take time to calm down, sit back, change gear. Nice to just let things come out and sit on paper for a while. Not quite sure what track I'm on at the moment but don't worry something will come along in a bit. Good technique this. Doesn't matter. No one's going to read this later on – so don't worry about it – so can write anything. (Adam, medical student)

> I write without thinking much, trying to overcome all kinds of self-criticism, without stopping, without giving any consideration to the style or structure… only putting down on paper everything that can be used as raw material. (Llosa, 1991, p. 45)

Begin, like Llosa, by allowing the pen to write:

Six Minutes' Writing

1. Write whatever is in your head, uncensored.
2. **Write without stopping** for at least six minutes.
3. **Don't stop to think or be critical**, even if it seems rubbish.
4. Allow it to flow with no thought for spelling, grammar, proper form.
5. Give yourself permission to **write anything**. You need not reread it.
6. Whatever you write is **right**: it is yours, and no-one else need read it.

Lots might be written, or little. It might be lists, poetry, gobbledegook, spirited logical argument: anything at all. *Six minutes' writing* sometimes turns up gold, sometimes dross. It is always useful, however, for beginning to make marks on the page or screen: a difficult stage for any writer. It can help prevent 'What am I going to write?' by dumping mind-clutter onto the paper. Some will be useful – even *diamonds in the dustheap* (Woolf, 1979, p. 223) springing from seemingly nowhere, some only shopping lists or scurrilous moans. Stowed safely on paper, the mind is freed to continue. Awareness of anything other than the writing can inhibit the flow, so allow the writing to follow its own track and leave writing rules (grammar, logical sequencing, etc.) until later.

I'm clearing out the rubbish

I'm emptying my mind,

The trouble with this task is that

I don't know what I'll find.

I came because I want to write,

I wanted to move on,

And if I keep on writing,

Maybe I can move the stone.

Perhaps what lies beneath is ore,

Of course it may be dross,

But let the chance go just once more,

And all there'll be is loss. (Janet Tipper)

Six minutes

Here I am

Now.

A life, that is mine, I want

To be known – my heart it is

beating through gates that

are open. (John McAuley)

I always do my 6 minutes – complete and utter garbage – shopping list, weird exclama-
tions and verbal tics. I also have another current slowly going along in my mind –
deciding what to write about. Then I sit at the end of the six minutes and think, oh
THAT is what I am supposed to do. Sometimes I don't want to do it and I try to do
something different but it is the thing that has appeared in the six minutes that is very
insistent and demands to be written. (Helen Drucquer, 2004, pp. 203–4)

Stage 2: The Incident, Narrative, Story

**Forget about grammar, syntax, spelling – for now. They block the inspira-
tional flow. Correct them later.**

Six minutes' writing has given a generous sense of permission to write anything,
respect for whatever is written, and a realisation that words can satisfyingly appear
as if from nowhere. It's good to stay with the flow without rereading yet. Writing
immediately following *six minutes* is likely to be significant.

Write straight away about any time in your experience, telling the story simply and
allowing it to come in its own order. Focus on a particular occasion, chosen seemingly at
random. Try to write about the first event which comes to mind. The most vital thing to
write about might seem to be the most mundane. Alternatively a writing theme may have
arisen in *six minutes*. No one else need read this: what matters is capturing what is there.

Write in the same way as *six minutes*, allowing words to arrive on the page without planning or questioning.

Write with a focus: the story of an experience. Try not to block with questions like *Why this: it's not nearly important enough?!* Everything is important: try to ignore the niggling demon.

Choose the first event which comes to mind. The more anxiously the *right* account is sought, the more the really right one, the one thought of first, will slip away.

Allow yourself to write for as long as it needs, 20 to 40 minutes perhaps.

Thinking wastes time. Let the writing hand do the thinking.

Re-create the situation as memory gives it, with as many details as possible, rather than *what you would rather have happened*, or worrying about *getting the facts right.*

Consider it fiction. This can relieve embarrassment, confidentiality anxiety, fear of getting it wrong. It means it doesn't matter if you are uncertain your memory is right.

Spelling, grammar, syntax usually flow naturally in such vitally charged writing. If infelicities, repetitions or unclarities occur, they are correctable later.

Proper form does not matter. Life doesn't have proper beginnings, middles and ends; write this with the same glorious muddle of life. Let your pen muse on the event (e.g. what you should/should not have said), if it wants. The writing can be tidied up later, before anyone else has to make sense of it, or embarrassingly read innermost feelings. You will probably find it naturally gains a very appropriate pleasing form.

Allow the fingers to notice details: tone of voice, clothing, spoken words, seeming incidentals, and feelings. As the experience is replayed, vital details begin to emerge, even if you thought you hadn't remembered them. Write them ALL down.

Allow reactions, emotional responses, feelings.

Being judgemental about writing, or the event, will tend to block reflective thinking.

Types of writing, and topics for stage 2

Autobiographical narratives, fictional plotted stories, poetry, songs, drama, image exploration (Chapters 4, 5, 6); descriptive passages are all appropriate. Here are some themes generated by my groups:

changes
a conflict
in control
taking care
a dilemma
a celebration
a moment of joy
a sensitive subject
a time I took a risk
a clash of interests
a conflict of loyalty
a misunderstanding
a frustrated episode
a missed opportunity
a parting or beginning
a case for compassion
an evocative occasion
an extremity of emotion
the most dangerous time
a breach of confidentiality
a time when I was incapacitated
a time I felt powerful or powerless
the blowing of the pressure valve
a time my values were challenged
a time that inspired/surprised/shocked/upset me

Give the story your own title. Make it positive, so if the incident was problematic, try renaming it with a title more empowering to you (Fook, 2012).

Bev's story

Sister liked to control her flock of nurses, and also her flock of rams: her doctors. We were all in fear and awe of her; she had favourites and could be extremely sarcastic. The young mother was unmarried, scared to death, in labour for the first time, and in isolation because she was socially unacceptable.

(Continued)

(Continued)

Sister ordered an enema: 'high, hot and a hell of a lot'. We all stood on the periphery, observing what this youngster was subjected to. Sister's delivery was clinically correct and cold, cold, cold as ice, with no family support.

I don't know what trauma was taken away by this young girl. It had a profound impact on me about power, dominance, control, exclusion and the withholding of warmth to anyone in distress.

From another source years later I learnt that Sister had had a breakdown of some description. Part of me thinks this was divine retribution and another part reflects on what we do to ourselves as human beings when we become so rigid, fixed and inflexible.

Bev Hargreaves

Stage 3: Read and Respond

Trust the process; have faith in yourself.

Rereading writing to yourself is significant. This writing is created *in camera*, without us really being aware of the content. Reading is then like a dialogue with the self, hearing what the hand had to say, and being able to respond back to it. Reflexive interpretive thoughts might be written in response. Rereading privately, slowly and respectfully, with responses noted, gives insight.

When the first *dash* is written, reread everything (including *six minutes*) slowly, attentively, and appreciatively, adding or altering if you wish, but being only positive about your writing.

(a) Read with **attention yet openly, non-judgementally**, looking at content rather than form.
(b) Attend with an **openness to divergent connections** previously perceived as separate, or inappropriate together, especially links between *six minutes* and later writing.
(c) Be aware of **underlying links**, fresh understanding and awareness.
(d) **Write additions** and alterations, making deletions only if you must.
(e) Fill out with **as much detail as possible**, remembering we have **five senses**; smells and sounds can give vital clues, as can time of year, discomforts, intuitions, what people said, and the tone of voice they said it in.

Everything is significant.
Ask some of these questions, responding to them in writing:
  WHY do you think you chose this incident?
  What is **significant** about it for **you**?
  How does this account relate to **theory**?
  Did your actions fit your **theory** or **values**?
  Who or what holds **power**? Is this any different from what you assumed?
  Could **different interpretations** be made, from yours?
  Is it **puzzling**? Try to work out what and why.
  Is it **surprising**? Or different from what you expected?
  What did you **feel** at different points?
  Why do you think you **felt** this way?
  Are **contrasts** within the story significant?
  Does **officialese** or **jargon** conceal anything?
  What is **missed out**, whose **perspective** for example?
  Are there **assumptions or taken-for-granteds**? Look and reflect hard!
  At every opportunity ask: **WHY?**
  Try not to come to a final answer (closure) yet.

A participant in a multicultural course for social workers, run by Olwen Summer-scales (2006), commented on redrafting:

> firstly, a summary of the incident... then I redrafted it as a [fairy] story. Noticing how much more emotion came into it, I redrafted it again – this was really powerful, much more reflective. I could see I'd moved on.

Edward De Bono (2000) suggested we all think from six perspectives, which he related to colours:

- Neutral and factual: White
- Optimistic, positive, offers praise: Yellow
- Feeling/emotional, opinionated, intuitive: Red
- Cautious, offering critical judgements: Black
- Alternative, speculative, creative: Green
- Summarising, overviewing, acting as control: Blue.

Write an account of an event. Rewrite it up to six times, choosing a hat colour to give a different perspective. Always finish with blue, which will offer reflections on the previous five. Here is an example of Stage 3 writing:

A look from the past that communicates with nurses today

Mary was about 60 and had had a cerebrovascular accident. I was 19, in my second year of nurse training (1979), and 'in charge' one night, assisted by two nursing auxiliaries; senior staff supported from a distance. Mary had been incontinent of urine. I was angry and abrupt. I left Mary in a chair in the toilet while I changed the sheets. Mary sensed my frustration. I very clearly remember her looking into my eyes. She was anxious and I knew it. I do not remember reassuring her or offering any kind words of comfort.

I have never forgotten her look or my conduct that morning. It haunts me still. It is why I embrace critical reflection.

I was responsible for what happened that morning; reflecting on it has helped. I was exhausted, inexperienced and unprepared; I felt alone. These are not excuses, rather explanations. Mary's legacy has helped me be a better nurse. Perhaps she was hoping for that when she looked at me. I share this incident with students.

In my teaching, I discuss our experiences, question our actions, personal values and beliefs, and help us all develop new ways of being. Perhaps it is who we are that determines whether we are reflective educators or not. Perhaps it is the interactions we have had with others that shape us as educators. The 'betweenness' I referred to: in nurse education it must also include those in our care, such as Mary.

Caroline Ridley

Caroline has sought the positive in this account, found how it could empower her now in her job. You can do this similarly by adding some paragraphs which examine the words and therefore attitudes in the piece:

- Examine 'what was the **effect** of this (on me and others)?', in place of 'I **caused** this'.
- Try 'what **responsibility** can I take for this now?', instead of 'who was to **blame**?'.
- Focus on **care**, in place of feeling/remembering **guilt.**
- Rephrase as **active** (I *did*) rather than the powerless **passive** (this was done *to me*).
- Seek **success** in the account, rather than **failure.**
- And the **positive** in place of **negative.** (adapted from Fook, 2012, p. 158)

Stage 4: Sharing Writing with a Peer(s)

Your writing has the power to influence another, and they you.

Peers' responses can open up fresh avenues. They can support towards deeper levels of reflection, and perceive wider institutional, national, social and political contexts.

Reflecting on a critical incident is still within the confines of one's own perspective. Reflecting with another person, with the written incident before you, can bring added insights. (Jane)

Our discussion may focus on the thoughts, feelings and experiences which led to the piece, on the way it was crafted, or both. The trust we have developed means we may quickly move from empathising deeply with a writer's grief at the death of a loved one to suggesting their piece would be more powerful without the last sentence. (Maggie, Sheena, Clare, Mark, Becky)

Choose a colleague or fellow student with whom to share writing.

Be positive and supportive; negative opinions are more readily received when preceded by positive.

Comment on *writing*, not *writer*: considering writings as fiction can reduce hurt or loss of confidentiality.

Consider everything read and discussed as confidential.

Create your own ground rules.

Encourage others to ask WHY? as often as possible.

Your writing is as wonderful as everyone else's: apologetic competitions are unfruitful.

Enjoy deepening the reflective process, whether verbally or in writing.

Seeking just the right person or people to share your writing with can be worthwhile. E-contact can be a good substitute (see Chapter 3, p. 61). A colleague might be right, but they or a life-partner *might* be *wrong*: emotionally charged relationships may add non-useful complexities without offering different enough perspectives.

Boundaries and ground rules are significant. Finding just the right people (critical friends/trusted reader) to share this deep and emotionally involving journey with, is worth working on. We must trust and respect them, and feel they'll hold confidentiality; but often we can't know people well enough before we start out with them. If nurtured, however, the essential trust and respect does tend to develop. Students should be in the lucky position of having their choice of group or partner facilitated by a tutor, but they still need to form their group or partnership with care.

Sharing writing can take courage; the prospect can inhibit honest writing. The solution lies in groups (or pairs) creating their own ground rules in a safe-enough space with firm boundaries (see also Chapters 1, 2, 8, 11). Issues can be raised tentatively or hesitatingly, aired supportively, and then appropriately shared more widely. Many ingredients create appropriate boundaries to engender confidence and relative safety:

- responding to and critiquing the *writing*, not the *writer*
- taking each other as they experience them within the closed culture of the group

- relating to and supporting each other through discussions of the writing without seeking to question beyond the boundaries of that writing, and the group.

These help participants write about and share important issues. Participants do not relate to each other as *doctor* or *co-student*, but Saleet or Sai. They do not expose *themselves*, but their writing. They will have had time to write, reread and think about sharing their writing beforehand.

Remember the particular nature of the narrated 'I' (Chapter 5, p. 85). **It is not the writer who bares their soul but the narrator.** Discussions will then focus on what was written for the group to share, rather than on the whole personal hinterland of the writer. This can help protect the writer.

Writings are considered as fiction. There is no '*really*': characters do not walk beyond the page and do anything. A question will sometimes stray, but often accompanied by such as: 'I'm going to ask you this; please don't answer if you don't want to, but I think it might help.' A group respects a 'no', just as a decision not to read a piece because it feels too personal is respected. Trust, and a sense of safety, is fostered by *confidentiality*. Belonging to such a group, hearing important reflective material, is a privilege. The writings belong to the writers, and the discussions to the group; neither should be shared outside the group without express permission. I remember one group even requesting nothing be shared with life-partners.

- A sense of group *boundaries* helps create confidence. The group needs to set these at their first meeting. Many professional groups choose to focus solely upon work issues, for example.

Respect and mutual trust are facilitative. An attitude of 'unconditional positive regard' (Rogers, 1969) can be modelled by the facilitator (if there is one). A disagreement can be undertaken in a spirit of mutual respect. Discussions will be constructive and friendly if comments are either generally positive, or if negative elements are expressed gently, along with definite appropriate constructive suggestions.

> Sometimes reading my work feels exciting; sometimes gratifying; sometimes heart-breaking; sometimes even faintly dangerous. (Becky)

> Reading a piece aloud is like writing a song and singing it – it's not just your creation, it's your interpretation, it's putting your own voice out there. (Sheena)

> Reading in the group can give the writer the courage to examine painful events in a truthful way. The group holds the writer's hand through a raw and painful life event. (Mark)

> I've learned that reflective writing about a difficult event when I am a novice leaves me much more vulnerable than when I write about difficulties in something I am expert at. (Maureen Rappaport)

Bev reread her story (p. 139, above), and was comforted by her group that there was nothing she could have done to help the girl. The group encouraged her to write fictionally from Sister's perspective. Here is a fragment:

> The young girl (17 years?) was arrogant and demanding – I thought I'd soon knock the stuffing out of her, lick her into shape. She should not be with the married mothers so I decided I would look after her. I'm here to keep control – control of everything, I'm not here to be liked.
>
> Bev Hargreaves

Bev's group agreed this is not successfully enlightening fiction, and made further suggestions.

Stage 5: Developing Writing

You can't write the wrong thing. Whatever you write will be right: for you.

Writing developmental pieces can deepen and widen understanding. The writer explores: *what would it be like if…*; being the *other*; different endings; or altering other essential aspects. Here are some suggestions for a new piece developing the themes of your Stage 2 writing. A group or peer-mentoring pair will develop their own, appropriate to their own writing:

> **Give the story a title.**
> **Write about the same event** from the viewpoint of client or colleague: this person will become 'I'.
> **Try writing from a different, or opposing point of view**: observer, friend or foe.
> **Write from the perspective** of **omniscient narrator:** all characters become 'he', 'she', including you.
> **Try rewriting the story in the past**, if you wrote the initial story in the present (or in the present if you wrote it in the past).
> **Rewrite the story** with the gender of the main character(s) switched.
> **Write the next chapter.**
> **Write the previous chapter** (the backstory perhaps).
> **Write a commentary** on your own or another's text, either as yourself or as one of the characters.
>
> *(Continued)*

(Continued)

Retell the story with a different ending or focus, the ideal outcome perhaps.

Write what a character is thinking at any one moment.

Write about a (some) missing character(s). Like a photograph, a story is always an unreal and slim slice of reality: think beyond the frame.

Rewrite the story in a different style/genre: newspaper article/fable/ narrative poem/children's story/romance/detective/sci-fi/fantasy/fairy story (see Chapter 5).

Write *thought bubbles* for vital (or puzzling) characters at significant points in the narrative.

Rewrite the story with the locus of control/power altered.

You are a reporter: interview a character from the story.

Take a character who's just left the action; describe what they might be doing/thinking.

Write a letter to a character, expressing puzzlement/anger/sympathy. Write their reply.

Write a letter or transcribe a telephone conversation between two characters.

List the objects/colours in the story. Are they significant?

List assumptions held by any of the characters in the story.

What themes or patterns relate to other experiences in your life?

What is missed out of this story (perhaps the painful or emotional bits)?

Write a film/dust-jacket blurb for the story.

Continue the story six months/a year later.

Consider asking someone from the *real* situation to write their own version; or interview them.

Explore the area which puzzles you.

Ask what if? Invent your own!

Ask why?

These techniques make a channel in the sand with a stick,

Water comes right up from underneath immediately,

Sometimes faster than others.

Like discovery rather than creation.

Clare

Writing a further piece can feel difficult, especially if the first has been done in a group, and the second at home/work. Some find it easier to write in their own time and space; others find it awkward or cannot maintain the momentum. Two students once wrote great pieces during a session, received interesting suggestions for development, but merely typed out their original pieces with a few amendments. They came from a culture, I think, where imaginative flair was not expected of students, and could not maintain it in their own time and space without group encouragement.

Reread the new pieces, and the original one. Here are some elements to look for, reflect upon, and write further about:

- Social, organisational or personal context and background of the incident
- Main themes or patterns
- Ways or methods of communication
- Labels (of people or groups)
- Binary opposites (white/black; nurse/doctor; member-of-the-public/police)
- People or organisations not in the account, but affected by the situation
- Individual or organisation perspective which is missing, distorted or devalued
- Interpretations or explanations made, by whom, and their influence
- Different interpretations or explanations which could be made now
- Any assumptions or taken-for-granteds (e.g. about treatment or pedagogy)
- What are the power relations in the story? (developed from Fook, 2012, p. 107)

Bev's final story

Once there was a bubbly, friendly 5-year-old called Mary Ellen Rose. Joe became my sweetheart and lifetime partner. Nursing was hard work in those years, but I always wanted to care for anyone who was sick.

And then the war came and Joe marched off with the rest. I haven't let myself dwell on our last time. I hurt more and more after the news came, a bone-deep coldness that I couldn't shake off – the same coldness I felt when I had the miscarriage which was never spoken of. Life had to go on; I never again met anyone to be close to, and buried myself in my work.

Bev Hargreaves

This fragment shows how past events influence present action, in sometimes puzzling and damaging ways. Insight like Bev's can ease relations in the present, and support developmental change.

Developing the Five Stages

These five stages are described and exemplified in an ideal order. They might be undertaken in many different ways and orders. And having experienced all five, reflective writers develop their own adaptations of the stages. There is no set way of doing it. There are also many more ways writing can be used. Here are four examples.

Lists

Sally Jane Shaw needed to decide whether to change from practitioner to lecturer. She made a list of things which prevented her, ranging from *Is it really what I want to do?* and *Would I be jumping out of the frying pan into the fire?* to *Would I miss my patients?* and *Don't want to travel.* Under each heading she wrote arguments for and against. As she wrote, more and more insights occurred to her. She realised there were other role change options other than the two she had felt stuck between, such as remaining a practitioner while developing her additional role of educator. Having thoroughly examined pros and cons, her confidence in her role and ability was reinforced.

Unsent Letters

Sally Jane also wrote to help cope with anger and frustration with a colleague ('Tom') not pulling his weight. She wrote a pair of letters, to and from Tom (with no intention of sending them). Here is how she expressed feeling afterwards:

> Reading the reply from Tom has made me cry. I don't know why. I'm crying writing this. I'm overcome with how Tom feels and I think I can identify with how he feels having to keep things locked inside and not lying but not being honest.
>
> I feel like I have opened a wound on Tom.
>
> I feel like I have been cruel not in my letter to him but the thoughts I have had and also some of the discussions I have had with the other team members. I know what we have discussed is right but should we say it to Tom.
>
> I did not cry when I was writing the reply but when I read it back to myself, from the point where, in my fictional letter, Tom says 'I just need you there for a little longer, Sal'. (Sally Jane Shaw)

Sally was able to build a supportive yet developmental relationship with Tom, with him accepting her appropriately pushing him, yet not leaning on her. Experiencing feelings fully, crying even, on reading back often happens. Writing can seem to place experiences outside the writer, so rereading seems like hearing an outside communication. Dialogue can create reflexive distance (Crème, 2008), easing embattled work relationships by paradoxically bringing the *other* closer, more accessible.

Such writing, whether unsendable fictional letters, or writing as if a playscript, can help towards insight and empathy. Examples are 'Oh I see! He wasn't trying to put me down, but was upset', 'She's not pulling her weight because she doesn't know what she should be doing, and I can help' and 'She seems bossy but like my sister this is her way of coping with lack of confidence'.

Dialogue to Develop Aspects of Ourselves

Writing can enable proper listening to ourselves. Our rushed world tends to cut us off from wider aspects of ourselves. Once different sides are heard, they can be worked with harmoniously, leading to enhanced integrity (with the parts of the self integrated). Thinking of us as containing different voices can be helpful. For example, people say 'I was in two minds about it', 'I don't know what got into me', 'I didn't know I had it in me', 'I was able to cope because it was as if it happened to someone else', 'As soon as the music starts my sober self disappears and I party like mad', 'When the time came I just couldn't do it, though I knew beforehand I could', 'I heard myself being really judgemental just like my mother', 'There's this voice tells me all the time I'm rubbish' and 'The knowledge of just what to say came out of the blue'.

Writing can enable contact with these hitherto enigmatic selves, to understand their role in my single-seeming self. It can enable us to draw consciously upon the strong elements of ourselves, and find strategies for dealing with the inhibiting and negative.

Internal Mentor

We all have an internal mentor, the wise self who gives helpful guidance and support. Writing from the point of view of the 'internal mentor' can be powerfully reflexive, tapping into our own trustworthy wisdom, too often ignored, or even worse undetected. 'One piece of self-advice is worth a hundred tips from someone else' (Tarrant, 2013, p. 84). Others take this further, saying that we only really listen to our own advice (Roffey-Barentsen and Malthouse 2013, p. 23). Russell's mentor is his journal:

I value reflection 'sorting my head out' enormously. Although it has taken almost six years to become part of me, it has transformed my research and work role. I thoroughly enjoy writing longhand, and this freedom to let my reflection take me where it will, as unfettered as possible (Etherington, 2004).

(Continued)

(Continued)

I see a pattern I would not otherwise have spotted. The occasions when I feel I am being a lump (avoiding the world and not researching at all) almost always result in a journal entry that captures 'eureka' moments, sudden break-throughs in my analytical work.

Freely writing told me the link between down days of sloth and subsequent productivity. Instead of berating myself, I can sift through and harness what has been happening, to influence future actions. Now I cannot think of any other way to discover and utilise those times when my brain is working busily away, beyond immediate notice, than reflective writing. I have learnt to embrace the brief periods of inactivity, keeping my journal close by to capture anything that comes to mind. I feel more confident that something fruitful can emerge from periods of seeming little productivity, that these are not self-sabotage.

Russell Delderfield

Linda Garbutt: Finding the internal supervisor

Linda has taken the value of a wise inner self a stage further. As a practising therapist and supervisor of other therapists, she researched a theory of the *internal supervisor*.

The internal supervisor can meet the challenge of management of practice between external supervisions, and be useful for professionals without external supervisors.

An internal supervisor (Casement, 1990) collects together knowledge, skills, and awareness from training, practice and supervision. This resource can also be accessed and consulted when with a client or supervisee. It can take time to develop confidence using an internal supervisor. I evolved a three-stage model using reflective writing:

Stage One is a piece of generic reflective writing (see Stages 1 and 2 above).

Stage Two introduces a direct question, such as 'What do you have to say about that, *Internal Supervisor?*' promoting a dialogue between the therapist and their inner self, thoughts and feelings.

Stage Three develops reflexivity, creating necessary distance and space to encourage additional and alternative perspectives. This involves returning to a previous reflection and asking questions including 'What else...? What was I thinking...? What was I feeling when...? Why...?' which stimulate reflexivity.

This three-stage model offers one means of becoming a reflective practitioner and developing an internal supervisor at the same time.

Linda Garbutt

Internal Saboteur

There are also negative selves who narrate our life-story, who can be powerfully influential, yet tricky to recognise and tackle. The *Internal Saboteur* habitually tells stories to the professional's detriment, for example: 'I made a blunder yet again…'. More positive and constructive narrators can be written who don't just mete out blame and guilt but might tell the same story, for example thus: 'that didn't go very well, but circumstances were difficult and I think I can see how I can learn from the disaster'.

Writing can also help those who conversely employ consistently self-justificatory narrators, failing to perceive learning opportunities. One professional found his *Inner Saboteur* wrote 'my new staff member is as bad as the others'. He was able to play with different perspectives and found a constructive 'subpersonality' (Rowan, 1990) narrator who approached it thus: 'if all my staff are obtuse and obstructive, perhaps I need to think about how I ask them to do things?' He struggled to listen to this positive voice, and deny the dominant but unhelpful one: unlearning old skills is harder than learning new ones. Reflexive development was difficult with writing, instead of impossible, however.

The *Internal Justifier* is part of the *Saboteur*. This part of ourselves can feel helpful at the time, consistently finding reasons why everything was ok, reasons we don't have to change. It makes us feel comfortable with the status quo, finding that problems were somebody else's fault: no need for us to do anything. This is the opposite of the reflective practice project.

Being aware of, and even at times choosing, the narrator of life stories both written and told is also a powerful reflexive process (Chapters 1, 5). These are imaginative uses of fiction to help professionals to stand outside themselves reflexively.

Writer's Block

Even the most experienced writers suffer from this. And we all read the news online and respond to emails, clean the car or house, or sweep up leaves to delay starting writing. All this is as much part of writing as putting words on paper or screen. How do we deal with it?

Discipline: writing isn't always a joyous ride, and we do sometimes have to use psychological glue to stick our bottoms to the chair. The best glue is knowing that this stage will pass, and the writing will happen. Before you are experienced, you just have to take my word for it: you can do it, and you will get there. Sit and write.

Time management: small chunks of time are great for reflective writing, even five minutes. Writing for a short period regularly is much better than waiting for a big time-space. Procrastination breeds anxiety. Frequent writing breeds confidence, self-respect and trust (see Caroline Hadley, Chapter 9, p. 161).

Understand your writer-self: all writers have an inner saboteur waiting to destroy confidence and authority. A student described the critical reader of their writing as: 'A dark presence, some kind of teacher… rather stern, want[ing] excellence. I want them to… change their colours, literally to "lighten up"' (Hunt, 2013, p. 21).

We also all have an internal mentor itching to advise, and a strong, wise self who knows how to write, and just can't wait to do so. Writing a letter to the internal writer, asking him or her how best to support the writing process, AND WRITING the reply, is a powerful strategy. At least one writer I know writes these letters every time she sits down to start, to help her get going. She also has a block she can activate on her computer, to stop her accessing the internet and wasting time.

Exercise: a writer's tip is to go for a walk when the going gets tough. Coleridge and Wordsworth tramped up the highest Lakeland fells; Ian Sinclair 'burns fresh neural pathways' thus (2012).

Time and place: Writing somewhere different and at a different time of day can release the block, as can writing by hand instead of on screen (or the reverse). Experiment: find what suits you. Listen to this reflective writing course evaluation:

> It was a new experience for me to share written experiences in a trusting and stimulating place. I was surprised how easy it was to write about previous experiences, and, once the setting was right, how the ideas flowed. Over the months we laughed, cried and discussed our work together and I found I gained confidence both in my ability to write but also the value of it. Somehow writing it down enabled me to get to the essence of past experiences and events in a way that discussion alone cannot. From the beginning Gillie encouraged us to write whatever came into our heads; this felt very different from the prescriptive writing I had been doing as part of my Masters.
>
> I discovered I wrote about the more profound and painful experiences and sometimes wondered if I wanted to share them; however, whenever I did it was very valuable. (Shirley)

Having explored and explained how to write, the next chapter gives advice on starting and keeping a reflective and reflexive journal, using the above writing methods.

 Read to Learn

Branch, W.T., Higgins, S., Bernstein, L., Manning, K., Schneider, J., Kho, A. and Brownfield, E. (2011) Through the looking glass: how reflective learning influences the development of young faculty members, *Teaching and Learning in Medicine*, **23**(3), 238–43.
An excellent example of the use of reflective writing in professional development.

King, S. (2000) *On Writing: A Memoir of the Craft.* New York: Simon and Schuster. Stephen King is a most reliable and readable guide to writing. This is a text about how to write, and how to be a writer, rather than being specifically about fiction, or any genre within fiction.

Lawrence, H. (2013) Personal, reflective writing: a pedagogical strategy for teaching business students to write, *Business Communication Quarterly*, **76**(2), 192–206.
Holly Lawrence explains how she uses reflective writing strategies effectively, and gives sample exercises.

   ## Write to learn

For *How To* do this writing, please see *Write to Learn,* Chapter 1 (Chapter 8 for fuller advice). Do a *six-minute-write* about anything to limber up, before starting on the exercises below. Writings can be shared fruitfully afterwards with a group or confidential trusted other, if this seems appropriate, once the writer has read and reflected on it first.

8.1 Through the mirror

1. Write for *six minutes* following the flow of your mind, as above, without stopping and without rereading till you've finished.
2. Follow-on writing: write for about 20 minutes about 'A Time in My Experience' as above. Remember this is for you; if you wish to share it you can redraft it first if you wish. Try to choose the first event which comes to mind, even if you have no idea why. Your writing will tell you why it is important. Trust it to do that.
3. Read all your writing to yourself, and alter or adapt as seems good. Are there any connections between the *six-minute-write* and this follow-on? Note any reflections which occur to you as you read.

8.2 Your wise internal mentor

1. Write a letter to your wise internal mentor. This being observes what is going on all the time, supports, comforts, and can advise on difficulties and problems. It might be modelled on a real person, yet has a fictional name, rather than the name of a real person you know. Write: 'Dear...'
2. Write their reply.
3. Continue the correspondence.
4. You could do this by email. Write an email to your internal wise adviser (to your own email address), save it to a special file on arrival in your inbox, and only open, read and write your reply after a predetermined time (e.g. a week).

(Continued)

(Continued)

8.3 Giving advice

1. A young person entering your profession has asked your advice.
2. Write back to them, remembering what it was like when you started out, the kind of letter you would have liked to receive.
3. Write the young professional's reply.
4. Write a letter to yourself reminding yourself of the best advice anyone ever gave you.

8.4 Really perceiving a person

1. Describe a client/colleague you know well. They will never see this, so you can write anything (if working with a collegial group choose someone they do not know).
2. Write phrases, describing these characteristics:

gesture or movement   way of walking or sitting   turn of phrase, or saying

habitual greeting   quality of speaking voice   their clothes   a colour

a sense of touch (handshake)   smell   sounds other than voice   a taste

anything or anyone they remind you of   what they make you feel   and so on ...

if they were an animal what animal would they be? (phrase)

if they were a piece of furniture what would they be?

If a season/weather?   food?   a drink?   flower?   a form of transport? and so on ...

3. Write as if by this person: a poem, story, letter to someone other than you (for example to their child, mother, or the local newspaper), shopping list, things-to-do list...

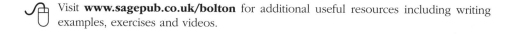

Visit **www.sagepub.co.uk/bolton** for additional useful resources including writing examples, exercises and videos.

CHAPTER 9

REFLECTIVE PRACTICE JOURNALS

Journals are experimental stations for reflective practice writing, using the practical methods of Chapter 8. The difference between logs, diaries and journals is explained; ethical values relating to journals are discussed, what to write on and with, how to write (4 stages of journal writing), and when, where, for and with whom, are explored. How journals can be incorporated into courses is discussed.

The periods when I undertake writing can be unsettling just as much as they can be therapeutic. They are vehicles for me to test out the very basis of my assumptions and re-evaluate significant portions of both personal and professional life. (Sonya, a senior practitioner)

Unless [my students] feel sufficiently free to write things in their journals that they would be embarrassed for me to read, then they are probably not using their journals sufficiently well for them to be good examples of reflection. (David Boud, 2001, p. 16)

An unbending tree is easily broken. Students say afterwards to wise tutors: we did it ourselves. (Adapted from Lao Tsu, 1973)

Reflective practice journals give space for regular, frequent, private, explorative and expressive writing. Journals can be where all first draft reflective writing is undertaken, where no-one else will read it until the writer is ready. Reflective practice journals are essentially private, yet parts can fruitfully be shared with confidential trusted others in the ways suggested in Chapter 8. And parts can be extracted to be put forward for assessment, if a course requires learning journals be kept. Here are three students' astonished reactions to journal writing:

To have the chance to write what we really think rather than just quote some other old dude? Unheard of! Students actually have original thought that is worth reading? Never! And to think that a lecturer was interested in my opinion of class, and my reflections on the topic is really rather empowering and invigorating…

It amazes me that I took this paper because I wanted an easy ride this semester. Well what a ride it has been. Twelve weeks down the track, and I am a different person. I am a person with a purpose, but also a person who recognises that I am in charge of my own destiny. I recognise that I have faults, but I also recognise that they are fixable, adaptable and that they are worth working on…

It's funny to think that a class I nearly withdrew from in the first week has resulted in a change of life: I am now volunteering and choosing a different career path that has low pay but much more enjoyment. Two things that six months ago, I would never have picked. (Pavlovich et al., 2009, pp. 54–6)

Organic exploration rather than product, journals engage critical faculties to tussle with the 'basic practical-moral problem in life [which] is not what to do but what kind of person to be' (Cunliffe, 2009a). The most vital enquiry seeks even more specific and dynamic questions which arise from existing questions. This chapter covers learning journals: why, what and how, with examples from practitioners, students and lecturers (facilitation is discussed on the website (www.sagepub.co.uk/bolton); assessment Chapter 10). The chapter explains the four stages of starting and keeping a journal.

A learning journal asks a writer directly or indirectly to enquire into:
What you:
and **others did** on any particular occasion

thought, and what **others might** have thought

felt, and what **others might** have felt

believe, and **how** these beliefs are carried out in your practice

are **prejudiced** about, take for granted, and unquestioningly assume

can do about **how all** of the above affects **yourself** and **others**.

I initially chose to have my students report *just the facts*, then I slowly found myself more interested in the Journals of students who had violated the rules and strayed into the subjective meadow. The entries were both enlightening and in many instances poignant. I began to see the Journal entries as a mirror of a student's ever-increasing awareness of the act of teaching… I have [also] found that without prior training, entry content is likely to be observational and reactionary rather than reflective. (Trotter, 1999)

Journals give writers' perspectives on issues discussed, described, challenged, engaged with in whatever way. They cannot give a final objective picture, and are always open to further interpretation (like narratives, see Chapter 4).

We write to:

- communicate with and advise the self: about overcoming personal prejudices perhaps
- clarify beliefs and goals: how current thinking is partly formed by family of origin and past history, perhaps
- make and evaluate decisions
- be self-indulgent
- reflect upon dreams and disappointment
- rehearse future behaviour
- reflect on current events, situations and people
- work towards clarity and order where appropriate
- exercise self-responsibility, and reinforce self-trust, -respect and -confidence
- reflect upon and reinforce value of occasions when things went right
- be expressive and creative
- examine areas hard to voice with others
- respond to, and reflect on how to apply, professional theory. (adapted from Wright and Bolton, 2012, pp. 7–8)

I think I can see how I changed as well, how I've learnt more self awareness, I've learnt more acceptance, I'm not so rattled by other people's response to me, even if it's unexpected, I think I can accept it and um it's been very, very useful for me to be writing it in a journal. (Student, in Wright, 2005, p. 516)

It was only through reading *Writing Cures* (Bolton et al., 2004) that I discovered that what I had been doing for years as a personal resource was called 'Reflective Practice'. I simply have a large loose-leaf notebook, and take five minutes – or an hour – to write down what's on my mind: anxieties, dreams, experiences, bits from books, puzzling psychotherapy sessions, relationships, ideas… you name it.

The main benefit is that I stop obsessing or ruminating about them, because I begin to disidentify with what's bugging me – get it out of my head and down onto the page; and then I can begin to understand. If I'm too upset, it doesn't work, or I just can't bring myself to write. (Nathan Field)

Logs, Diaries and Journals

Although these words are often used interchangeably, it is useful to explore their characteristics.

Logs straightforwardly record events, calculations or readings as aide-mémoires, like ships' logs. Anorexics, for example, might keep logs of food intake and symptoms.

Diaries, at the other extreme, can contain anything, be confidantes like Anne Frank's (1947) or Virginia Woolf's (1977, 1978, 1980). Diaries started in Japan in the eighth century (Heehs, 2013). One of the oldest literary forms in the West, diaries were traditionally kept by women who, being more confined, needed confidential interlocutors. Diaries can be confessor or special friend (Anne Frank called hers Kitty) for confined women; or a place of creation, such as those of writers (for example, Virginia Woolf). They contain stories of happenings, hopes and fears, memories, thoughts, ideas, and all attendant feelings. They also contain creative material: drafts of poems, stories, plays or dialogues, doodles and sketches (Bolton, 2014).

Journals are records of experiences, thoughts, and feelings about particular aspects of life. Journals can record anything, and in any way. These documents (some virtual), might be drafts to be worked on to share with a wide audience. Politicians, and some artists, intend publication, but most are drafts for documents to share with tutor, mentor, portfolio group, degree cohort, or examiner. Journal writing has a range of uses. Politicians' journals record their years in office. Victorian travel journals were popular; travel writing still uses this intimate personal form. Qualitative research journals can record material, be a data source, or a process of enquiry itself.

> I now feel quite sad about this journal which represents for me the space which this course has given me for my 'whole' life so far. It has given me intellectual space and opportunity – physical space from work and social group – spiritual space... also psychological space to rethink my responses, reactions, motivations, expectations and hopes... (this passage cut from journal, for personal reasons). I'm more able to take risks and I have thought of things I'd like to do which I've previously not thought as possibilities in the past... (Elaine, Master's student)

> The writing has been a real eye-opener for me. I was sceptical at first, partly because the *reflective journal* has almost become a cliché in nursing education, but also because I was anxious about others reading my gibberish... I will continue to write because Gillie was right. Things come out differently when written down. Feelings and thoughts can creep up and surprise you in writing. I will always be grateful to this course for giving me the space to discover this. And when you discover something for yourself you use it! (Ann, Master's student)

The Reflective Practice Journal: an Explanation

Cornerstones of reflective practice and critical reflexivity, journal elements can be discussed with peers, mentors or supervisors, or redrafted for portfolios. Solitary private writing can enable tentative or bold expression and exploration of past, present and future, the discovery of hitherto unknown areas, some even cathartic (Shepherd, 2004; Sutton et al., 2007). 'Writing things down without worrying what other people think is the most powerful thing' and 'those who are better able to notice and feel their successes learn more' (Beveridge, 1997, p. 42). A student said: 'I must say I like this idea of keeping track of your thoughts.'

A dynamically rewarding process (Boud et al., 1985; Farrell, 2013), reflective journal writing requires commitment, energy, and sometimes courage; it also requires expert facilitation so students know what to do (Dyment and O'Connell, 2010; O'Connell and Dyment, 2011), and to help with the problem of 'variable levels of commitment and competence, in particular with regard to probing review' (Cowan, 2013, p. 9).

Keeping a professional reflective journal pushed Attard (2008) to question what he previously took for granted, realising that at times 'the more I write, the more confused I feel'. He eventually could tolerate uncertainty sufficiently to appreciate a 'reflexive suspended state of not knowing'.

> By keeping a personal-professional journal you are both the learner and the one who teaches. You can chronicle events as they happen, have a dialogue with facts and interpretations, and learn from experience. A journal can be used for analysis and introspection. Reviewed over time it becomes a dialogue with yourself. Patterns and relationships emerge. Distance makes new perspective possible: deeper levels of insight can form. (Holly, 1989, p. 14)

Such insight is not lightly obtained, and could not be facilitated by verbal discussion with colleague or mentor alone. It is essentially self-dialogic, and can be deeply reflexive (Hickson, 2011). Writers are face to face with themselves, examining vulnerable areas, their own cutting edge. And it brings its own rewards.

> From the first few entries I was struck by how quickly I was able to recognize emerging patterns, for example in individual behaviour; similarities in the way meetings were conducted, who led the discussions and who remained silent; how decisions were made and by whom. This information when combined together helped me develop a holistic picture of the organization which helped me understand how it worked. (Shepherd, 2004, p. 202)

Qualitative research journals can also be reflective: a process of enquiry itself, including findings, thoughts and feelings, colloquial quotes, quantitative data such as tables and figures, and descriptions of focus groups or interviews, or narratives. Extracts might be publicly shareable data, or personal and private (Etherington, 2004). The research journal itself can be an essential part of the research method (Richardson and Adams St Pierre, 2005; Watson 2006). Jasper (2005) found a reflective research journal facilitated creativity, critical thinking, analysis, innovative discovery and provided a trustworthy audit trail. Shepherd (2004) developed reflective PhD journals to deepen, enrich and enhance research.

> Masters in Higher Education students were encouraged to keep research diaries of observations and interpretations of their teaching; accounts of thinking in response to discussions; critical responses to literature; evaluative comments about the course itself and so on. Private documents, no one else, including the tutors, had any rights of access. The material might be used in informal course seminars; as a basis for later publications; or to identify issues for further exploration with other participants or course tutors… Participants should see their own regular writing as a fundamental part of the enquiry process. (Rowland and Barton 1994, p. 371)

Reflective Practice Journals and Ethical Values

Reflective practice journals significantly develop and enhance awareness of ethical values used in practice, helping them to congruence with espoused values. 'The students are helped to realise there is no magic formula for ethical decision-making. Instead, the process of writing followed by group discourse enables the analysis of relevant and important factors to be considered in morally challenging decisions' (Durgahee, 1997, pp. 140–1). Fins et al. (2003) used journals similarly with palliative medicine students; observing and reflecting on psychosocial and ethical issues and patient-centred advocacy in 'highly empathic and emotional' (p. 308) journals, students share unique perspectives with peers. Journals facilitated reflection upon emotional response to family medicine (Howard, 1997). These practices counteract a tacit medical and healthcare attitude of detachment and inhumanity (Shem, 2002).

Discovering values-in-practice, by examining assumptions underlying actions, can be uncomfortable (assumptions might prove to be prejudices). Privacy in journal-writing helps this genuinely to take place. The writer gains courage to enter normally no-go reflexive areas, relinquishing certainty for a time in Winnicott's (1971) 'play' or 'transitional space': a place between innermost thoughts and feelings, and the world of actions, events and other people. Normally we protectively hide private thoughts and feelings. But can play with them in this gap between imagination and reality.

Journal writers become *bricoleurs* (brick-layers) (Levi-Strauss, 1966) or stone-wallers, choosing bits from their thoughts and experiences, fisting them for size and shape, and creating possible constructions and models. In speculating about ideas which are neither right nor wrong, writers try out experimental ideas, values, positions. They discover possible selves.

Journals can be 'a process of integration' for *containment*, and *therapeutic space*: a 'space to explore and confirm' (Best, 1996, p. 298) experiences and emotions, however bad. These might be reread and reflected upon more safely later: the writer will have moved on and be able bravely to reassess the situation, their feelings and thoughts.

Life is busy, with a full time job, my Diploma in Counselling, and being Secretary of my local Samaritans branch. However, before I go to sleep at night I always, without fail, write my journal. How do I manage this, when for years I had more free time and never did? I'm not sure, but I've made it a pattern of my day, and do it to feel creative and stretch myself and unwind.

I've tried writing at different times, but it suits me to write at night. I always write a letter about what's happened to me that day. It helps to frame the day and get any grumbles or worries out of my system, which might otherwise fly around my head. When I'm home late from my course, it settles and soothes me.

I don't like to get into a rut, and try various techniques. I have read about gratitude journals, so for the last few months I have listed three things that I have been grateful for during the day, such as a friend cooking me a meal or being welcomed home by my cats. I also include quotes and pieces of writing that call to me, and do drawings and doodles. If I go to the cinema or theatre, I stick in the tickets to remind me of the memory.

More recently I have been capturing three feelings each day. Although I have no problem in feeling things, I can find it hard to describe them, and doing this is helping me.

Finally, I produce a small piece of descriptive writing every day. I enjoy the awareness of noticing something and playing with words to try and capture it. These examples are about work:

Sitting at my desk I quickly type up pages from the notebook with the inky blue cover, trying to decipher the pencil scribbles.

I sit in the quiet office, focused on filling in the forms. My pen scratches across the paper. The clock ticks. Time passes.

Our office reverberates to the sounds of sneezes, snuffles and blowing noses. My throat begins to tingle and my head to ache.

Caroline Hadley

The Thing

A reflective journal is an object, a possession. I recommend appropriate and pleasurable investment. Mine are A5 notebooks, neat and contained for unruly thoughts and adventures. In the past I used A4 loose-leaf folders containing handwritten or typed sheets, letters, newspaper cuttings, journal papers, pictures, and all sorts. I write with 2B rubber-tipped pencils: I never rub out, but I might; a soft pencil whispers to the page. One nursing group had between them: a suede-covered book, one decorated with bright children's pictures, one plain but a glorious red, another a shocking pink folder and pen.

Pen feels more permanent than pencil, fountain pen more professional and sophisticated than biro. Coloured pens and paper for particular emotions and feelings can take writing in unforeseen directions, as can different sizes of paper: A1 for anger, shopping list pad for low confidence. Typing can create different reflections from handwriting: watching print appear on the screen can invite organised and deliberate analytic revision. I prefer handwriting because I'm from the pre-computer age; younger people find keyboard-writing facilitative. Discover what's best for you.

I feel comfortable writing longhand when it's about me, my personal stuff. When I'm on the keyboard it's for somebody else to read, it's an essay, it's an assignment it's a letter and that's how I kind of keep a demarcation between my stuff and more public stuff. (A student, in Wright, 2005, p. 517)

Types of Writing

A reflective journal can contain any writing, in any order, for no reason other than the writing comes out that way. It might contain free-flow *six minutes'* writing (see Chapter 8, p. 136), stories of practice, fiction, poems, musings or reflections on why, what, how, when, who, why, dialogues with the self, fictional dialogues with others such as clients, analysis of motives and actions, philosophising on for example ethics, evaluation or assessment of practice, description, fantasy used to aid insight, cathartic writing, unsent letters, extended metaphors, visualisation, ethnography, mindmaps, sketches, cartoons, descriptions of dance or diagrams. Or it might be drawings, or collage (cut out pictures or extracts from magazines and so on). Experiment! These methods are explained in different chapters of *Reflective Practice*. Experienced journal writers allow the most appropriate to present themselves naturally.

Ownership and responsibility for writing enable development of understanding. Rereading, and reflecting, are significant, and sometimes challenging. 'At one point, I noted a pattern in my journals: I was saying how tired I was every week. I knew that, but seeing it in the journal weekly really hit the point home. Re-reading these journals today as a collection shows a lot more fatigue, emotional upset' (Farrell, 2013, p. 468).

Some journal writers leave space to return and make reflexive notes in a different colour, others reread and continue to write on later fresh pages. A left-hand column reflective journal (Argyris, 1991) records events in two columns: the right focuses on the event, the left on what did not happen – thoughts, feelings or impulses to action.

Fook (2012, p. 48) recommends rereading journals 'looking for gaps, biases, themes and missing themes'.

Management consultancy coaching

A recent and very bright graduate, working on a complex and difficult business change project was often overwhelmed with the challenges of becoming a consultant, the change between work and studying and staying away from home at the client site as well as understanding the company he was working for and the complexity of organisational politics. The journal I encouraged him to keep became a survival mechanism and rich source of learning. This free word association extract gives a strong sense of how his perception of the culture of the company merges with his own state of mind:

NewCo pointless old tired stale dark cold unfriendly confusion anxious bleak stagnant slow protracted conflict going round in circles repeat same old parochial trivial dread going through the motions denial escape fight withdraw individual shell distance myself scared bitten stress pedantic process machine automation indecisive conflict avoidance stupid panic macho picking holes unhelpful barrier don't care apathy ridiculous smallminded prejudiced siloed blinkered unappreciative arrogant waste of space obstruction denial deaf clueless machine hierarchical fragment disintegrate plural infighting political playing games Machiavellian agenda effort failure antagonism conflict embarrassment hide away secretive behind closed doors inefficient paperpushing overly complex dispersed resentful bitter stuck repeat.

Angela Mohtashemi

How to Write: the Four Stages

Writing strategies outlined in previous chapters are appropriate to the reflective practice journal. Each journal writer develops appropriate format and ordering. Spaces might be left for later reflections in a different colour, or previous writings might be interrogated on fresh later pages.

Journal writing stage 1

Do the six-minute mind clearing exercise (see Chapter 8, p. 136).
   Now write an account of an experience (10–20 minutes).
   Allow an event to surface in your mind, rather than reaching for the most *critical*. Often the routine, everyday, or seemingly insignificant episode most needs dwelling upon. Paradoxically, and crucially, these might be harder to focus upon than the significant. Or it might be a puzzling occasion.
   Write about the occasion as descriptively as you can, including all detail.
   Give it a title as if it were a story or film.

It's 4 o'clock in the morning when I get the pen and paper out. The sheer cultural complexity of the University of the South Pacific: race, gender, sexuality, status and other I'm meeting every day as a counsellor, and the lack of professional consultation and isolation from counsellors with Codes of Ethics and Practice keeps me awake. So, I write it all down. The feelings of inadequacy, of excitement, the confusion and doubts, contradictions and discoveries.

Some I've kept, some torn into very small pieces, too awful and negative to reread. Scribbling it in complete privacy was a safety valve. I could be my own

(Continued)

(Continued)

'supervisor' and avoid the worst of the isolation. I also suggested writing to some staff and students. Some were using their third language, English, to speak to me and were thousands of miles from their village in another remote part of the Pacific. The writing gave us the possibility of a bridge.

Mustn't grumble, that so very English maxim is turned on its head. You must grumble, I say, but on paper and in your own language.

Jeannie Wright

Journal writing stage 2

Reread all you've written and ask questions like these:

What strikes you particularly about this story? Why?

What have you missed out? Go back and put it in, however insignificant it seems. Why do you think you missed it out?

What do you feel (and felt then)? Why?

What did you think (and thought then, but perhaps did not say)? Why?

What assumptions have you made? Why?

What does it tell you about your ethical values in action (for example, respect for the disadvantaged)? Why?

How is power handled, and the relative status and roles of those involved? Why?

How has any power imbalance affected you, or the other person? Why?

What is the balance of responsibility between peers; how could it be different? Why?

What do misunderstandings or non-understandings tell you about communication? Why?

What do you find challenging? Why?

My teaching journal collects moments from the [infant] school day (drawing, photograph, child's work or quote) with questions or reflections.

A child's note: 'I don't want to sit next to Russell, not today.'

My note: 'Russell's mum gave me this note in the morning: he'd been upset by it. Why didn't I make time to deal with it? I wanted to speak to the boy myself: but didn't have time. This bothered me.'

I discovered the note-writer thought writing would soften the blow for Russell. How words can be unkind and upset others, mixed with the thinking that writing softens their impact, is typical of how children explore the complexities of friendships and relationships with others. I was able to explore this more with the whole class, feeling it was in line with my developing teaching principles.

The journal became a space where I could capture elements otherwise lost, put them on hold for later, and slow my thinking. It is very easy to forget the social and emotional side – the human dimension – of working with children. My journal opened my eyes to how little time I spent on the social and emotional side, and gave me courage to do more.

My teacher identity, priorities, and principles were highlighted and shaped by what I was (and was not) including in my journal. This reflection helped me understand these friendship issues are as (or more) important as curriculum matters, and developed my respect for children's individual circumstances.

Teresa Smith

Journal writing stage 3

Write a further account, attempting to gain wider perspective, by trying activities such as these:

Write the story again as if from the point of view of the other person (student, client, patient, colleague, other).

Or, if there is no other significant person, or far too many, write a further account from an omniscient observer, such as from the perspective of your coffee mug, who observes everything.

Or invent your own way of re-storying, or choose another from the list in Chapter 8, p. 139; 145–6.

Ask similar questions to those in stage 2.

Remember repeatedly to ask WHY? This is the critical reflexive question.

Journal writing stage 4

Reread your journal (the next day or after perhaps three months) and ask yourself some of these:

Where has this taken you? Why?

What patterns can you perceive, such as repeated behaviour? Why?

What do you notice about the language, particularly about non-peers? Why do you think you used it?

(Continued)

(Continued)

Is there a *destructively* self-critical voice in your writing? Why? Make it *con-structively* critical.

Where might further explorations go? Why do you choose these?

Why, how, when, with whom?

What challenges does all this present you with? Why?

What I am learning about writing and reflecting – and sharing and conversing – does not simply lie in the world of work, professional development, somehow distanced and divorced from me. It is very much about me, who I am as a person and professional, my vocation in life. So what we have been doing is actually very personal and existential. It has been about my relationship with myself, how that relationship finds its way into my work is a place to begin and perhaps end – at least for professional development purposes. But the real work/gift is the change going on within me – my sense of self.

I remembered the Rilke quote – to live the questions. I have learned a lot and learned things I knew but know again: to trust the knowledge of the heart, trust what I know, speak what I know, to take what I have to offer the world seriously (world being my profession, my discipline, communities, students, colleagues, meetings where I live so much of my life, the classroom).

Kathleen Russell

When keeping a journal, remember:

- This is for *you*: write somewhere private.
- This is for *you*: use materials you enjoy using, and feel free with.
- Date entries: you will not remember.
- Try different writing forms: explorative, descriptive, lists, devil's advocate, story (Chapters 4, 8), poetry (Chapter 5), metaphor exploration (Chapter 6), anecdote, reflective musing, vignettes, portraits, lists, interview yourself…
- Fill out notes from teaching/learning sessions; ask why.
- Develop previously half-expressed arguments or opinions.
- Changes of opinion are significant; explore them.
- Examine things difficult to understand or do.
- Ask WHY? of everything and anything: this is the critical reflexive question form.

When, Where, For and With Whom to Write a Journal

When you want to, when you need to. Any or every time you can find five minutes or more without interruption. The most creative times might paradoxically be when your cognitive powers are at lowest ebb: midnight or 4 a.m.

'Aren't you going to bed *yet* Mum? Are you *still* working?'

'No, I'm not working. I'm just writing.'

Write about an event at the right time for you. Left too late, events lose impact and interest: attempted too soon they may be too raw:

If the experience is very close, I feel inhibited… If the closeness of the real reality, of the living reality, is to have a persuasive effect on my imagination, I need a distance, a distance in time and space. (Llosa, 1991, p. 44)

For and with whom: a reflective journal is primarily for its writer: as internal dialogue for their own reflexivity, reflection, and therefore development. There are three possible responders to journals: self, peer, and/or tutor.

Journals can be used in mentoring relationships, and can contain reflections on personal objectives set in association with mentor or supervisor (Gray, 2007). Journals available for reading by another, or even for assessment, are qualitatively different from private arenas for students or professionals to engage in critical reflexivity and reflection: it is 'misleading, confusing and risky' to treat all forms of journal writing as equivalent to each other (Boud, 2001, p. 16).

Co-peer mentoring (paired support), each confidentially reading other's material and supportively commenting is valuable (see Chapter 3). My students shared and discussed otherwise undiscussably confidential material, coming close to personal boundaries. Not only extremely satisfying to students, who met over coffee somewhere nice, it took the pressure off their fully stretched tutor. Small, trusting, trusted confidential groups or pairs can offer developmental possibilities (Crème, 2008). Some courses use web-based participant sharing (see Julie Hughes, Chapter 3, p. 54). Boud (1998) suggests peer-feedback is valuable and closely related to self-assessment.

Peers discussing journals need to be clear about their purpose. These are sensitive areas, requiring agreed boundaries and scope. They need to be critical and confronting enough without mimicking assessors, and they need listening and empathetic responding skills. Peer-sharing of learning journals becomes a route of learning essential interpersonal skills as well.

Write anywhere: by a lake, in bed, perhaps difficult on a bike. This, from an academic counselling department head, was written in a café:

A student tells me she is experiencing severe insomnia, and I feel helpless, feeling only inner compassion. A colleague, in the canteen, looking ashen, laments his own bureaucratic burden and his impotence about finding any end to it. Again, I can only feel for him, sit in silent solidarity. Sometimes, with a client, while listening to a complex narrative of inescapable suffering, I will become aware of some stillness, in me, between us, a sensed original sanity. Is this what is meant by a wounded healer? Wounded, yes. Healer, I'm not so sure. If counsellors become tame, professionalised, 'audit-minded' rule-keepers, how can they be free? If I can't overturn my adversity, de-oppress myself, practise what I teach, and practise what I feel, who can? (Feltham, 2004)

Journal writing enables an ongoing self-dialogue with otherwise quiet or silent voices within (see Chapter 7, 8; Bolton, 2014; Rowan, 1990): knowledge, intuition, analysis, inspiration and feelings. It enables standing back, taking a long reflective look, and allowing fresh views to form: a route to *loving and living the questions themselves* (Rilke, [1934] 1993).

This writing process is really helpful. It enabled me to find a synthesis of all those things going round and round in my head. (Priti)

Journals as a Course Element

Reflective practice journals, cornerstones of reflective practice and critical reflexivity, are often required for courses or portfolios, and require skilful facilitation (see website). Journals only support reflection and reflexivity when writers have authority over and responsibility for their journal. Educator's roles are therefore to introduce the subject fully, yet be carefully consistent about who owns both writing process and product.

What began as a pre-requisite for my counselling training has become so much more. Through my writing I have discovered intelligence greater than intellect, teaching more than any other could do. I have become my own therapist, supervisor, and author of my own experience. Over many years, I have documented significant events, relationships, thoughts and feelings, becoming the observer of my own process.

Writing gave me the insight and the courage to believe in myself, as I uncovered parts of my personality which had lay dormant for most of my life. Reading through my entries helped me to recognise themes and patterns, which I began to address and change. I was able to question without feeling shamed, and I learned to explore my thoughts and feelings as they emerged, in the knowledge that I was free from judgement. I found the freedom to express myself, and as I delved deeper, I discovered many aspects of myself who questioned, and challenged all I thought was true.

As I re-read my journals today, I am reliving a professional nightmare, feeling the rage inside me for the harm that was done. This allows me to process my emotions in the present, and finally integrate this experience.

Writing continues to be my road to consciousness, as I weave the many layers of my personality together using words and images and reflective material spanning many years.

Sue McDonald

Deeply reflective writing does not always come easily to graduates of our schools and universities. Morrison successfully introduced higher degree students to in-depth reflective journal writing. 'They were initially prisoners of their own expectations and perceptions, [yet] the process has been an enabling and liberating experience' (Morrison, 1996, pp. 323–4). Introduced and facilitated with knowledge and skill, journals repay the time and effort. Students need facilitation in how to write (see Chapter 8) to begin to grasp the rewards, and lessen their fear. University tutors who kept learning journals reported how experienced facilitation had significant positive impact on learning (Cowan and Westwood, 2006).

A company's employees kept 'thinkbooks': 'to record significant events, make observations on their performance, analyse their actions, draw conclusions, note learning points, and make suggestions for further action' (Rigano and Edwards, 1998, p. 436). Realising the journal's impact after three months, Vincent's daily entries changed from 'organising daily routine… to a process of reflection leading to growth' (ibid. p. 440). The researchers concluded Vincent's success stemmed from owning the process. Realising he needed to share his reflections to develop further, Vincent's company offered facilitated reflective writing in work time.

Students are too rarely taught and supported in how to write reflexively (e.g. Trotter, 1999), and are often given structures to work within, and sometimes over-leading and repetitive prompts which show lack of respect, and inhibit honesty and imagination because they only lead to certain types of answers (e.g. Hobbs, 2007).

Seven experienced university teachers gained significant personal and professional development, writing similar journals to those they required of students: 'I have found that being required to put pen to paper encouraged me to spend more time on my reflection and to structure my thinking more carefully' (Cowan and Westwood, 2006, p. 65). Practising what they preached significantly improved their organisation and facilitation of students' reflection. A colleague refused to join the experiment, although he required written reflection from his students, saying: 'I can write a journal in my head when I am gardening or even in bed or sitting in a traffic jam – if this works for me does it need to be written?? [sic]' (ibid. p. 64). The paper's authors make no comment as to how successful this colleague was at teaching journal-writing.

Journal writing needs to be understood at first hand to be facilitated. Legal educators are advised to keep journals (Hinett, 2002). Lecturers applying to be registered practitioners of the UK Higher Education Academy are required to keep reflective journals. Kuit et al. (2001) report a successful journal keeping 'action learning set' for academic staff.

Dialogue journals are different from those discussed in the rest of this chapter. Students are in confidential, trusting, non-inspectorial relationships with tutors who read and respond within the journal sensitively, with awareness and experience (Carson and Fisher, 2006; Cunliffe, 2004; Wright, 2005; Gray, 2007; Kathpalia and Heah, 2008; Hughes, 2010, 2012). Chris developed her understanding from her own journal-writing experience, then worked out how to use dialogue with her students and their journals:

My own journal enabled me to make visible transient thoughts hard sometimes to pin down and then examine; however, this only ever *initiated* the reflective process. Even though I could apply critical and searching questions, the process still remained viewed from my own perspective.

I recognised that dialogue could create a crucial stage for my students to think beyond their own assumptions and beliefs and expose their ideas to scrutiny and challenge: their perceptions are tested and exposed to different ways of thinking. I had to establish a form of dialogic communication which worked for both my students and me.

We were then able to challenge assumptions around the universality of events, where what is seen in one context is assumed to be the norm, and a new awareness of the professional role was gained. In the early stages of developing students' reflective writing, my role therefore is about asking questions to develop curiosity and consider assumptions and underpinning beliefs. The *process* of guided dialogue brings us insight.

Chris Neanon

Journal dialogue can foster critical thinking, and can be useful in cross-cultural communication and increasing language facility (Hancock, 1998). And listen to Julie's dynamic experience:

'I didn't have a voice until I joined this group'

Journal dialogue with all new teachers individually was handwritten, personal and dated, sometimes with coloured pens, stickers or illustrative drawings. A sense of expectancy and trust emerged, facilitative to reflection. In the second semester two students per week shared their journals with the group, writing for self and each other. The dialogue reflection and refraction represented multiple perspectives and perceptions, suggesting resistance to the reproduction of self as mirror image. In adopting different narrative voices and genres students were able to challenge and talk back to themselves reflectively, though some writers felt it was their role to 'entertain' their readers with comedic narrative style. Some writers struggled with content and writing style: dialogue can be intrusive, enforcing censorship. Sensitivity is vital to encourage honest reflection and risk-taking. Language choices, individual and social identities, and assumptions were challenged, sometimes destabilising former certainties. Boundaries and literacies are blurred. Dialogue journals offer recognition of the plural and multiple text, and challenge institutional norms of reflective writing. There is no 'getting it right', they *get it differently*. (Julie Hughes, see also Chapter 3, p. 54)

Modelling Critical Reflexivity

'Unearthing and questioning assumptions is often risky. It's important teachers first model how they try to unearth and research their own assumptions. There's something essentially false about asking learners to do something you haven't done first' (Brookfield, 2013, p. 23). Student journals can push *tutors* to meaningful reflexivity. Ann Cunliffe describes an experience:

> It means being critically reflexive about our own teaching practices and the voices we might silence... The journal excerpt below caused me to do some critically reflexive questioning of my own:

> The process of questioning one's assumptions and values is disconcerting and tortuous. It is uncomfortable to truly look inwards and then reflect on all the assumptions and values that one has built over almost a lifetime. I have always assumed that my values and goals were just right for me and proceeded almost with single-minded purpose to achieve them. There was no reason for me to question them. Yet, I have been *forced* to be conscious [italics added [in original]] of this process over the past weeks.

> Although this student talked about the relative and non-absolute nature of knowledge and voice, the language he used struck me: have I 'forced' others? Have I acted inconsistently by claiming students must consider multiple perspectives? I need to look at my own teaching practices to ensure I am enacting the values I espouse. (Cunliffe, 2004, p. 419)

Learning journals can be the locus of effective learning. Yet can professional and academic course leaders and facilitators find out if their students are learning and developing, and if so, how much? Teaching a wide-ranging, deeply personal process like this is problematic; how do tutors know they are teaching well?

Read to Learn

Bassot, B. (2013) *The Reflective Journal.* Basingstoke: Palgrave Macmillan.
A straightforward, helpful introduction, with inspired exercises.

Hargreaves, J. and Page, L. (2013) *Reflective Practice.* Cambridge: Polity Press.
A brief, clear, straightforward introduction to beginning to reflect in healthcare, with excellent imaginative exercises (Page is a playwright). It covers areas appropriate to its subject healthcare, such as safeguarding vulnerable people, whistleblowing, and how to write an essay.

Wright, J.K. and Bolton, G. (2012) *Reflective Writing in Counselling and Psychotherapy.* London: Sage.
Jeannie Wright, supported by Gillie Bolton, gives a readable and enlightened route into the kind of writing which is appropriate for a reflective practice journal.

Write to Learn

For *How To* do this writing, please see *Write to Learn,* Chapter 1 (Chapter 8 for fuller advice). Do a *six-minute-write* about anything to limber up, before starting. Writings can be shared fruitfully afterwards with a group or confidential trusted other, if this seems appropriate once the writer has read and reflected on it first.

9.1 Have a proper look

1. Describe entering your office or place of work.
2. What do you observe? Note everything, remembering you have five senses.
3. Mark five things which strike you most for some reason known or unknown.
4. Choose one to write more about.
5. Write a further reflective piece about what you would like to change about:

   (a) things in this space
   (b) the way you use or respond to this space.

9.2 Take an even closer look

1. Write about entering the workroom or place of a colleague you admire.
2. What do you observe? (Remember you have five senses.)
3. Mark the five things which strike you most: do not ask 'why these'?.
4. Choose one, write more about it.
5. Compare this with your own work space observations. What do you think and feel?

9.3 Rethinking your space

1. Think of an object you have on your desk or near it (picture, ornament, shell...).
2. Describe it.
3. Write why you think you have it there.
4. Now imagine: this object is in another room, different from yours. Describe the room, and how it feels for you to be in it.
5. Do you prefer the imagined room? Why? If not, why not?

9.4. Significant learning

1. At the end of a work day: list in your journal:

   (a) 5 things I've learned today
   (b) 5 things I'd still like to learn.

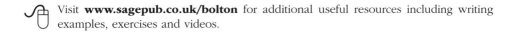 Visit **www.sagepub.co.uk/bolton** for additional useful resources including writing examples, exercises and videos.

CHAPTER 10

ASSESSMENT AND EVALUATION

What assessment is and could be for reflective practice is the focus of this chapter. The many moral, ethical and practical issues raised by facilitators, examiners and students are discussed, as are a range of assessment solutions created by them to deal with the problems. The fascinating area of evaluation is explained and discussed with innovative and effective methods described.

The Latin root of the word assessment [is] 'to sit beside', reflect[ing] the values being promoted in critically reflective learning as collaborative rather than inspectorial. (Brockbank and McGill, 1998, p. 100)

What I wanted, in contrast to faux evaluations, was something that could sink its hooks into my classes, something with wings and talons that could sweep down and snatch both me and my students by the shoulders and shake us out of our collective passivity to the point that we either shrieked with pain at the terror of plummeting to our deaths or else clung to it for survival until we could glide back down to some more stable literary terra firma. (Babcock, 2007, p. 513)

Assessment is a complex moral and ethical act, needing to be just, accurate, fair, impartial, and based upon appropriate criteria. Assumptions need to be examined about students' prior knowledge and attitudes; different cultural, spiritual and faith beliefs will affect what is reflected upon, how, and why (Scaife, 2010). Knowing something is to be examined can change its nature, as well as attitudes to it; the very process of examination can also change it, a principle common in many disciplines including sciences. The problem is to assess, while keeping students' focus on learning rather than on achieving a high assessment. Educative processes work best when they drive assessment, rather than the other way round. It is probably the biggest conundrum in curriculum development.

There are many approaches to reflective practice, and a wide range of aims and objectives, many of which are for specific purposes within defined areas of curricula or professional development. Some do not need assessment, some only need evidence that reflection has been undertaken, some have clearly enunciated agreed assessment criteria. Why and how assessment might be feasible, useful, ethical and moral is discussed in this chapter. The discussion centres on summative assessment. Formative assessment undertaken throughout, however, can be a valuable dialogue with the tutor giving students feedback on how they're doing.

Evaluation, a way for lecturers to gain feedback from students on courses and programmes (summative), and which can enable communication between tutor and students to improve student experience (formative), is far less ethically loaded. This chapter looks at various strategies.

Assessment of Reflective Practice Journals

Assessment of reflection and reflexivity is not straightforward because reflection and reflexivity are process based, and assessment is product based: a paradigmatic *muddle in the model*. Reflective practice is complex and multifaceted, involving feelings and emotions, varied personal, cultural (including faith) and disciplinary perspectives, making assessment problematic (Tummons, 2011). Awareness of assessment can corrupt reflection or reflexivity. How assignments are constructed and communicated to students also affects their attitude to assessment and reflection itself (Segers et al., 2006; Bos et al., 2013). Collins (2013) found it led to antagonism towards reflective assignments perceived as having little intrinsic meaning at the beginning of training. Involving students in the assessment process can help alleviate this negative impact.

Reflective practice is itself self-enquiry leading to a form of self-assessment. An element of it could reasonably be development of assessment criteria. But assessment is in danger of becoming a 'tick box' exercise contrary to the development of critical thinking (Wilson, 2013), leading to a vulnerable disengagement and deskilling (Collins, 2013).

If students are fully aware of assessment requirements and criteria and that these are in keeping with course aims and objectives (even better if students develop criteria themselves) then many authorities consider the process can be positive (Sutton et al., 2007; Pavlovich et al., 2009). Other authorities go further, saying students will not value reflection and reflexivity without assessment (Bulman and Schutz, 2013). This feeling was endorsed by some of Wright's students (Wright and Bolton, 2012), though her earlier students expressed vehemently anti-assessment feelings, for example, 'there's a lot of information I could have used, but withheld because I don't want anyone else reading it' (Sutton et al., 2007, p. 396). Yet private un-assessed writing can lead to significant insight, materially and positively affecting final assessments (Carson and Fisher, 2006).

Crème (2005, p. 290) identifies guidelines for assessment. A good record of study, she claims, is: (a) comprehensive, as it meets requirements of an introduction, conclusion and demonstrates syllabus coverage; (b) shows understanding of the material, with the ability to select, summarise, analyse and show relationships between concepts, both within the course and outside of it; (c) shows self-awareness of the writer as learner, both in relation to the ideas on the course, and to course activities, processes and colleagues; and (d) demonstrates that the writer is prepared to take risks with the material in relation to their own political and intellectual position. Embedded in these guidelines is a mix of cognitive skills in knowing what content should be selected as important, while also writing in a manner that emotionally and holistically connects the student with the context.

Moon (1999) maintains detailed assessment criteria can play a central part in the success of journal writing, providing structure and foundation for what is expected. This is an example of assessment driving the educational process. She lists assessment criteria and discusses the 'need to decide whether the student is being assessed on content or on the writing, the process of the writing, or the product of the learning' (1999, p. 34). Roffey-Barentsen and Malthouse (2013) draw on Moon and others to offer analysis of 'levels of reflective writing' for assessment purposes. The problem with these is that students are likely to frame their writing to fit the criteria.

Assessment: Queries, Problems and Pitfalls

Journals can develop students' ability to question their actions, knowledge, ideas, feelings, prejudices, assumptions, espoused values, and so on. Dialogic journals can enhance communication and understanding between tutor and student (see also 'Evaluation' below).

Assessment design is tricky but many consider it possible when exposure of personal issues is not expected, there is a clear focus towards a specific shared area of experience, and if it is undertaken in a manner consonant with the pedagogical principles of the course (Stevens and Cooper, 2009). Portfolios containing reflective and reflexive elements are considered effective for assessment (for example, Groom and Maunonen-Eskelinen, 2006), giving good access into students' thinking and quality of learning. Students invest personality and self-image (Varner and Peck, 2003) and are asked to use individual voices honestly and take risks in journals' contents (Crème, 2005).

There are problems, however, when the extrinsic motivation of assessment takes over from the intrinsic desire to improve reflection in order to develop practice. Scaife quotes a radiography student: 'Reflective practice: I hate it. I don't know what it is. I passed it last year though' (2010, p. 227).

Journals can be read inappropriately or even assessed by line managers (see Chapter 9). Perceived enforced confession or disclosure of professional or personal material can lead to discomfort, lack of trust, or 'laundered' material (Ghaye, 2007; Sinclair-Penwarden 2006; Sutton et al., 2007). Lillis found students disguised black identity, fearing discrimination (2001). Nursing students may create reflective material retrospectively for assessment (Clegg et al., 2002, Chapter 9). Some students are negative about 'forced RP [and so] fake it' (Hobbs, 2007, pp. 409, 411; Hargreaves 2004). Knowing they are to be assessed, students can fear writing honestly (Hansen 2012), tend to write 'strategic journal entries' (Pecheone et al., 2005), display journal entries to please tutors (Hobbs, 2007), or create reflective material retrospectively (Clegg et al., 2002).

Hargreaves (2004) is disturbed that in her study of assessed nursing students' journals, only three story-forms are considered to be legitimate and given marks. In *valedictory* narratives, the narrator recognises a crisis, responds appropriately and 'wins the day'. Condemnatory narratives have negative outcomes, the narrator 'loses the day' and feels guilty and/or angry. In redemptive narratives, the student-writer-hero learns from mistakes (or inappropriate values) and thus improves professional practice. In order to pass the assessment, students alter their accounts to fit within these frames, while signing to say their work is a true, faithful reflection of their practice. She concludes: 'exploring the value of fictional narratives may reveal a powerful medium for the development and understanding of professional practice' (2004, p. 199); they would be expected to write fictionally rather than pretending their accounts were absolutely accurate reflections of thoughts, feelings and actions (see Chapter 5).

Journals are in danger of being positively harmful when written for assessment, if the process is not handled with experience and care founded on congruent pedagogical principles (see Chapter 9). Some 'assessment regimes… kill off the qualities that the work itself was designed to foster' (Crème, 2005, p. 291). And 'learning journals cannot be successful if students write them with the sense that they will be judged in the same way as an essay' (Crème, 2005, p. 294). Students can see required assessed journals as a waste of time with 'no real meaning for themselves' (Hobbs, 2007, p. 412).

Brookfield also sees a danger in that 'students come to see journals as mandated disclosures focused on eliciting the right kind of revelations' (1995, p. 100). Macfarlane and Gourlay (2009) go even further and liken the creation of reflective products for assessment to television reality shows: students are required to expose emotions, insecurities, inabilities, how they discovered the true road to redemption, and their remorse at the error of previous ignorance. 'Governance of the soul' is demanded, and fictional conformism is the likely result.

Marking of journals is therefore reported as time-consuming and difficult, forcing uncomfortable value judgements (Varner and Peck, 2003), as their subjective nature defies the standardised criteria of more objective forms of assessment (Pavlovich et al., 2009). Brookfield (1995) says journal material is and should be non-assessable.

How does my own experience help me to help students relish learning; they are so focused on qualification, they stifle opportunities for enjoying the quirky, often circuitous, genuinely surprising experience of learning. Reflection has helped me to understand this first hand. What is worthy of our enjoyment and commitment is not the end of the journey: it is the journey itself.

My reflective journal combining the personal with the professional, which has no 'rules', has led to valuable insights into my process of learning. It is the journey that dismays, delights and transforms us. 'The experiences gained in the course of the journey(s) are the prize, not some final Shangri-La of knowledge at the end of the road.' (Alvesson and Sköldberg, 2000, p. 260)

(Russell Delderfield)

Issues with Grading Reflective and Reflexive Writing

Many consider graded assessment inappropriate because it can prevent genuine examination of feelings, thoughts, ideas, prejudices, attitudes. Teachers, coaches or counsellors should only have access to whatever thoughts or feelings reflective practitioners choose to reveal; assessment destroys reflection, disabling students from involving themselves in the 'raw' process (Boud et al., 1985).

'There is a real danger that creating assessment criteria will have the effect of killing off the spontaneity and individuality of the exercise' (Beveridge, 1997, p. 42). Beveridge feels tutors are in a cleft stick: without assessment students do not see the process as being sufficiently worthwhile; the effect of it, however, can be to prevent them from expressing themselves freely. Students with non-English mother tongue write journals in English so they can be assessed, thereby reducing the expressive nature of the document (Wright, 2005). Scott does not mince words: 'Reflection *can be* a particularly invasive means of reinforcing institutional authority... Those who assign and assess reflective writing should be mindful of the dispositions toward authority that this practice might foster in time' (2005, p. 27); a reminder of muddle in pedagogical principles.

We can see from the above, that there is divergence of opinion in what reflection is, what model of pedagogy it works within, and therefore what model of assessment, assessment substitute or none at all is appropriate.

The method of assessment (if there is assessment) has to be appropriate, and in harmony with the curriculum (Wright, in Wright and Bolton, 2012). Redmond maintains: 'the appearance of *the ability to reflect* as an assessable category on a competency checklist can only be regarded as a retrograde step, lacking any basic comprehension of the concept' (2006, p. xiii, emphasis in original). Ixer adds:

If reflection is to be regarded as a core facet of individual professional competence, then we need to know far more about its structure, substance and nature... none of the work on reflection thus far has effectively tackled issues of oppression in the teaching and learning environment...

A particularly loud note of caution must be sounded that some commentators still inherently endorse reflection as a skill or competence that can be learnt through instrumental reasoning. This leads to the assumption that course planners need only structure assessment in such a way as to encompass a new outcome called 'reflection'... The nature of reflection [clearly] does not fit the competence model... The fear is that reflection will become seen as a self-indulgent or 'soft' subject that cannot be afforded, that standards will fall, and that users will receive a poorer service as a result. (1999, p. 514)

And:

Will the habits of reflection that we seek to develop..., become devalued simply because they are difficult to evaluate, summarise, and report? (Ward and McCotter 2004, p. 244)

A very significant question.

Assessment Solutions

Many consider *self and/or peer assessment* can be effective and is also a reflective process in itself (Bryan and Clegg, 2006; Hinett, 2002; Wright in Wright and Bolton, 2012; Vu and Dall'Alba, 2007; Hansen, 2012). Allowing students to develop their own assessment criteria is perceived by some as a reflective extension of the reflective practice process. Hattie found self-assessment to be most effective, from an analysis of 800 meta-analyses of 50,000 studies relating to educational achievement (2009). Giving and receiving feedback on others' writing is a skill which can be taught and developed, as is taking a critical stance concerning one's own. Ken Martin and his students agree their assessment criteria, and their work is then submitted to three-way *triadic assessment* by (a) self, (b) peers and (c) tutors:

Class discussions defining criteria are usually terrific; each group seems to bring out something new, though students find it difficult. The usual criteria are flagged up but debating definitions drives home the problems with interpretation of language and difficulties with objectivity and validity [my experience of positive engagement in this tussle is similar]. This term's exercise produced two new points: one was the use of metaphors in critical analysis.

Self-assessment is usually quite acceptable to students, though many find it difficult criticising peers, and being self-critical initially; some find it empowering. However, many students get very thoughtful, honest, accurate and insightful about their own work very quickly. It can help refine ideas and boost esteem. The standard of reflective practice and reflexivity is certainly helped by self-assessment. In a small way, perhaps, triadic assessment opens that 'secret garden' of assessment to some scrutiny and collaborative analysis.

Ken Martin

Self- and peer-learning can develop students' understanding of, and ability to reflect, if they are supported adequately. Peer assessment needs careful handling not to undermine peer cooperation (Boud, 1995). Students can find suggestions for criteria helpful. Here, based on advice in previous chapters, are some:

- description based on detailed observation of events, places, people, including:

  o   use of all the senses (e.g. her breath smelt of alcohol)
  o   feelings (discomfort, fear, etc.) as evidenced vocally and by body language of the other (e.g. patient/client/colleague)
  o   characteristic movements of the other (e.g. not meeting the eye)
  o   examples of exact or characteristic words used by the other

- narratives of events including:

  o   where, when, to/with whom, how, and why what happened
  o   level of empathy, lack of, or other feelings about the other
  o   feelings before, during, after
  o   what information was given, and what deduced

- further narratives exploring the experience of the incident from the point of view of the other, etc.
- the way this incident relates to other experience
- what assumptions are evidenced and/or challenged by the incident; how they were addressed
- what strategies etc. of the organisation (e.g. school, hospital) were brought into question; how they were addressed
- what principles and ethical values were evident in this incident

  o   whether these were consonant with espoused values/theories

- how theories of practice are demonstrated or brought into question by the incident
- critical examination of why actions were taken, or why they weren't (by the writer); critical investigation as to why specific feelings were experienced; evidence that a series of further 'why' questions have been critically enquired into.

The critical nature of these enquiries ensures the process is entered into fully, rather than just to pass the assessment.

My Master's in Medical Science students drew upon private journals and writings for ungraded assessment without submitting 'raw reflection' (Boud, 1998). The reflective course element was formative, only needing to prove they'd kept a journal. With a manageable-sized group, I was able to perceive the fruits of their reflection, offer support and facilitation where needed, and be satisfied they were using critical reflection and reflexivity appropriately for their needs and wants. For graded assessment on the rest of the course, they discussed and set criteria themselves with tutors, giving them authority and some degree of ownership over the process. Where students are involved in criteria development, there is greater congruence between student and tutor mark (Hinett, 2002).

Patchwork text assessment is Winter's solution (2003). A series of fragments created over time from students' learning experience is synthesised into a final submission: 'an essentially creative process of discovering [and presenting] links between matters that may seem to be separate' (Winter, 2003, p. 121). Tutors in business, social work, nursing, sociology and Greek tragedy say this developed academic rigour, commitment, motivation-driven learning rather than to pass examinations, willingness to take risks and tackle complexities and dilemmas, ability to think independently and present critical arguments, integration of personal and professional issues, critical reading and varied writing abilities. It also allows assessment of the *process* of learning, as well as the *product* (Smith and Winter, 2003), though 'the most difficult aspect has been persuading myself to "let go", release students to really take ownership' (McKenzie, 2003, p. 160).

We can see there is considerable disagreement concerning assessment of reflective practice. Many with long experience of teaching and researching it point to its many dangers. Given the ethical and moral nature of both reflective practice and assessment itself, each course/programme developer has to take all this into consideration. They make their own decisions based on their own values, in order to ensure any assessment methods they use do not compromise the principles upon which reflective practice is based.

Evaluation

Evaluation involves the attempt to understand the principles, methods, processes and outcomes of a particular programme. Bloom et al. (1956) identified evaluation as the highest form of achievement in their *taxonomy of education objectives*. It is used in education to gain feedback on programmes from students (summative) and communication between tutor and students to improve student experience (formative). Summative evaluations give participants' experience of the whole course; formative evaluations are undertaken at the end of each session, and help form the remainder of the course.

Recent prominence given to student evaluation of their teachers has led many to perceive a danger of teachers being motivated by concern to maximise student satisfaction rather than educational values. This development poses some threat to evaluation of programmes. However, the following discussion takes evaluative enquiries to be genuinely undertaken in order to develop courses and programmes.

Formative evaluation enables students to tackle and share thoughts and feelings regularly, rather than brood and complain too late. Facilitators gain valuable insight about students' responses to courses from learning journals, metaphor exercises (Linn et al., 2007; see also Chapter 13), and other journals such as for practice attachments (Svenberg et al., 2007). Co-peer mentoring (see also Chapter 3) can enable participants to communicate and discuss ideas and feelings with one peer before sharing with tutor and/or group. I gave my Master's students unstructured reflexive space at the end of each session, working with the (occasionally) very rough, with the (occasionally) very smooth and everything in between. Patricia Hedberg (2009) describes and illustrates similar periods.

Brookfield illuminatively describes his critical incident questionnaire (CIQ) (1995, 2009), an end-of-session written reflexive evaluation. Participants have to focus critically upon specific elements (incidents) within the course, responding to the following questions:

- At what moment did you feel most engaged?
- At what moment were you most distanced?
- What action of teacher or student did you find most affirming or helpful?
- What action did you find most puzzling or confusing?
- What surprised you most?

Brookfield analyses, feeds back and discusses responses with students. The group then decides on appropriate changes and developments to the course. Because these CIQs are written, students feel able to express more freely than in verbal evaluation. Because they are a regular course element, students develop critical reflexivity, attitudes which spill over into other work. Because they feel directly involved, and their judgements and feelings are respected, students are engaged and learn more from the course. Students at the year's end collate elements of their CIQs into their summative portfolio, a self-assessment process. They also learn good reflective practice from the way their teacher models it in his teaching. Brookfield even shared his own reflective journal writing with students when he felt this would help them to understand his pedagogic motives etc.; such modelling can teach better than any amount of other pedagogic strategies. I have used Brookfield's evaluatory questions for years, and find the final two most productive, I think because people don't expect to be asked: 'what was puzzling?' and 'what was surprising?'.

Hattie's study (2009) showed how facilitators who constantly seek feedback and model enquiring reflective attitudes, created learning environments where students could feel safe to make, and learn from, mistakes.

Matt Babcock developed a 'liberating and destabilizing tool for pedagogical intervention' (2007, p. 514) similar to Brookfield's, for a university introductory literature course. His 'Learning Log... if implemented consistently, not only enhances the personal political and ideological communion of teachers and students but also raises the collective awareness concerning classroom dynamics and methods to higher levels'. For 5–10 minutes at the end of each class he and his students freewrite 'What have I learned or not learned today?' (p. 514), and then read their statements to each other. Initially the students offer 'meek verbatim summaries' (p. 515), then by week three there develops the 'class's transformation into symbiotic community of learners and teachers which depends on each individual's willingness to take up, cast off, and exchange those titles at any moment' (p. 516). Of course 'the teacher's reactions to log entries are crucial'. He responded to students' submissions, dialoguing with them dynamically and critically reflexively addressing his own teaching and course design, with positive results. 'The Log... intervened and transformed the physical, intellectual, and interpersonal environment in which my students and I read, wrote, lived, and learned' (p. 518).

For summative evaluation, my short-course participants wrote anonymously what was good, on one paper, and on another, what could have been better. When we have sufficient time, they spread the sheets out so everyone can read them, marking their agreement or disagreement on each (Rowland, 1993). Comments can be transferred to flip chart or typed up and fed back as part of final evaluation. Or they write brief (10-minute) evaluative stories, using the same approach for evaluation as for the course. We read back with no comments, an affirming and warm way to end: the stories tend to refer to the life of the group as a whole. An anonymous form to be handed in is needed to elicit negative points.

Drawing formative evaluations, pioneered in Sydney universities for a range of disciplines and courses (McKenzie et al., 1998), gave different information, inventively and informatively, from participants' written evaluations. One drew a juggler juggling a variety of commitments, another drew someone falling at the last of a succession of high hurdles. Anonymity can be obtained by, for example, a postbox to collect evaluations. I think the evaluation process needs to be useful to participants, rather than just a chore.

Students' reflective writing can itself offer course evaluation and material for tutor reflexivity. Beveridge developed course structures in the light of students' reflective journal material (1997). Here is an example of tutor reflexivity, enabled by reflective journals used as a form of evaluation:

> What we have learned about our students led us to take action on the elementary science methods course... Interestingly our finding that methods students lack an understanding of first graders' abilities mirrors our lack of understanding of the pre-service teachers. While our students were observing, writing about, and discussing the actions of first graders and their teacher, we were learning about them. (Abell et al., 1998, p. 506)

A simple evaluation I have used at the end of a residential is: invent a word which describes this course; now invent a short dictionary definition. Here are some:

Spontographarsis: release through instant writing

Refreat: a place and time to think and write

Connectifection: the process of finding and connecting realities in the search for truth

Cariyumminess: the process of writing to reveal one's inner thoughts and feelings: the revealing of one's soul (from the Welsh *caru*: to love)

Writology: writing one's thoughts down on paper as a way of exploring feelings

Writtance: the process of putting one's thoughts on paper and getting rid of them

Inkathinkalink: with the ink from our pens we think and link our memories and lives with our friends and mentors in a chain of magic pens. The tutor waves her magic wand and says INKATHINKALINKA! (Royal College of General Practitioners (East Anglia Faculty) annual course).

Reflective practice must be one of the most difficult (many would say impossible) areas of education to assess. We turn from the learning of individuals to the learning of teams. Reflective practice writing can have significant development impact on single- or multi-disciplinary practice teams.

Read to Learn

Brookfield, S.D. (2009) Engaging critical reflection in corporate America, in J. Mezirow, E.W. Taylor and Associates (eds), *Transformative Learning in Practice: Insights from Community, Workplace and Higher Education*. San Francisco, CA: Jossey Bass. pp. 125–36.
Brookfield's Critical Incident Questionnaire, a brilliantly effective evaluation method, is itself a critically reflective process.

Rowland, S. (1993) *The Enquiring Tutor*. Lewes: Falmer.
Rowland brilliantly explains his evaluation method in Chapter 7, and explores the dangers of students measuring satisfaction in terms of enjoyment. He also discourses valuably on how to be a reflective and reflexive tutor in the rest of the book.

Shiel, C. and Jones, D. (2003) Reflective learning and assessment: a systematic study of reflective learning as evidenced in students' learning journals, in, *LTSN BEST Annual Conference, 911 April 2003, Brighton*. (Unpublished) Available at: http://eprints.bournemouth.ac.uk/1390/1/Shiel_Output_1.pdf (accessed 13 April 2014).
A summary of research exploring reflective learning through journals with business students. The authors developed a strong analytic framework, and developed criteria for assessment marking.

Tummons, J. (2011) 'It sort of feels uncomfortable': problematising the assessment of reflective practice, *Studies in Higher Education*, **36**(4), pp. 471–83.
Tummons and Wilson explore the problematic nature of assessment of reflective practice, issues which are due to its very nature.

Wilson, G. (2013) Evidencing reflective practice in social work education: theoretical uncertainties and practical challenges, *British Journal of Social Work*, **43**(1), pp. 154–72.
Wright, J. (2012) Chapter 12: Assessment, in J. Wright and G. Bolton, *Reflective Writing in Counselling and Psychotherapy*. London: Sage.
Jeannie Wright looks at the successes and pitfalls of assessment of reflective journals for counselling and psychotherapy students.

   Write to Learn

For *How To* do this writing, please see *Write to Learn*, Chapter 1 (Chapter 8 for fuller advice). Do a *six-minute-write* about anything to limber up, before starting. Writings can be shared fruitfully afterwards with a group or confidential trusted other, if this seems appropriate once the writer has read and reflected on it first.

10.1 Assessment and spiders' webs

1. Write 'assessment', in the middle of a page.
2. Write words or phrases which arise in relation to this word anywhere on the page, allowing them to cluster; these elements might be all sorts: frustrations, facts, opinions...
3. Read your spider to yourself, adding, deleting or filling out as you wish; list the words/phrases, or join them up into a piece of prose.
4. Note down any thoughts arising about this knotty subject as a result.
5. This method can be used with any *key* word in the centre.

10.2 Evaluations

1. Do this with groups at a course end.
2. Participants each write a list in response to: 'You are leaving this course now and going on a journey. What are you packing in your bag to take with you from here?'
3. They might include things such as 'a full notebook', or abstract elements, for example 'learning'.
4. I have often finished a course with this, and started with:

'What do you bring with you to the start of this course?'
Participants might write 'a pen' or 'hope'. They then each read out, so those who have only thought of practical items gain insight. They are then prepared imaginatively for the final evaluation 'bag packing' exercise.

10.3 Summative evaluation

1. What engaged you most?
2. What was helpful?
3. What was unhelpful?
4. What were you surprised by, or was unexpected?
5. What was puzzling?
6. What did you give to yourself?
7. What will you take back for the future?

 Visit **www.sagepub.co.uk/bolton** for additional useful resources including writing examples, exercises and videos.

CHAPTER 11

REFLECTIVE WRITING AND TEAM DEVELOPMENT

Chapter 11 presents the power of reflective practice writing in team development. In-depth examples show this gaining of team communication, understanding and strength, and how individual practitioners learn also from the process.

Shape clay into a vessel;

It is the space within that makes it useful. (Lao Tsu, 1973, p. 11)

Sunlight's a thing that needs a window

before it enters a dark room.

Windows don't happen. (Thomas, 1986, p. 53)

We get to know each other through the writings in a way we are never normally privileged to do. (Medical student)

Reflection in teams and groups I have come to term 'refractive practice'. Just as a stick refracts or appears to bend when placed in water, so a new member of a team refracts when placed in the medium of the team. Reflection is here conceived as a shared or distributed activity. (Bleakley, 2002)

A significant element of reflective practice writing is sharing with specific others. Such collaborative learning is deeply educative, facilitative of empathetic listening and communication, and can therefore be powerfully team-building (Wills and Clerkin, 2009). The writing and discussion processes facilitate frankness and openness when a safe-enough environment is created for elements of relationships and organisations to be faced and reconfigured. Barry et al. (1999) have persuasively written of their use of reflective writings in developing their team researching doctor-patient communication. Another example is *the patchwork text* reflective course assessment process which aids team development (Illes, 2003). In this chapter I describe a course for senior social workers, and one for community health work. Descriptions of further team-developing reflective courses follow.

The Growth of a Team

Six officers-in-charge of this and nearby old people's homes and I met in a huge-windowed room. Unlike me, they were used to the warm atmosphere, where old people shuffle between tea table and television. They were all strangers to me; their area manager wanted to bring these isolated professionals together into a collaborating supportive group. They shared initial perplexity, asking, as so many others have: 'Writing is so difficult, why can't we just discuss these issues with each other?' One member commented in her final evaluation:

> First day – not too keen. Did not know what to expect – wasn't going to be really clever – I am not an academic type person.

They were almost immediately plunged into the process. For six minutes we wrote whatever came into our heads in whatever jumbled order, without stopping. Since this writing was not to be shared, the morning's irritations, a shopping list, diatribes against an impossible colleague/family member, last night's unshareable nightmare were all possible subjects. Nobody ever has nothing in their head.

This *six minutes* put writing on the paper. It also allowed the busy business of everyday concerns to surface, be recorded and, hopefully, put on one side; or perhaps a flash of insight to be recorded. We immediately wrote a story about *a time when something vital was learned*, for a further 10–20 minutes. Once more: no stopping to think; thinking can block inspiration and flow. We would share all or part of this writing with each other, if appropriate.

Resting aching fingers, all six realised they could write; pens had scribbled frantically. Reading both pieces of writing privately with attention, to acquaint ourselves with the writing, and to look for previously unnoticed connections, was next.

Some Boundaries

Before we read our pieces aloud, we shared anxieties and hopes; everyone wanted to be warm and involved, yet cautious and almost afraid of being curious about each other. We established initial ground rules:

- We will be trying to tease out professional and possibly personal issues embedded within writings, and draw out related, underlying themes of concern to writer and group.

- We will do this in a spirit of support and respect for each other.
- A thoughtful silence often arises after a piece has been read. As facilitator, I will not break it: I could easily do all the talking. The silence may feel supportive and reflective, or unnerving to the waiting writer. Someone must take responsibility for breaking it.
- While you are listening, be formulating provisional discussion queries/points. They might be questions, suggestions, or requests for further information.
- When you read you may feel hesitant, but the group will not perceive the imperfections of your writing as you do. They will be interested and involved.
- Everyone's thoughts are of value; yours *and* theirs must be heard.
- Careful timekeeping will ensure everyone has their fair share of time to read and have their writing discussed.
- We will discuss our **writings**, not **ourselves**. These pieces are fictions, although they may slide along a fiction–faction–reality continuum: the extent of this is not readers' and listeners' business. Fiction preserves confidentiality because we discuss the characters and their situations, not the writer themselves: we cannot ask 'what happened next, what did you actually think, etc., because there is no 'next' or 'actually': our discussion focuses upon the writing itself. Writers may wish to share more during or after the session.
- Confidentiality is essential; anything written or said in the group belongs to the group and cannot be spoken of outside without express permission.

Everyone read out all their writing, or a paragraph. The discussion was wide-ranging and rewarding, if careful, after our boundary-creating session. Group-members were generous in sharing personal information about their demanding, stressful work. Most felt afterwards: I can do this, and I *think* I might even enjoy it. The unanimously experienced shadow, felt then and expressed later, was, *everyone but myself is a brilliant writer*.

Time was running out; they decided to keep journals. Everyone was to bring a new piece in any form, next time. I suggested a topic (*A Clean Sheet*, literal or metaphorical); subsequently all topics were created by them.

One writer felt uncertain about writing at home, but overcame fears by setting her alarm for 15 minutes. The group had many discussions about staff relationships with residents, being concerned that there should be grace and loving care. One writer brought a wise yet humorous slant on all this, as her contributions always did.

More Stories; Evaluation

All participants read their pieces: 'like opening windows on themselves for each other'. Headings for ensuing pieces included: 'dilemmas', 'leadership', 'changes', 'aspirations', 'perceptions', 'a conflict of loyalties' and 'a frustrating episode'. One participant thought fate had laid calamitous events to create writing topics. We decided it was probably always so, but the course made them aware, and able to deal with them.

Time was found to write about past, unsorted-out issues, such as clients' suicide. This led to a long discussion about dealing with death in a dignified and loving way. I was impressed, time and again, by thoughtful and caring professional attitudes. Though there was always insufficient time for discussion.

Brief formative evaluations reviewing ground rules, format and content concluded each session. In these, and their summative evaluation they told me they'd gained confidence exponentially, writing and sharing things difficult or impossible to take elsewhere. Group trust led to supportive relationships radically altering their working experience, particularly those fresh to it, or taking on role changes. Each had been struggling with daily problems such as inspections, disciplinaries, all of which were now shared. And they gained confidence in the hated job of writing regular reports. They arranged meetings beyond the course.

> Coming each week has been a great source of strength and support to me. Sometimes I have come away feeling a more valued member of 'the team'.

There was formerly no 'team', only a handful of people in the same area doing much the same job. One fear was: 'I hope we don't lose it all!'. I heard that they continued to support each other through problems and challenges, using writing.

More Team-building Stories

The Soup Kitchen for Homeless People in the Community

I run the Kitchen along with other volunteers, and in our own way 'party!' with music, plays, poetry, and painting. I soon realized what was missing was developed practice underpinned with knowledge, and introduced a training programme that would involve ourselves and our guests in learning to share and trust each other. In groups of about twelve, we follow the five stages (see Chapter 8). Something powerful and meaningful happens when a group start to write down their thoughts.

After and during the sessions each volunteer is encouraged to develop their own Soup Kitchen Reflective Handbook with three sections *Think book, How to book, Need to know book*. Introducing this to incredulous volunteers is challenging, but allows each to develop at their own pace and interest. Grasping these opportunities to write and talk together about what we do and why has significantly

(Continued)

(Continued)

increased the participation of volunteers in new initiatives and engaging meaning-fully with our guests. Here is Rachel, volunteer leader of the guests' art class:

> I usually write when I am emotional. I think about stuff and when I write it is not in my head anymore. This is from my six minute writing: 'Need to change my life, confused, frustrated, not happy at work, I need to make a decision, I am in a rut.' In my 20 minute write I wrote the story about being bullied at school. I hit the bully and ran home.
>
> In the writing sessions I am able to put together my random thoughts and feelings and come to a conclusion or a decision about things.
>
> I feel that, through my writing, I can confirm that something really did happen (as with the bully) and it really did have a positive outcome.
>
> Writing is my way of making sense of random memory. It can help me see my present circumstances with more clarity and insight.
>
> I call reflective writing at home 'my brain'. I write what I think at the time. Recall actual events. Then write good and bad lists, action plans, compare my current relationship with previous relationships. It is about my life, where to go, where to live, it is a place where you can ask 'could I have done it differently?'
>
> For me this process of reflection increased my confidence and has helped me in many aspects of my life.

In the Painted Hall, Royal Naval College Greenwich, London, you can look in a mirror at the vast ceiling. At first I could only see a bright reflection of myself. Then I looked beyond to see figures telling their story of the past. This ability to see beyond myself is the essential learning in reflective practice. We try, we fail, we try and we try again. Reflection as individuals and as a team gives us the opportunity to recount that process and play it again and move from the initial overture, the serenade and the full explosion of theatre, music and song.

Martin Stone

Community Health Project Team

This team invited me to help reflect upon their stressful work with disadvan-taged communities, meeting in a room animated by children's artwork. Derek Snaith reflected upon feedback he received which gave him:

[T]he realisation that I am doing something right within my work. She said that I was a *key worker* because I helped start a social club for adults with learning difficulties. I had never realised my work made a difference to people. I could tell from the passion in her voice that 'The Millennium Club' is something she and others have been looking for for years. I still am shocked when positive feedback comes from those involved helping to run the sessions and those who come along to enjoy it.

This simple statement, and the subsequent realisation of the impact of my work has helped my confidence in my own abilities and views. I think I will be able to be myself more at work and be more assertive dealing with difficult people. Because I now know that I have made a difference to people who are in need, it means I can stick my neck out and say more of what I think clearly, rather than a watered down mish-mash that is often not understood. (in Bolton 2003, p. 19)

We *never* normally *talk* to each other like this about what we *feel* and *think* about our work and the lives of people with whom we work. (Derek Snaith, in Bolton 2003, p. 19)

Many of the group shared feelings, hopes and anxieties, which surprised the others. They were amazed Derek needed feedback to assure him of the value of his work, and were able to reinforce it. A staff member wrote about a negative encounter knocking her confidence: her colleagues were surprised at her uncertainty, and offered real support.

Interdisciplinary Team

I delivered three reflective writing sessions after work (local unitary council for whom I worked) with 12 strangers of diverse professions. Discussion added dimensions to the benefits of reflection. Participants felt safe to discuss their issues, and could share alternative views and possible future options. Even though participants worked in different areas they described common themes and situations.

I tried to give group members experience of as many reflective practices as possible. Each session started with participants giving a single word to describe how they were feeling, followed by 5 minutes' free-fall writing. Both moved people to an internal focus, and brought them together.

Writing exercises connected past, present and future experiences. The helpfulness of poetry or story, and examples, were discussed to encourage people

(Continued)

(Continued)

to express thoughts (W.H. Auden's *Funeral Blues*, Jo Cannon's *Performance* [Chapter 5]). No one had written poetry before but were pleased and amazed with the haiku they wrote and shared.

Evaluation confirmed the feelgood factor, lowering of stress levels, and the spreading of reflective writing to colleagues or family: 'It did more for me personally than anything I have tried before, uplifting'; 'Triggered much discussion back at work'; 'It felt like unloading'; 'It provided some answers'; 'I know why it happens now'.

Maria Garner

Therapeutic Team

Carry Gorney, family therapist, and Joolz Mclay, art therapist, in an NHS child and family therapy team, practised reflective writing together. This developed mutual understanding and teamwork:

Carry: We created a safe space to develop and explore through writing in the art room. This 'peer-supervision' felt a confidential process, mirroring the therapeutic process, developing our interest in language, images, metaphor, poetry and stories.

We agreed to write alone and meet to listen to each other's words and the spaces between words, then reread each piece silently. Conversations evolved around the children, the effect of the writing on each other and on our subsequent work. Then we wrote more.

At first our writing was stiff and professional, calmly and cognitively placing our practice within a context of intelligent observation. Then as we trusted each other more our writing began to flow from somewhere else. Sometimes it seemed to pour out of our hearts, our guts, our fingertips and our imaginations. It moved in a circle of unexpressed, previously unidentified responses to the children we saw.

Joolz: For me, it's been untangling the professional from the personal and private self. By writing without constraint, without fear of judgement about clinical practice I have begun to rediscover and to nurture the inner voices of my private self. These voices have been strengthened through writing, through being heard, and through conversation. They have engaged me in dialogues with neglected and forgotten parts. They have drawn attention to things overlooked, ignored and misplaced. They have made me laugh and cry and feel I am not alone. (Carry Gorney and Joolz Mclay)

Management Teams

As a management consultant I help organisations become more effective through better communication and engagement with their employees, I introduce reflective writing for teamwork, learning and development and coaching. The workplace is a tough, manipulative environment where people are often expected to comply without challenge, to 'live the company's values', to 'display the right behaviours' and even to adopt the corporate language. One's sense of self can become fragile and this limits potential. Groups and individuals say writing can bring a sense of liberation and that they are getting to the heart of things.

Free writing, although very simple, is often a revelation. A number of participants went to their action learning sets keen to use it to explore organisational issues before discussing them. They were excited about the patterns that emerged and about the honesty of a conversation with one's self. One wrote to me later:

> I spent almost 2 hrs writing up how I felt during our discussion and how I intended to change my behaviour as a result, which I found surprising, as I have, until now, been avoiding writing down anything about how I feel – so Thank You!

An activity I have found very effective for team-building is writing group poems. With my own team, we started by listing words that came to mind about our team. Each individual then wrote about how they felt as a member of the team, while I composed some linking lines. The group was moved by the commonality of themes and echoes of words and yet the distance between the different individual paths, in terms of both content and form.

When I first began this work I feared the response would be cynicism and doubts about its relevance. After all, most workplaces are based on rational and 'scientific' management practices: plans, budgets, facts, timelines, blueprints, etc. There is little place for emotion and individual expression. Yet every time the response has been very positive and unleashed the power people can have when they bring their whole selves to work. One team member said the writing was 'one of the most exciting, interesting and engaging things I've done since I've been with the firm'.

Angela Mohtashemi

Even a one-off session can positively affect later working relationships. A single session with a leading UK university academic medical department led to excited, exciting writing and discussion. More than one reported to me years later how they could still sense the improved working relationship engendered that morning. Critical reflective writing has been seen to be powerfully team-building as well as professionally developing individuals.

The evidence here suggests the impact of reflective practice beyond a course. There is little longitudinal research exploring this. Such research could strengthen the case for reflective practice in training, professional development, and team development. We are nearly at the end of our reflective and reflexive journey. Chapter 12 presents final pictures of the process at work.

 Read to Learn

Allan, J., Fairtlough, G. and Heinzen, B. (2001) *The Power of the Tale: Using Narratives for Organizational Success*. Chichester: Wiley.
Allan et al. demonstrate how stories have led to learning, dilemma resolution and organisational development.

Jude, J. and Regan, S. (2010) *An Exploration of Reflective Practice in a Social Care Team: A Qualitative Review*. Children's Workforce Development Council (CWDC). Available at: http://dera.ioe.ac.uk/2764/1/Microsoft_Word_-_PLR0910013Jude_Regan_proofed.pdf (accessed 25 February 2014).
This is an illuminating account of a social work team benefiting from reflection. Unusually they used four methods of reflection, including role play, visual aids, soft play and toys. They report that strong management support is required for this valuable professional development to take place.

Oelofsen, N. (2012) The importance of reflective practices, in *Health Service Journal*. Available at: http://www.hsj.co.uk/resource-centre/best-practice/flexible-working-and-skills-resources/the-importance-of-reflective-practices/5048994.article#.UwS8N2J_uCY (accessed 25 February 2014).
Oelofson describes how a modest investment created strong outcomes. The healthcare teams who benefited from reflective practice reported better decision making, better and more humane care, increased staff wellbeing and engagement and fewer incidents and complaints.

 Write to Learn

For *How To* do this writing, please see *Write to Learn,* Chapter 1 (Chapter 8 for fuller advice). Do a *six-minute-write* about anything to limber up, before starting. Writings can be shared fruitfully afterwards with a group or confidential trusted other, if this seems appropriate once the writer has read and reflected on it first.

11.1 Abstract to concrete

1. Write four concrete nouns, e.g. bicycle, daffodil, horse, carrots.
2. Choose one, then write a list of the qualities of this object.
3. Reread it, thinking of it as parallel with your work. Write what it says about your view of your work.

E.g.: 'My bicycle is my friend: versatile, adaptable, light and easy to carry, goes really well over bumpy ground as well as smooth, can be wheeled through one way streets, doesn't need a parking spot but can be chained safely to any railing, is waiting for me when I get back, has never had a puncture, means I meet all sorts of people who are really nice whereas in a car I'd be isolated, riding it I can see scenery and feel the air, I can ride along river or canal bank instead of always on roads, can dart around London traffic. The only problems are complex junctions, like in front of Buckingham Palace: to be avoided.' Reading this replacing *bicycle* with *my work*, adjusting a few other words as well, made me feel very positive about my work.

11.2 Asking questions

1. Discuss with your team group which of these questions might be useful as a heading for writing.

   (a) Why did you become a [your profession]?
   (b) What does your profession mean to you?
   (c) Describe your job as if to a child.
   (d) When someone says 'Oh that's just like a [your profession] ... !', about you, what do they mean?
   (e) What do your clients/patients/students think of you?
   (f) Describe your ideal service-user/parishioner/member of the public.
   (g) What are your professional ambitions?
   (h) What would you like to hear your boss say in his speech when you retire?

11.3 Letter to Santa

1. Write a wish list letter to Santa; include dreams and hopes and realistic items.
2. Write Santa's reply.
3. Reread reflectively before sharing with your team group.

 Visit **www.sagepub.co.uk/bolton** for additional useful resources including writing examples, exercises and videos.

CHAPTER 12

REFLECTION ON REFLECTION

Reflective Practice concludes with examples demonstrating how reflective practice writing can enable critically reflective and reflexive development. Practitioners can be enabled to let go and rewrite assumptions, ossified notions of themselves, and take greater responsibility for actions, thoughts and feelings, even those of which they were previously unaware. They can perceive what needs changing in their organisations, or other social or political structure, and gain the authority to do something about it. Going *through-the-mirror*, rather than staring at the self reflected back-to-front in the glass, can effect significant change and development.

Courses like this might help you get what you said you wanted from the profession in the beginning. (A practitioner, in Bradley Smith, 2008, p. 462)

Life never does more than imitate the book, and the book itself is only a tissue of signs, an imitation that is lost, infinitely deferred. (Barthes, 1977, p. 147)

'Would you tell me, please, which way I ought to go from here?'

'That depends a good deal on where you want to get to,' said the Cheshire Cat.

'I don't much care where – ' said Alice.

'Then it doesn't matter which way you go,' said the Cat.

'So long as I get *somewhere*,' Alice added as an explanation.

'Oh, you're sure to do that,' said the Cat, 'if you only walk long enough.' (Carroll, [1865] 1954, p. 54)

Certain uncertainty is an oxymoron at the heart of reflective practice, as we saw in Chapter 2. The only way to get anywhere in reflection and reflexivity is to do it, trusting the journey. We have faith in and respect for ourselves and our abilities to reflect as well as to practice, and generosity and positive regard for fellow travellers such as clients and colleagues. We are open to reassessing our values-in-practice, and formerly strongly held assumptions. As Barthes (1977) pointed out, even the meaning of language slips about offering no safe hold in an unsafe world.

We do not know our destination, and never reach a definitive *somewhere* anyway, just as Alice got to the Mad Hatters' Tea Party – an illuminating experience – but had to move on again. She later met the Mock Turtle who helped her realise that the most productive journeys are undertaken without set purpose ('porpoise': Carroll, [1865] 1954, p. 88) (see also Aristotle, 1953). Writers might make surprising discoveries, quite possibly from insignificant-seeming, rather than critical-seeming, incidents.

Setting out into reflective practice with an open questioning mind, rather than previously determined goals, can lead to fresh dynamic territory, which at the same time is 'to arrive where we started/And to know the place for the first time' (Eliot, [1936] 1974, p. 222). Reflective practice helps makes a great deal more sense of where we are. On the journey we come across what seem to be stumbling blocks. Ancient eastern wisdom says: 'the boulder in your path IS your path'. The methods suggested in this book take writers *through-the-mirror*, turning stumbling blocks into stepping stones, albeit sometimes awkward slippery-seeming ones.

We gain a width of perspective and knowledge of responsibility, partly because the critical process has helped us find our own authoritative voices. We might be able only to change small things initially, perhaps, but they might be significant. For example, I might realise I previously reinforced situations unwittingly which silenced or ignored colleagues. Or I accepted decisions which ignored human beings because they were viewed as costs, effects and benefits (Cunliffe, 2009b; MacIntyre, 1985). We may be leaders of many, or of extremely few: whichever it is, we learned that leadership is an ethical act (Pellicer, 2008).

Our practice puts moral requirements upon us. Those beginning the adventure of their career know that although they might have perceived themselves as powerless, no-one is powerless unless they *choose* to be. All our actions and utterances are our responsibility. Our life and work are precious, we have the authority to act ethically and wisely. Through reflective writing Bradley Smith's Australian students (2008) found they rediscovered the profession they had hoped to enter at the beginning of their careers.

This enquiry process takes a *thoughtfully unthinking* approach, using creative methods to take us deeply into intuitive knowledge; the vast area behind the stage of our everyday life (Chapter 1). This is similar to the way footballers are taught, and Gaugin's experience that effective painting technique develops intuitively (Bolitho and Scott, 2010).

> I am engaged in thinking an idea struggling to have me think it (Bollas, 1987, p. 10).

> 'I think – ' began Piglet nervously. 'Don't,' said Eeyore' (Milne, [1928] 1958, pp. 240–1).

Letting go of hard and fast notions of myself, assumptions, taken-for-granteds, allows responsibility for a greater range of actions, thoughts and feelings, even those I was previously unaware of. We live in a culture where everything is considered to be somebody's fault: somebody has to pay; someone has the duty to sort me out: doctor, police officer, priest, therapist, counsellor, lawyer. Colluding in this means I do not take responsibility for myself. Who is my self anyway? I am no longer surrounded by a consistent nexus of family, neighbours, priest, the same boss and employees: these figures unreliably shift and change. I can change my body with plastic surgery or drugs, and invent different persona with bell-bottoms, mini-skirt, cheongsam or sari.

An outward consistent sense of self cannot be relied upon. Instead I invent myself anew all the time by telling and writing stories about myself: to make some kind of sense. And I locate and shift this growing self alongside others: through discussion and hearing their stories, and in the wider world through reading and discussing as many relevant texts as I can. '"I" doesn't exist; one constructs oneself' (Simone de Beauvoir, quoted in Guppy, 2000). 'The unfinishedness of the human person [in] a permanent process of searching' (Freire, 1998, p. 21). Perhaps *me* is not a noun, but a verb, a process: *to me*, rather like the word *being*. 'The illiterate of the 21st century will not be those who cannot read and write, but those who cannot learn, unlearn, and relearn.' (Alvin Toffler, quoted in Osterman and Kottkamp, 2004, p. 51). This can only be undertaken by the whole practitioner in a holistic aesthetic creative process, not flinching from the range of human experience, as Warner describes in this passage:

> The states of mind or feelings that art can excite have been helpfully distinguished in Sanscrit aesthetics, where they are called *rasas*, from a word meaning 'juice' or 'essence'. A fully achieved work of art should flow with all nine of them: their names might be transposed in English as wonder, joy, sexual pleasure, pity, anguish, anger, terror, disgust and laughter. (1998, p. 7)

Reflective practice offers enlightening provisional answers. If final solutions are sought, and seemingly found, we are probably ignoring the vital questions they pose and the further potential learning from exploring them.

Now we turn to a doctor and then an education academic evaluating their reflective and reflexive practice work. Their stories review and evaluate the writing and discussion processes recommended in *Reflective Practice Writing*.

A Participant's Story of a Course

'Sheila' deeply affected me. Exactly the same age as me, she had lived a very different life from mine, including spells in prostitution, in prison for drug running and serious opiate addiction. We really liked each other. The other group members remember other problematic 'Sheilas'. They gently probe why I may have chosen this particular story. What role does her age have, might I have a special empathy with people my age? Does Sheila's experience relate to my life, giving clues why I apparently became embroiled in her story-web?

By opening myself and my emotions to the group through the writing, I remained in control of what I disclosed and how deeply I wanted to go. The continued process of sharing my writing usually gets down to other levels which individual, personal reflection never approaches. The other doctors are not competitive or aggressive; they will not laugh at me for getting something wrong, or leave me feeling exposed when delicate emotions are touched on.

The group leader patrols the boundaries and asks the 'naive questions' no one else dares ask, pretending to know little about general practice. There are no conclusions, diagnoses or certainties. Various things are considered, mulled over and the enquiry moves on. This is very different from formal, often aggressive bog-standard medicine, where the drive for evidence-based, cost-effective interventions and the like leaves little room for philosophical ruminations, experimentation, or following of feelings or hunches.

I felt I really could understand Sheila's life at greater depth, and the interaction between her and me during consultations. I learnt as much about myself during the group session as I did about Sheila, bringing up quite disturbing things, which may need resolution elsewhere. Selective, intensive work of this nature does help me to understand what may be going on for people whom I have some responsibility to try to help: a valid and important training for all my work. It might also help me in my way of being with other people (specifically my own children) at important times of decision.

Why write?

Writing Sheila's story helped me empathise. Exact details or chronological precision didn't matter: indeed I fantasised and embroidered some events and forgot or changed others to make it into a story rather than a case history. Importantly, I saw the world through her eyes for a while. That clarified many

(Continued)

(Continued)

things. What must it be like to live your entire life with a major regret? The feelings of guilt, self-loathing, remorse, hatred and despair were immediately transmitted through writing from Sheila's own life directly way into my consciousness. The written product is not especially brilliant, but responds to human dimensions.

By writing it, I acknowledged the story's importance, and considered what happens when two human beings meet. Sheila's life is now understandable and accessible to me and to others who read or hear it.

In the group

We have developed a way of working together that looks at institutional, structural, and especially personal strains involved in our jobs. Our writing focuses naturally on events and situations that have affected us. The process of writing gets me in touch, very directly, with my feelings. Writing, the flow of words and ideas, thoughts and inner feelings… and then the editing and rewriting, polishing as best I can for presentation to the group, is a ritual I now know will help me sort out and organise my feelings. It has become less scary to bring these private efforts and lay them bare before the others. The group seems able to accept each other's imperfections and are relieved and strengthened to find that many of them are shared… and that all of them are understood by the group.

The levels of discussion following presentations acknowledge the human being within the professional concretions; discuss the feelings behind the descriptions; empathise with the situation; try to get to the nub of the problem; joke as well, to relieve some of the intensity. All this seems to have been developed unselfconsciously together and they have arrived at levels of intimacy which are indeed supportive.

When I next met Sheila I felt a warmth and understanding had developed and deepened. I felt emboldened to suggest things that might never have been tried if I had not felt the support of this group.

Tom Heller

A Story about Writing

On the train, I was jittery about the workshop I had organised for the following day; and meeting Gillie, whose ideas pretty much underpin my whole thesis, was unexpectedly daunting. I began to write, just as Gillie had taught me: six minutes, don't take your hand off the page, let your writing hand work. Years of saying this to groups and yet I had to remind myself to trust the process. The drivel poured from my pen. Then I remembered how Gillie said that when stuck, play with writing. Pick a story you loved when young. Imagine yourself in it. Write yourself into it. Write it from another point of view.

My writing hand speeded up excitedly. *The Hobbit* (1937). My hand began to remember how I feel small and deliberately invisible in my work. Working with groups, creating spaces to energise people, to help them transform their lives: feels like a series of reluctant adventures. Given my fearfulness, the work is heroic: I am the Hobbit.

I opened *Writing Cures* (Bolton et al., 2004) and flicked the pages of her heavily highlighted chapter. In the riffle of pages something registered: 'people have no idea before they start what they are going to write – like Bilbo in Tolkein's The Hobbit, putting one foot in front of the other when he set out, not knowing where his adventure would lead him' (Bolton et al., 2004, p.109).

Telling Gillie (emotionally) about how my son had said I was a wonderful parent for always attending his football matches, she responded: 'Wouldn't it be interesting to hear your students' equivalent of Dara's speech?'. There was a firing of ideas all in a minute and things came together in a mess of thought: teacher-self, parent-self, hobbit-self. All the way home, the grime of the train mattered not to me, for I was busy writing and writing and writing a chapter of my research that meant something to me, one that I could live with and build on, one that freed my energy and my pen.

David McCormack

The Ekoi people of Nigeria (Gersie, 1992), have a tradition of *story children* from long ago. Each story has to be told and heard for both *child* and hearers to be nourished and run free. Once heard and known, however, the wisdom in each story can never be unheard or unknown: therein lies its power. Listening to and telling such stories changes teller and listener irreversibly. Reflective practice can enable us to be authorities over our own lives, within our organisations, over 'the continual wrenching of experience':

> They were not the same eyes with which he had last looked out at this particular scene, and the brain which interpreted the images the eyes resolved was not the same brain. There had been no surgery involved, just the continual wrenching of experience. (Adams, [1984] 1995, p. 493)

Write to Learn

12.1. Three wishes

If you could have three wishes for your work, what would they be?

12.2. Gains, positive and negative?

1. List what you've gained by having undertaken effective reflective practice.
2. List what you have left behind.

12.3. What my work means to me

Karol Silovsky, family physician, and emergency care doctor, shares an exercise with you:

'The exercise was to list the contents of my work bag, and then pick one of the "bits". My pen decided for me(!) to write about the bag itself. We then had to ask the object the questions below. My poem showed, I believe, that we may be a small package on the outside, but contain an immense amount of knowledge and secrets on the insides, accessible to others if they know how.

The Dr's bag

Red bag with a large sign DOCTOR, so people let me in.

What do you do for me?

I hold your professional life together.
I am your ID, security blanket and your barrier.
Sometimes the only clean place to sit on in a house.
I am your "bag of tricks", and can allow you to perform your magic.

How do you do it?

I am big/small/just the right size to hold it all in.
I have multitudes of zipped pockets, to find things quickly
I have a depth and secrets which can always amaze.
I am RED!

When do you do it?

I do it in an emergency. I do it routinely.
I am the first thing that you grab when you arrive on "scene".
I do it every day and all the time.
I only relax when you are finished and re-organizing my insides.

Where do you do it?

I do it on the road; I do it on the street.
I do it in the house, be it bedroom or en suite.
I do it on the pavement; I do it on the grass.
I do it everywhere, you just have to ask.

Who do you do it for?

I do it for the patient, that is number one.
I do it for the relatives, when they see you've come.
I do it for your colleagues, when the fear sets in.
I do it to reassure all even if only a bit.

Why do you do it?

I do it as I need to; I do it as I can.
You designed me this way, you allowed me that.
I do it as I need to; I do it all the time.
I help to save lives.
I buy people time.'

 Visit **www.sagepub.co.uk/bolton** for additional useful resources including writing examples, exercises and videos.

REFERENCES

Abell, S.K., Bryan, L.A. and Anderson, M. (1998) 'Investigating preservice elementary science teacher reflective thinking using integrated media case-based instruction in elementary science teacher preparation', *Science Teacher Education*, **82** (4): 491–510.

Abse, D. (1998) 'More than a green placebo', *The Lancet*, **351**, 362–4.

Adams St Pierre, E. (with Richardson, L.) (2005) 'Writing: a method of inquiry', in N.K. Denzin and Y.S. Lincoln (eds), *Handbook of Qualitative Research*. 3rd edn. London: Sage. pp. 923–47.

Adams, D. ([1984] 1995) 'So long and thanks for all the fish', in D. Adams, *A Hitch Hiker's Guide to the Galaxy: A Trilogy in Five Parts*. London: Heinemann.

Aeschylus (1999) *The Oresteia*. Trans. T. Hughes. London: Faber & Faber.

Alarcon, G.M. and Lyons, J.B. (2011) 'The relationship of engagement and job satisfaction in working samples', *The Journal of Psychology*, **14** (5), 463–80.

Alexander, B.K. (2005) 'Performance ethnography: the reenacting and inciting of culture', in N.K. Denzin, and Y.S. Lincoln (eds), *Handbook of Qualitative Research*. 3rd edn. Thousand Oaks, CA: Sage Publications.

Alighieri, Dante (1985) *Dante's Inferno*. Trans. T. Philips. New York: Thames & Hudson.

Allan, J., Fairtlough, G. and Heinzen, B. (2001) *The Power of the Tale: Using Narratives for Organisational Success*. Chichester: Wiley.

Alvesson, M. and Sköldberg, K. (2000) *Reflexive Methodology: New Vistas for Qualitative Research*. London: Sage.

Argyris, C. (1991) 'Teaching smart people how to learn', *Harvard Business Review*, **63** (3), 99–109.

Aristotle (1953) *The Nichomachean Ethics*. Trans. J.A.K. Thomson. Harmondsworth: Penguin.

Aristotle (1995) *Poetics*. S. Halliwell (ed.). 1457 b 6–9, p. 105. Cambridge, MA: Harvard University Press.

Attard, K. (2008) 'Uncertainty for the reflective practitioner: a blessing in disguise', *Reflective Practice*, **9** (3), 307–17.

Babcock, M.J. (2007) 'Learning logs in introductory literature courses', *Teaching in Higher Education*, **12** (4), 513–23.

Bager-Charleson, S. (2010) *Reflective Practice in Counselling and Psychotherapy*. London: Sage.

Barnett, R. (2007) *A Will To Learn. Being a Student in an Age of Uncertainty*. Maidenhead: Open University Press.

Barry, C.A., Britten, N., Barber, N., Bradley, C. and Stevenson, F. (1999) 'Using reflexivity to optimise teamwork in qualitative research', *Qualitative Health Research*, **9** (1), 26–44.

Barthes, R. (1977) *Image, Music, Text*. London: Fontana/Collins.

Barthes, R. (1987) *Criticism and Truth*. Trans. and ed. K.P. Keuneman. Minneapolis, MN: University of Minnesota Press.

Baruch, J.M. (2013) 'Creative writing as a medical instrument', *Journal of Medical Humanities*, **34** (4), 459–69.

Bassot, B. (2013) *The Reflective Journal*. Basingstoke: Palgrave Macmillan.

Bay, U. and Macfarlane, S. (2011) 'Teaching critical reflection: a tool for transformative learning in social work?', *Social Work Education*, **30** (7), 745–58.

Beaty, L. (1997) *Developing your Teaching Through Reflective Practice*. Birmingham: SEDA.

Belenky, M.F., Clinchy McVicar, B., Goldberg, N.R. and Tarule, J.M. (1997) *Women's Ways of Knowing: the Development of Self, Voice and Mind*. New York: Basic Books.

Beowulf and Grendel (1973) Trans. M. Alexander. London: Penguin.

Berger, J.G. (2004) 'Dancing on the threshold of meaning: recognising and understanding the growing edge', *Journal of Transformative Learning*, **2**, 336–51.

Best, D. (1996) 'On the experience of keeping a therapeutic journal while training', *Therapeutic Communities*, **17** (4), 293–301.

Bettelheim, B. (1976) *The Uses of Enchantment*. London: Penguin.

Beveridge, I. (1997) 'Teaching your students to think reflectively: the case for reflective journals', *Teaching in Higher Education*, **2** (1), 33–43.

Blake, W. (1958) *Songs of Innocence (The Divine Image)*. A. Lincoln (ed.). Harmondsworth: Penguin.

Bleakley, A. (1999) 'From reflective practice to holistic reflexivity', *Studies in Higher Education*, **24** (3), 215–330.

Bleakley, A. (2000a) 'Adrift without a lifebelt: reflective self-assessment in a postmodern age', *Teaching in Higher Education*, **5** (4), 405–18.

Bleakley, A. (2000b) 'Writing with invisible ink: narrative, confessionalism and reflective practice', *Reflective Practice*, **1** (1), 11–24.

Bleakley, A. (2002) 'Pre-registration house officers and ward-based learning: a "new apprenticeship" model', *Medical Education*, **36** (1), 9–15.

Bleakley, A. (2005) 'Stories as data, data as stories: making sense of narrative analysis in clinical education', *Medical Education*, **39** (5), 534–40.

Bloom, B. (ed.) (1956) *Taxonomy of Educational Objectives: The Classification of Educational Goals: Handbook I: The Cognitive Domain*. New York: Longman.

Boggs, J.G., Mickel, A.E. and Holtorn, B.C. (2007) 'Experiential learning through interactive drama: an alternative to student role plays', *Journal of Management Education*, **31** (6), 832–58.

Bolitho, S. and Scott, M. (2010) *Gaugin, Maker of Myth Exhibition Curation Notes*. London: Tate Modern Gallery.

Bollas, C. (1987) *The Shadow of the Object: Psychoanalysis of the Unthought Known*. London: Free Association Books.

Bolton, G. (1999) 'Reflections through the looking glass: the story of a course of writing as a reflexive practitioner', *Teaching in Higher Education*, **4** (2), 193–212.

Bolton, G. (2003) 'Riverside Community Health Project: experiences told by workers', in J. Kai and C. Drinkwater (eds), *Primary Care in Urban Disadvantaged Communities*. Oxford: Radcliffe Press.

Bolton, G. (2009) 'Writing values: reflective writing for professional development', *The Lancet*, **373**, 20–1.

Bolton, G. (2014) *The Writer's Key: Introducing Creative Solutions for Life*. London: Jessica Kingsley Publishers.

Bolton, G., Howlett, S., Lago, C. and Wright, J. (2004) *Writing Cures: An Introductory Handbook of Writing in Counselling and Psychotherapy*. London: Brunner-Routledge.

Booker, C. (2004) *The Seven Basic Plots: Why We Tell Stories*. London: Continuum.

Borkan, J., Reis, S., Steinmetz, D. and Medalie, J. (1999) *Patients and Doctors: Life Changing Stories from Primary Care*. Madison, WI: University of Wisconsin Press.

Bos, J., van Opijnen, J. and Zomer, P. (2013) 'Are you talking to me? Assessing discourses on reflection', *Reflective Practice*, **13** (5), 621–35.

Boud, D. (1995) *Enhancing Learning Through Self-assessment*. London: Kogan Page.

Boud, D. (1998) 'Use and misuse of reflection and reflective practice', paper presented at seminar at Sheffield University, February.

Boud, D. (1999) 'Avoiding the traps: seeking good practice in the use of self assessment and reflection in professional courses', *Social Work Education*, **18,** 121–32.

Boud, D. (2001) 'Using journal writing to enhance reflective practice', in L.M. English and M.A. Gillen (eds), *Promoting Journal Writing in Adult Education*. San Francisco, CA: Jossey-Bass. pp. 9–18.

Boud, D. and Walker, D. (1998) 'Promoting reflection in professional courses: the challenge of context', *Studies in Higher Education*, **23** (2), 191–206.

Boud, D., Keogh, R. and Walker, D. (1985) *Reflection: Turning Experience into Learning*. London: Kogan Page.

Bradley Smith, S. (2008) 'This sylvan game: creative writing and GP wellbeing', *Australian Family Physician*, **37** (6), 461–2.

Branch, W.T. (2005) 'Use of critical incident reports in medical education: a perspective', *Journal of General Internal Medicine*, **20**, 1063–7.

Branch, W.T., Frankel, R., Gracey, C.F., Haidet, P.M., Weissmann, P.F., Cantey, P., Mitchell, G.A. and Inui, T.S. (2009) 'A good clinician and a caring person: longitudinal faculty development and the enhancement of the human dimensions of care', *Academic Medicine*, **84** (1), 117–26.

Branch, W.T., Higgins, S., Bernstein, L., Manning, K., Schneider, J., Kho, A. and Brownfield, E. (2011) 'Through the looking glass: how reflective learning influences the development of young faculty members', *Teaching and Learning in Medicine*, **23** (3), 238–43.

Brett-MacLean, P.J., Cave, M.T., Yiu, V., Kelner, D. and Ross, D.J. (2010) 'Film as a means to introduce narrative reflective practice in medicine and dentistry: a beginning story presented in three parts', *Reflective Practice*, **11** (4), 499–516.

Briggs, C.L. and Lovan, S.R. (2014) 'Nursing students' feedback to a spiritual health reflection', *Journal of Holistic Nursing*, DOI: 10.1177/0898010113519288 (site visited 29 January 2014).

Brimacombe, M. (1996) 'The emotional release of writing', *GP*, 13 December.

Brockbank, A. and McGill, I. (1998) *Facilitating Reflective Learning in Higher Education*. Buckingham: Open University Press.

Brockbank, A. and McGill, I. (2004) *The Action Learning Handbook*. London: Routledge Falmer.

Brookfield, S.D. (1990) *The Skilful Teacher: On Technique, Trust and Responsiveness in the Classroom*. San Francisco, CA: Jossey-Bass.

Brookfield, S.D. (1995*) Becoming a Critically Reflective Teacher*. San Francisco, CA: Jossey-Bass.

Brookfield, S.D. (2005*) The Power of Critical Theory for Adult Learning and Teaching*. Milton Keynes: Open University Press.

Brookfield, S.D. (2009) 'Engaging critical reflection in corporate America', in J. Mezirow, E.W. Taylor and Associates (eds), *Transformative Learning in Practice: Insights from Community, Workplace and Higher Education*. San Francisco, CA: Jossey Bass. pp.125–36.

Brookfield, S.D. (2012) *Teaching for Critical Thinking: Tools and Techniques to Help Students Question their Assumptions*. San Francisco, CA: John Wiley.

Brookfield, S.D. (2013) *Powerful Techniques for Teaching in Lifelong Learning*. Maidenhead: Open University Press.

Bruce, L. (2013) *Reflective Practice for Social Workers*. Maidenhead: Open University Press.

Bruner, J. (2002) *Making Stories: Law, Literature, Life*. Cambridge, MA: Harvard University Press.

Bruster, B.G. and Peterson, B.R. (2013) 'Using critical incidents in teaching to promote reflective practice', *Reflective Practice*, **14** (2), 170–82.

Bryan, C. and Clegg, K. (eds) (2006) *Innovative Assessment in Higher Education*. Abingdon: Routledge.

Bullough, R.V. (1991) 'Exploring personal teachers' metaphors in pre-service teacher education', *Journal of Teacher Education*, **42** (1), 43–52.

Bulman, C. and Schutz, S. (2013) *Reflective Practice in Nursing*. 5th edn. Oxford: Wiley-Blackwell.

Bulpitt, H. and Martin, P.J. (2005) 'Learning about reflection from the student', *Active Learning in Higher Education*, **6** (3), 207–17.

Burch, V. (2008) *Living Well with Pain and Illness: The Mindful Way to Free Yourself from Suffering*. London: Piatkus.

Burney, F. ([1778] 1898) *Evelina, or the History of a Young Lady's Entrance into the World*. London: George Bell & Sons.

Byatt, A. (2004) 'Happy ever after', *The Guardian Review*, 3 January, pp. 4–6.

Campbell, C. (1999) 'Empowering pedagogy: experiential education in the social work classroom', *Canadian Social Work Review*, 16, 35–48.

Campo, R. (1997) *The Desire to Heal: A Doctor's Education in Empathy, Identity, and Poetry*. New York: Norton.

Cancienne, M.B. and Snowber, C.N. (2003) 'Writing rhythm: movement as method', *Qualitative Inquiry*, **9** (2), 237–53.

Carroll, L. ([1865] 1954) *Alice's Adventures in Wonderland*. London: Dent & Sons.

Carson, L. and Fisher, K. (2006) 'Raising the bar on criticality: students' critical reflection in an internship program', *Journal of Management Education*, **30** (5), 700–23.

Casement, P. (1990) *Further Learning from the Patient*. London: Routledge.

Cavallaro-Johnson, G. (2004) 'Reconceptualising the visual in narrative inquiry into teaching', *Teaching and Teacher Education*, **20**, 423–34.

Chambers, P., Odeggard, E.E. and Rinaldi, E. (2007) 'Risk-taking and reflective learning', *Reflective Practice*, **8** (2), 163–76.

Charon, R. (2000) 'Medicine, the novel and the passage of time', *Annals of Internal Medicine*, **132** (1), 63–8.

Charon, R. (2006) *Narrative Medicine: Honouring the Stories of Sickness*. New York: Oxford University Press.

Cherry, D. and Spiegel, J. (2006) *Leadership, Myth and Metaphor*. Thousand Oaks, CA: Corwin Press/Sage.

Chi, F.-M. (2013) 'Turning experiences into critical reflections: examples from Taiwanese in-service teachers', *Asia-Pacific Journal of Teacher Education*, **41** (1), 28–40.

Chretien, K., Goldman, E. and Faselis, C. (2008) 'The reflective writing class blog: using technology to promote reflection and professional development', *Journal of General Internal Medicine*, **23** (12), 2066–70.

Chuang Tsu (1974) *Inner Chapters*. Trans. Gia-Fu Feng and J. English. London: Wildwood House.

Cixous, H. (1991) *Coming to Writing and other Essays*. D. Jenson (ed.). Cambridge, MA: Harvard University Press.

Cixous, H. (1995) 'Castration or decapitation?' in S. Burke (ed.), *Authorship from Plato to the Postmodernists: A Reader*. Edinburgh: University of Edinburgh Press. pp. 162–77.

Clandinin, D.J. and Connelly, F.M. (1990) 'Narrative experience and the study of curriculum', *Cambridge Journal of Education*, **20** (3), 25–37.

Clandinin, D.J. and Connelly, F.M. (1994) 'Personal experience methods', in N.K. Denzin and Y.S. Lincoln (eds), *Handbook of Qualitative Research*. London: Sage.

Clark, P.G. (2002) 'Values and voices in teaching gerontology and geriatrics: case studies as stories', *The Gerontologist*, **42**, 297–303.

Clegg, S., Tan J. and Saeideh, S. (2002) 'Reflecting or acting? Reflective practice and continuing professional development in HE', *Reflective Practice*, **3** (1), 131–46.

Clifford, J. (1986) 'Introduction: partial truths, and on ethnographic allegory', in J. Clifford and G.E. Marcus (eds), *Writing Culture: The Poetics and Politics of Ethnography*. Berkeley, CA: University of California Press. pp. 1–26 and 98–121.

Clutterbuck, D. (1998) *Learning Alliances*. London: Institute of Personnel and Development.

Clutterbuck, D. and Megginson, D. (1999) *Mentoring Executives and Directors*. Oxford: Butterworth-Heinemann.

Cocteau, J. ([1930] 1968) *Opium: The Diary of a Cure*. London: Peter Owen.

Coleridge, S.T. ([1798] 1969) *Poetical Works (The Rime of the Ancient Mariner)*. Oxford: Oxford University Press.

Coleridge, S.T. ([1817] 1992) *Biographia Literaria*. London: Dent.

Coleridge, S.T. ([1834] 1978) *The Rime of the Ancient Mariner*. New York: Harper & Brothers.

Collins, C. (2013) 'Trainee counselling psychologists' experiences and understanding of reflective practice and its impact upon personal and professional development', Professional Doctoral Thesis in Counselling Psychology, University of East London. (A thesis submitted in partial fulfillment of the requirements of the University of East London for the degree of Professional Doctorate in Counselling Psychology, Claire Collins, September 2013.)

Collins, S., Arthur, N., and Wong-Wylie, G. (2010) 'Enhancing reflective practice in multicultural counselling through cultural auditing', *Journal of Counseling and Development*, **88**, 340–7.

Connolly, D.M. and Clandinin, D.J. (2000) 'Teacher education: a question of teacher knowledge', in J. Freeman-Moir and A. Scott (eds), *Tomorrow's Teachers: International and Critical Perspectives on Teacher Education*. Christchurch, NZ: Canterbury University Press and Christchurch College of Education. pp. 89–105.

Cook-Sather, A. (2008) '"What you get is looking in the mirror, only better": inviting students to reflect (on) college teaching', *Reflective Practice*, **9** (4), 473–83.

Copley, S. (2011) *Reflective Practice for Policing Students*. Exeter: Learning Matters (Sage).

Copping, A. (2010) 'Watching me, watching you, aha! Developing reflection and practice through the use of video', *TEAN Journal*, **1** (2), December. Available at: http://194.81.189.19/ojs/index.php/TEAN/article/viewFile/60/72 (accessed 10 December 2013).

Cowan, J. (2013) 'Noteworthy matters for attention in reflective journal writing', *Active Learning in Higher Education*. Published online 27 December 2013. DOI: 10.1177/1469787413514647.

Cowan, J. and Westwood, J. (2006) 'Collaborative and reflective professional development: a pilot', *Active Learning in Higher Education*, **7** (1), 63–71.

Creese, A. (2008) 'Linguistic ethnography', in K.A. King and N.H. Hornberger (eds) *Encyclopedia of Language and Education*. 2nd edn. Vol. 10. New York: Springer Science+Business Media LLC, pp. 229–241.

Crème, P. (2005) 'Should student learning journals be assessed?', *Assessment and Evaluation in Higher Education*, **30** (3), 287–96.

Crème, P. (2008) 'Student learning journals as transitional writing: a space for academic play', *Arts and Humanities in Higher Education*, **7** (1), 49–64.

Crow, J. and Smith, L. (2005) 'Co-teaching in higher education: reflective conversation on shared experience as continued professional development for lecturers and health and social care students', *Reflective Practice*, **6** (4), 491–506.

Cunliffe, A. (2008) *Organisational Theory*. London: Sage.

Cunliffe, A.L. (2002) 'Reflexive dialogical practice in management learning', *Management Learning*, **33** (1), 35–61.

Cunliffe, A.L. (2004) 'On becoming a critically reflexive practitioner', *Journal of Management Education*, **28** (4), 407–26.

Cunliffe, A.L. (2009a) 'Reflexivity, learning and reflexive practice', in S. Armstrong and C. Fukami (eds), *Handbook in Management Learning, Education and Development*. London: Sage.

Cunliffe, A.L. (2009b) 'The philosopher leader: on relationism, ethics and reflexivity – a critical perspective to teaching leadership', *Management Learning*, **40** (1), 87–101.

Cunliffe, A.L. and Jun, J.S. (2005) 'The need for reflexivity in public administration', *Administration and Society*, **37** (2), 225–42.

Cupitt, D. (1991) Interviewed by Neville Glasgow, BBC Radio 4, 8 September.

Daloz, L. (1999) *Guiding the Journey of Adult Learners*. 2nd edn. San Francisco, CA: Jossey-Bass.

DasGupta, S. and Charon, R. (2004) 'Personal illness narratives: using reflective writing to teach empathy', *Academic Medicine*, **79** (4), 351–6.

David, S., Clutterbuck, D. and Megginson, D. (eds) (2013) *Beyond Goals: Effective Strategies for Coaching and Mentoring*. Farnham: Gower.

De Bono, E. (2000) *Six Thinking Hats*. London: Penguin.

Dehler, G.E. and Edmonds, K.E. (2006) 'Using action research to connect practice to learning: a course project for working management students', *Journal of Management Education*, **30** (5), 636–69.

Denyer, S., Boydell, L., Wilde, J. and Herne, U. (2003) *Reflecting Leadership: Leadership for Building a Healthy Society*. Dublin and Belfast: Institute of Public Health in Ireland.

Denzin, N.K. (2014) *Interpretive Autoethnography*. London: Sage

Deshler, D. (1990) 'Metaphor analysis: exorcising social ghosts', in J. Mezirow (ed.) *Fostering Critical Reflection in Adulthood*. San Francisco, CA: Jossey-Bass.

Desmond, J. (2012) 'Stepping into the unknown: dialogical experiential learning', *Journal of Management Development*, **31** (3), 221–30.

Dewey, J. (1933a) *How We Think: a Restatement of Reflective Thinking in the Educative Process*. Boston, MA: DC Heath & Co.

Dewey, J. (1933b) *Children, Power and Schooling: the Social Structuring of Childhood in Schools*. Stoke-on-Trent: Trentham.

Dirkx, J.M. (2008) *Adult Learning and the Emotional Self: New Directions for Adult and Continuing Education No 120*. San Francisco, CA: Jossey-Bass.

Diski, J. (2005) 'Your dinner is the dog', *The Guardian Review*, 15 January, p. 31.

Doty, M. (1996) *Atlantis*. London: Jonathan Cape.

Douglas, K. and Carless, D. (2009) 'Exploring taboo issues in professional sport through a fictional approach', *Reflective Practice*, **10** (3), 311–23.

Doyle, W. and Carter, K. (2003) 'Narrative and learning to teach: implications for teacher-education curriculum', *Journal of Curriculum Studies*, **35** (2), 129–37.

Drucquer, H. (2004) in, Bolton, G., Allan, H.S. and Drucquer, H., 'Black and blue writing for reflective practice', in G. Bolton, S. Howlett, C. Lago and J. Wright, *Writing Cures: An Introductory Handbook of Writing in Counselling and Psychotherapy*. London: Brunner-Routledge.

Duffy, A. (2013) 'Opening the door to personal metaphor within organisations: a study of everyday metaphor in the workplace', Dissertation for City University London, MSc in Innovation, Creativity and Leadership.

Durgahee, T. (1997) 'Reflective practice: nursing ethics through story telling', *Nursing Ethics*, **4** (2), 135–46.

Dyment, J.E. and O'Connell, T.S. (2010) 'The quality of reflection in student journals: a review of limiting and enabling factors', *Innovation in Higher Education*, **35**, 233–44.

Dymoke, S. (ed.) (2013) *Reflective Teaching and Learning in the Secondary School*. 2nd edn. London: Sage.

Eagleton, T. (1983) *Literary Theory: An Introduction*. Oxford: Basil Blackwell.

Eagleton, T. (2008) 'Coruscating on thin ice', *London Review of Books*, 24 January, pp. 9–20.

Eastaugh, A. (1998) 'The pursuit of self knowledge through a study of myself as a member of a group of co-tutoring facilitators', unpublished MA dissertation.

Einstein, A. ([1929] 2002) Interview with Sylvester Viereck 1929, Berlin. Quoted by K. Taylor (2002) 'When fact and fantasy collide', *Times Higher Educational Supplement*, 20/27 December, p. viii.

Einstein, A. (1973) *Ideas and Opinions*. London: Souvenir Press.

Eisner, M. (2000) 'A villanelle: writing in strict form', in G. Bolton (ed.), 'Opening the word hoard', *Journal of Medical Humanities*, **26** (1), 55–7.

Elbasch-Lewis, F. (2002) 'Writing as enquiry: storying the teaching of self in writing workshops', *Curriculum Enquiry*, **32** (4), 403–28.

Eliot, T.S. ([1936] 1974) *Collected Poems*. London: Faber & Faber.

Elkind, A. (1998) 'Using metaphor to read the organisation of the NHS', *Social Science Medicine*, **47** (11), 1715–27.

Engel, J.D., Pethel, L. and Zarconi, J. (2002) 'Hearing the patient's story', *Sacred Space*, **3** (1), 24–32.

Engel, J.D., Zarconi, J., Pethtel, L.L. and Missimi, S.A. (2008) *Narrative in Health Care: Healing Patients, Practitioners, Profession and Community*. Abingdon: Radcliffe.

Epstein, R.M. (1999) 'Mindful practice', *Journal of the American Medical Association*, **282** (9), 833–9.

Eraut, M. (1994) *Developing Professional Knowledge and Competence*. London: Falmer Press.

Etherington, K. (2004) *Becoming a Reflexive Researcher: Using Ourselves in Research*. London: Jessica Kingsley.

Exley, H. (ed.) (1991) *A Writer's Notebook*. Watford: Exley.

Farber, S.K. (2005) 'Free association reconsidered: the talking cure, the writing cure', *Journal of the American Academy of Psychoanalysis and Dynamic Psychiatry*, **33** (2) 349–73.

Farrell, T.S.C. (2013) 'Teacher self-awareness through journal writing', *Reflective Practice: International and Multidisciplinary Perspectives*, **14** (4), 465–71.

Feltham, C. (2004) *Problems Are Us: Or Is It Just Me?* Felixstowe: Braiswick.

Ferguson, H. (2005) 'Working with violence, the emotions and the psycho-social dynamics of child protection: reflections on the Victoria Climbié case', *Social Work Education*, **24** (7), 781–95.

Feynman, R. (1995) *Six Easy Pieces: The Fundamentals of Physics*. London: Penguin.

Fins, J.J., Gentilesco, B.J., Carber, A., Lister, P., Acres, C.A., Payne, R. and Storey-Johnson, C. (2003) 'Reflective practice and palliative care education: a clerkship responds to the informal and hidden curricula', *Academic Medicine*, **78** (3), 307–12.

Flax, J. (1990) *Thinking Fragments*. Berkeley, CA: University of California Press.

Fogel, A. (2009) *The Psychophysiology of Self-awareness*. London: Norton.

Fook, J. (2012) *Social Work: A Critical Approach to Practice*. London: Sage.

Foucault, M. (1997). 'Technologies of the self', in P. Rabinow (ed.), *Ethics: Subjectivity and truth. Essential works of Foucault 1954 – 1984*. (Vol. 1, 223–252). London: Penguin.

Frank, A. (1947) *The Diary of Anne Frank*. London: Macmillan Children's Books.

Frank, A. (1995) *The Wounded Storyteller: Body Illness and Ethics*. Chicago, IL: University of Chicago Press.

Frank, A. (2004) 'Asking the right question about pain: narrative and phronesis', *Literature and Medicine*, **23** (2), 209–25.

Freire, P. (1998) *Pedagogy of Freedom: Ethics, Democracy, and Civic Courage*. Lanham, MD: Rowman & Littlefield.

Freud, A. (1950) Foreword, in M. Milner (eds), *On Not Being Able to Paint*. London: Heinemann Educational.

Freud, S. (1900) *The Interpretation of Dreams*. Standard Edition. 4: 1–610.

Freud, S. (1985) *The Complete Letters of Sigmund Freud to Wilhelm Fleiss. 1887–1904*. Trans and ed. J.F. Masson. Cambridge, MA: Harvard University Press.

Freud, S. (1995) 'Creative writers and day-dreaming', in S. Burke (ed.), *Authorship from Plato to the Postmodernists: A Reader*. Edinburgh: University of Edinburgh Press. pp. 54–62.

Gao, X. (2009) Interview by M. Jaggi. *The Guardian Review*, Saturday 2 October, pp.10–11.

Gardner, K., Bridges, S. and Walmsley, D. (2012) International peer review in undergraduate dentistry: enhancing reflective practice in an online community of practice, *European Journal of Dental Education*, **16** (4), 208–12.

Garro, L.C. and Mattingly, C. (2000) 'Narrative as construct and construction', in C. Mattingly and L.C. Garro (eds), *Narrative and Cultural Construction of Illness and Healing*. Berkeley, CA: University of California Press.

Garvey, B., Stokes, P. and Megginson, D. (2014) *Coaching and Mentoring: Theory and Practice*. 2nd edn. London: Sage Publications.

Geary, J. (2011) *I is Another: The Secret Life of Metaphor and How it Shapes the Way we See the World*. New York: Harper Collins.

Geertz, C. ([1973] 1993) *The Interpretation of Culture*. London: HarperCollins.

Gerber, L. (1994) 'Psychotherapy with Southeast Asian refugees: implications for treatment of western patients', *American Journal of Psychotherapy*, **48** (2), 280–93.

Gerber, L. (1996) 'We must hear each other's cry: lessons from Pol Pot survivors', in C. Strozier and F. Flynn (eds), *Genocide, War, and Human Survival*. New York: Rowman & Littlefield. pp. 297–305.

Gersie, A. (1992) *Storymaking in Bereavement*. London: Jessica Kingsley.

Gethin, R. (2011) 'On some definitions of mindfulness', *Contemporary Buddhism: An Interdisciplinary Journal*, **12** (01), 263–79.

Ghaye, T. (2007) 'Is reflective practice ethical? (The case of the reflective portfolio)', *Reflective Practice*, **8** (2), 151–62.

Ghaye, T. (2011) *Teaching and Learning through Reflective Practice: A Practical Guide for Positive Action*. 2nd edn. Abingdon: Routledge.

Gherardi, S. and Turner, B. (2002) 'Real men don't collect soft data', in A.M. Huberman and M.B. Miles (eds), *The Qualitative Researcher's Companion*. London: Sage. pp. 81–101.

Gibbs, G. (1988) *Learning by Doing: A Guide to Teaching and Learning Methods*. London: FEU.

Gibran, K. ([1926] 1994) *The Prophet*. London: Bracken Books.

Glaister, L. (1999) *Sheer Blue Bliss*. London: Bloomsbury.

Goethe, J.W. von (1998) *Goethe's Way of Science: A Phenomenology of Nature*, eds D. Seamon and A. Zajonc. New York: SUNY Press.

Goodson, I. (1998) 'Storying the self', in W. Pinar (ed.), *Curriculum: Towards New Identities*. New York and London: Taylor & Francis. pp. 3–20.

Goodson, I. (2004) 'Representing teachers', *Teaching and Teacher Education*, **13** (1), 111–17.

Goodyear, R.K. (2007) 'Toward an effective signature pedagogy for psychology: comments supporting the case for competent supervisors', *Professional Psychology: Research and Practice*, **38** (3), 268–75.

Gordon, D.R. (2001) 'Identifying the use and misuse of formal models in nursing practice', in P. Benner (ed.) *From Novice to Expert: Excellence and Power in Clinical Nursing Practice*. Upper Saddle River, NJ: Prentice Hall Health.

Gough, N. (1998) 'Reflections and diffractions: functions of fiction in curriculum inquiry', in W. Pinar (ed.), *Curriculum: Towards New Identities*. New York and London: Taylor & Francis. pp. 91–129.

Graham, E., Walton, H. and Ward, F. (2005) *Theological Reflection: Methods*. London: SCM.

Graham, L.J. and Paterson, D.L. (2010) 'Using metaphors with pre-service teachers enrolled in a core special education unit', *Teacher Education and Special Education*. In press.

Gray, D.E. (2007) 'Facilitating management learning: developing critical reflection through reflective tools', *Management Learning*, **38** (5), 495–517.

Groom, B. and Maunonen-Eskelinen, I. (2006) 'The use of portfolios to develop reflective practice in teacher training: a comparative and collaborative approach between two teacher training providers in the UK and Finland', *Teaching in Higher Education*, **11** (3), 291–300.

Gully, T. (2004) 'Reflective writing as critical reflection in work with sexually abusive adolescents', *Reflective Practice*, **5** (3), 313–26.

Guppy, S. (2000) 'Feminist witness to the century', *Times Educational Supplement*, February, p. 27.

Hallet, E. (2013) *The Reflective Early Years Practitioner*. London: Sage.

Hamberger, R. (1995) 'Acts of parting', *New Statesman*, 24 November, p. 49.

Hamberger, R. (2007) *Torso*. Bradford: Redbeck Press.

Hancock, P. (1998) 'Reflective practice: using a learning journal', *Nursing Standard*, **13** (17), 37–40.

Hansen, A. (2012) 'Trainees and Teachers as Reflective Learners', in Clough N., Copping, A, Davenport, H, Dudley, P, Gowing, E, Hansen, A, McVittie, E, Murtagh, L, and Pezet, M. (eds) *Reflective Learning and Teaching in Primary Schools*. London: Sage.

Hanson, C. (2013) 'Exploring dimensions of critical reflection in activist–facilitator practice', *Journal of Transformative Education*, **11** (1), 70–89.

Hargreaves, J. (1997) 'Using patients: exploring the ethical dimension of reflective practice in nurse education', *Journal of Advanced Nursing*, **25**, 223–8.

Hargreaves, J. (2004) 'So how do you feel about that? Assessing reflective practice', *Nurse Education Today*, **24**, 196–201.

Hargreaves, J. and Page, L. (2013) *Reflective Practice*. Cambridge: Polity Press.

Hattie, J.A.C. (2009) *Visible Learning: A Synthesis of over 800 Meta-analyses Relating to Achievement*. London: Routledge.

Hawkins, P. and Shohet, R. (2013) *Supervision in the Helping Professions*. Maidenhead: Open University Press.

Heaney, S. (1980a) *Selected Prose 1968–1978*. London: Faber & Faber.

Heaney, S. (1980b) *Selected Poems*. 'Digging'. London: Faber & Faber. pp. 10–11.

Heaney, S. (2008) 'To set the darkness echoing' (D. O'Driscoll interviewer), Guardian Review, 8 November, pp. 2–4.

Hedberg, P.R. (2009) 'Learning through reflective classroom practice: applications to educate the reflective manager', *Journal of Management Education*, **33** (1), 10–36.

Heehs, P. (2013) *Writing the Self: Diaries, Memoirs and the History of the Self*. London: Bloomsbury

Heel, D., Sparrow, J. and Ashford, R. (2006) 'Workplace interactions that facilitate or impede reflective practice', *Journal of Health Management*, **8** (1), 1–10.

Heller, T. (1996) 'Doing being human: reflective practice in mental health work', in T. Heller et al. (eds) *Mental Health Matters*. London: Macmillan.

Helman, C. (2006) *Surburban Shaman: Tales from Medicine's Front Line*. London: Hammersmith.

Herzog, W. (2011) 'The ecstatic flash' (interview by Hari Kunzru), *Saturday Guardian Review*, 16 April, p.18.

Hibbert, P. (2012) 'Approaching reflexivity through reflection: issues for critical management education', *Journal of Management Education*, **37** (6), 803–27.

Hickson, H. (2011) 'Critical reflection: reflecting on learning to be reflective', *Reflective Practice*, **12** (6), 829–39.

Hinett, K. (2002) *Developing Reflective Practice in Legal Education*. Coventry: UK Centre for Legal Education, University of Warwick.

Hobbs, V. (2007) 'Faking it or hating it: can reflective practice be forced?', *Reflective Practice*, **8** (3), 405–17.

Hogler, R., Gross, M.A., Hartman, J.L. and Cunliffe, A.L. (2008) 'Meaning in organizational communication: why metaphor is the cake, not the icing', *Management Communication Quarterly*, **21**, 393–412.

Hollinsworth, D. (2013) 'Forget cultural competence; ask for an autobiography', *Social Work Education*, **32** (8), 1048–60.

Holly, M.L. (1989) *Writing to Grow: Keeping a Personal-Professional Journal*. Portsmouth, NH: Heinemann.

Holman Jones, S. (2005) 'Making the personal political', in N.K. Denzin and Y.S. Lincoln (eds), *Handbook of Qualitative Research*. 3rd edn. Thousand Oaks, CA: Sage Publications.

Homer (1996) *The Odyssey*. Trans. R. Fagles. London: Viking Penguin.

Honey, P. and Mumford, A. (1992) *The Manual of Learning Styles*. London: Honey.

Hook, D., Franks, B. and Bauer, M.W. (2011) *The Social Psychology of Communication*. Basingstoke: Palgrave Macmillan.

Horowitz, C.R., Suchman, A.L., Branch, W.T. and Frankel, R.M. (2003) 'What do doctors find meaningful about their work?', *Annals of Internal Medicine*, **138** (9), 772–6.

Horsdal, M. (2012) *Telling Lives, Exploring Dimensions of Narrative*. Abingdon: Routledge.

Howard, J. (1997) 'The emotional diary: a framework for reflective practice', *Education for General Practice*, **8**, 288–91.

Howatson-Jones, L. (2013) *Reflective Practice in Nursing*. 2nd edn. London: Sage.

Hughes, J. (2010) '"But it's not just developing like a learner, it's developing as a person." Reflections on e-portfolio-based learning', in Sharpe, R., Beetham, H. and de Freitas, S. (eds), *Rethinking Learning for a Digital Age*. New York: Routledge.

Hughes, J. (2012) '"It's quite liberating turning up to a classroom without a pile of papers and equipment.' 'Pedagogic bungee jumping: a strategy to rethink teaching in a technology-rich age?' *Management in Education*, **26** (2), 58–63.

Hughes, J., Herrington, M., McDonald, T. and Rhodes, A. (2010) 'E-portfolios and personalized learning: research in practice with two dyslexic learners in UK higher education', *Dyslexia*, **17** (1), 48–64. Published online in Wiley Online Library (wileyonlinelibrary.com). DOI: 10.1002/dys.418

Hughes, T. (1967) *Poetry in the Making*. 'The Thought Fox'. London: Faber & Faber. pp. 19–20.

Hughes, T. (1982) Foreword, in S. Brownjohn, *What Rhymes with Secret?* London: Hodder & Stoughton.

Hughes, T. (1995) Interview, Paris Review. Available at: www.theparisreview.org/interviews/1669/the-art-of-poetry-no-71-ted-hughes (accessed 27 June 2014).

Humphrey, C. (2011) *Becoming a Social Worker: A Guide for Students*. London: Sage.

Hunt, C. (2013) *Transformative Learning through Creative Life Writing*. Abingdon: Routledge.

Huxley, A.J. ([1932] 1994) *Brave New World*. London: Flamingo.

Hwu, Wen-Song (1998) 'Curriculum, transcendence and Zen/Taoism: critical ontology of the self', in W. Pinar (ed.), *Curriculum: Towards New Identities*. New York and London: Taylor & Francis. pp. 21–4.

Illes, K. (2003) 'The patchwork text and business education: rethinking the importance of personal reflection and co-operative cultures', *Innovations in Education and Teaching International*, **40** (2), 209–15.

Inamdar, S.N. and Roldan, M. (2013) 'The MBA capstone course: building theoretical, practical, applied, and reflective skills', *Journal of Management Education*, **37** (6), 747–70.

Ixer, G. (1999) 'There's no such thing as reflection', *British Journal of Social Work*, **29** (4), 513–27.

Jasper, M.A. (2005) 'Using reflective writing within research', *Journal of Research in Nursing*, **10** (3), 247–60.

Johns, C. (2009) *Becoming a Reflective Practitioner*. 3rd edn. Oxford: Wiley Blackwell.

Jones, A. H., (1998) 'Narrative in medical ethics', in T. Greenhalgh and B. Hurwitz (eds), *Narrative Based Medicine: Dialogue and Discourse in Clinical Practice*. London: BMJ Books. pp. 217–24.

Jordi, R. (2011) 'Reframing the concept of reflection: consciousness, experiential learning, and reflective learning practices', *Adult Education Quarterly*, **61** (2), 181–97.

Joyce, J. (1944) *Stephen Hero*. T. Spencer (ed.). New York: New Directions Press.

Joy-Matthews, J., Megginson, D. and Surtees, M. (2004) *Human Resource Development*. 2nd edn. London: Kogan Page.

Jude, J. and Regan, S. (2010) *An Exploration of Reflective Practice in a Social Care Team: A Qualitative Review*. Children's Workforce Development Council (CWDC) Available at: http://dera.ioe.ac.uk/2764/1/Microsoft_Word_-_PLR0910013Jude_Regan_proofed.pdf (accessed 25 February 2014).

Kathpalia, S.S. and Heah, C. (2008) 'Reflective writing: insights into what lies beneath', *RELC Journal*, **39** (3), 300–17.

Keats, J. (1818) Letter to John Taylor, 27 February.

Kelley, A. (2007) *The Bower Bird*. Edinburgh: Luath Press.

Kemp, M. (2001) 'Fictioning identities: a course on narrative and fictional approaches to educational practice', *Reflective Practice*, **2** (3), 345–55.

Kerr, L. (2010) 'More than words: applying the discipline of literary creative writing to the practice of reflective writing in health care education', *Journal of Medical Humanities*, **31**, 295–301. DOI 10.1007/s10912-010–9120–6

Kinsella, E.A. (2010) 'The art of reflective practice in health and social care: reflections on the legacy of Donald Schön', *Reflective Practice: International and Multidisciplinary Perspectives*, **11** (4), 565–75.

Kipling, R. (1902) *Just So Stories*. London: Macmillan.

Kirkham, M. (1997) 'Reflection in midwifery: professional narcissism or seeing with women?', *British Journal of Midwifery*, **5** (5), 259–62.

Kirkham, M. (1999) 'The wisdom of nausea', *Midwifery Today*, **52**, 15.

Knausgaard, K.O. (2013) Quoted in Rachel Cusk, 'The book of self', *Saturday Guardian Review*. 19 January. pp. 2–4.

Knott, C. and Scragg, T. (2013) *Reflective Practice in Social Work*. 2nd edn. London: Learning Matters/Sage.

Kolb, D.A. (1984) *Experiential Learning: Experience as a Source of Learning and Development*. Upper Saddle River, NJ: Prentice Hall.

Kolb, D.A. and Fry, R. (1975) 'Toward an applied theory of experiential learning', in C. Cooper (ed.) *Theories of Group Process*. London: John Wiley.

Kuit, J.A., Reay, J. and Freeman, R. (2001) 'Experiences of reflective teaching', *Active Learning in Higher Education*, **2** (2), 128–42.

Kyeremateng, S. (2003) Jug, in G. Bolton (ed.), 'Opening the word hoard', *Journal of Medical Humanities*, **29** (2), 97–103.

Lakoff, G. (1991) 'Metaphor and war: the metaphor system used to justify war in the Gulf', *Viet Nam Generation Journal*, **3** (3) November. Available at: www2.iath.virginia.edu/sixties/HTML_docs/VNG_News_3&3_1.html (accessed 27 June 2014).

Lakoff, G. and Johnson, M. ([1980] 2003) *Metaphors We Live By*. Chicago, IL: University of Chicago Press.

Laming, H. (2003) *The Victoria Climbié Enquiry*. London: Stationery Office. Available at: www.publications.parliament.uk/pa/cm200203/cmselect/cmhealth/570/570.pdf (accessed 27 June 2014).

Landor, M., Kennedy, H. and Todd, L. (eds) (2015) *Video Enhanced Reflective Practice*. London: Jessica Kingsley Publishers.

Langer, T. (2012) 'Reflective practice: hidden beauty', *Patient Education and Counseling* **88** (2012), 354–55.

Lao Tsu (1973) *Tao Te Ching*. Trans. Gia Fu Feng and J. English. London: Wildwood House.

Lawrence, H. (2013) 'Personal, reflective writing: a pedagogical strategy for teaching business students to write', *Business Communication Quarterly*, **76** (2), 192–206.

Lemon, N. (2007) 'Take a photograph: teacher reflection through narrative', *Reflective Practice*, **8** (2), 177–91.

Lengelle, R., Meijers, F., Poell, R. and Post, M. (2013) 'The effects of creative, expressive, and reflective writing on career learning: an explorative study', *Journal of Vocational Behavior*, **83,** 419–27.

Levi, P. (1988) *The Wrench*. London: Abacus.

Levin, J. and Halter, C. (2013) *Creating and Using Multimedia as Artifacts for Mediating Learning*. University of California, San Diego. Available at: mmm.ucsd.edu/communication.html (accessed 27 June 2014).

Lévi-Strauss, C. (1963) *Structural Anthropology*. New York: Basic Books.

Lévi-Strauss, C. (1966) *The Savage Mind*. London: Weidenfeld.

Lévi-Strauss, C. (1978) *Myth and Meaning*. London: Routledge & Kegan Paul.

Lewis, C.S. (1961) *The Screwtape Letters*. New York: Macmillan.

Lillis, T.M. (2001) *Student Writing. Access, Regulation, Desire*. London: Routledge.

Linn, G.B., Sherman, R. and Gill, P.B. (2007) 'Making meaning of educational leadership: the principalship in metaphor', *NASSP Bulletin*, **91** (2), 161–71.

Livtack, A., Mishna, F. and Bogo, M. (2010) 'Emotional reactions of students in field education: an exploratory study', *Journal of Social Work Education*, **46** (2), 227–43.

Llosa, M.V. (1991) *A Writer's Reality*. Syracuse, NY: Syracuse University Press.

Lofthouse, R. and Birmingham, P. (2010) 'The camera in the classroom: video-recording as a tool for professional development of student teachers', *TEAN Journal*, **1** (2) December. Available at: http://194.81.189.19/ojs/index.php/TEAN/article/viewFile/59/70 (accessed 10 December 2013).

Loganbill, C., Hardy, E. and Delworth, U. (1982) 'Supervision; a conceptual model'. *Counselling Psychologist*. **10**: 3–42.

Longfellow, H.W. (1960) *The Song of Hiawatha*. London: Dent.

Lutz, L. and Irizarry, S. (2009) 'Reflections of two trainees: person-of-the-therapist training for marriage and family therapists', *Journal of Marital and Family Therapy*, **35** (4), 370–80.

Lyotard, J.F. (1984) *The Postmodern Condition. A Report on Knowledge*. Minneapolis, MN: University of Minnesota Press.

Lyotard, J.F. (1992) *The Postmodern Explained to Children*. London: Turnaround.

MacFarlane, B. and Gourlay, L. (2009) 'The reflection game and the penitent self', *Teaching in Higher Education*, **14** (4), 455–9.

MacIntyre, A. (1985) *After Virtue*. 2nd edn. London: Duckworth.

Mackay, M. and Tymon, A. (2013) 'Working with uncertainty to support the teaching of critical reflection', *Teaching in Higher Education*, **18** (6), 643–55.

Magos, K. (2011) 'Dina's Story: student teachers' intercultural education as a path of transformative learning'. *9th International Transformative Learning Conference, Athens*. Proceedings.

Mahoney, P. (2002) 'Freud's writing: his (w)rite of passage and its reverberations', *Journal of the American Psycholoanalytic Association*, **50** (3), 885–907.

Malcolm, J. (2003) 'The kernel of truth', *The Guardian Review*, Saturday 25 January. p.4.

Malcolm, J. (2011) 'A life in writing' (interview by E. Brockes), *The Guardian Review*, Saturday 4 June. pp.12–13.

Manning, K.D. (2008) 'A person of status', *Journal of the American Medical Association*, **300** (5), 483–4.

Maslow, A. (1954) *Motivation and Personality.* New York: Harper.

Matsuo, M. (2012) 'Leadership of learning and reflective practice: an exploratory study of nursing managers', *Management Learning*, **43** (5), 609–23.

Matthews, G.B. (1980) *Philosophy and the Young Child.* Cambridge, MA: Harvard University Press.

McKenzie, J. (2003) 'The student as an active agent in a disciplinary structure: introducing the patchwork text in teaching sociology', *Innovations in Education and Teaching International*, **40** (2), 152–60.

McKenzie, J., Sheely, S. and Trigwell, K. (1998) 'An holistic approach to student evaluation of courses', *Assessment and Evaluation in Higher Education*, **23** (2), 153–63.

McLean, S. (2014) *Creative Arts in Humane Medicine.* Toronto: University of Toronto Press.

Mezirow, J. (2000) 'Learning to think like an adult', in J. Mezirow and Associates (eds) *Learning as Transformation.* San Francisco, CA: Jossey-Bass.

Mezirow, J. (1981) 'A critical theory of adult learning and education', *Adult Education*, **32** (1), 3–24.

Mezirow, J. (1991) *Transformative Dimensions of Adult Learning.* San Francisco, CA: Jossey-Bass.

Mezirow, J., Taylor, E. W. and Associates. (2009) *Transformative Learning in Practice: Insights from Community, Workplace and Higher Education.* San Francisco: Jossey Bass. pp. 125–36.

Middlebrook, D. (2003) *Her Husband. Ted Hughes and Sylvia Plath: A Marriage.* London: Penguin.

Miller, J. (2009) Interview by N. Wroe, *The Guardian Review*, 10 January, pp. 12–13.

Milne, D. (2009) *Evidence-based Clinical Supervision: Principles and Practice.* Oxford: Blackwell.

Milne, A.A. ([1924] 1959) *The World of Christopher Robin (When We Were Very Young).* London: Methuen.

Milne, A.A. ([1928] 1958) *The World of Pooh (The House at Pooh Corner).* London: Methuen.

Modell, A.H. (1997) 'Reflections on metaphor and affects', *Annals of Psychoanalysis*, **25**, 219–33.

Moon, J.A. (1999) *Learning Journals: A Handbook for Academics, Students and Professional Development.* London: Kogan Page.

Mori, B., Batty, H.P. and Brooks, D. (2008) 'The feasibility of an electronic reflective practice exercise among physiotherapy students', *Medical Teacher*, **38** (8), e232–8.

Morrison, K. (1996) 'Developing reflective practice in higher degree students through a learning journal', *Studies in Higher Education*, **21** (3), 317–31.

Munno, A. (2006) 'A complaint which changed my practice', *British Medical Journal*, **332**, 1092.

Munro, E. (2010) 'Learning to reduce risk in child protection', *British Journal of Social Work*, 40, pp. 1135–1151.

Nakamura, Y.T. and Yorks, L. (2011) 'The role of reflective practices in building social capital in organizations from an HRD perspective', *Human Resource Development Review*, **10** (3), 222–24.

Nias, J. and Aspinwall, K. (1992) Paper presented at the Teachers' Stories of Life and Work Conference, Chester.

O'Connell, T.S. and Dyment, J.E. (2011) 'Health and physical education pre-service teacher perceptions of journals as a reflective tool in experience-based learning', *European Physical Education Review*, **17** (2), 135–51.

Oelofsen, N. (2012) 'The importance of reflective practices', *Health Service Journal.* Available at: http://www.hsj.co.uk/resource-centre/best-practice/flexible-working-and-skills-resources/the-importance-of-reflective-practices/5048994.article#.UwS8N2J_uCY (accessed 25 February 2014).

Orwell, G. ([1949] 1987) *1984.* London: Penguin.

Osborn, J. (1993) 'AIDS – science, medicine, and metaphor (editorial)', *Western Journal of Medicine*, **158** (3), 305–7.

Osterman, K.F. and Kottkamp, R.B. (2004) *Reflective Practice for Educators*. 2nd edn. Thousand Oaks, CA: Corwin Press (Sage).

Oz, A. (2005) 'The Devil's Progress', *Guardian Review*, Saturday 3 September. pp.4–5.

Patenaude, J., Niyonsenga, T. and Fafard, D. (2003) 'Changes in the components of moral reasoning during students' medical education: a pilot study', *Medical Education*, **37**, 822–29.

Paterson, D. (2010) 'Lust in action': Shakespeare's sonnets, *Guardian Review*. Saturday 16 October. pp. 2–4.

Pattison, S., Dickenson, D., Parker, M. and Heller, T. (1999a) 'Do case studies mislead about the nature of reality?', *Journal of Medical Ethics*, **25** (1), 42–6.

Pattison, S., Manning, S. and Malby, B. (1999b) 'I want to tell you a story', *Health Services Journal*, 25 February, p. 6.

Paula, C. (2003) 'Bubbles in a pond: reflections in clinical practice', *Clinical Psychology*, **27** (July), 27–9.

Pavlovich, K., Collins, E. and Jones, G. (2009) 'Developing students' skills in reflective practice: design and assessment', *Journal of Management Education*, **33**, 37–58.

Pecheone, R.L., Pigg, M., Chung, R.R. and Souviney, R.J. (2005) 'Performance assessment and electronic portfolios: their effect on teacher learning and education', *The Clearing House*, **78** (4), 164–76.

Pellicer, L.O. (2008) *Caring Enough to Lead*. Thousand Oaks, CA: Corwin Press (Sage).

Pennebaker, J.W. (2000) 'Telling stories: the health benefits of narrative', *Literature and Medicine*, **19** (1), 3–18.

Phillion, J.A. and Connelly, F.M. (2004) 'Narrative, diversity, and teacher education', *Teaching and Teacher Education*, **20**, 457–71.

Picasso, P. (n.d.) www.brainyquote.com/quotes/quotes/p/pablopicas402801.html (accessed 27 June 2014).

Pietroni, M. (1995) 'The nature and aims of professional education for social workers: a postmodern perspective', in M. Yelloly and M. Henkel (eds), *Learning and Teaching in Social Work: Towards Reflective Practice*. London: Jessica Kingsley.

Plato (1955) *The Republic*. Trans. D. Lee. London: Penguin.

Plato (1958) *The Protogoras and Meno*. Trans. W.K.C. Guthrie. London: Penguin.

Plato (1993) *Symposium and Phaedrus*. Trans B. Jowett. London: Dover.

Plato (2000) Apology of Socrates, in *Selected Dialogues of Plato*. Trans. B. Jowett. New York: Random House.

Pullman, P. (1995) *His Dark Materials*. London: Scholastic.

Purcell, D. (2013) 'Sociology teaching and reflective practice: using writing to improve', *Teaching Sociology*, **41** (1), 5–19.

Quality Assurance Agency (2001) *Guidelines for HE Progress Files*. Gloucester: QAA.

Redmond, B. (2006) *Reflection in Action*. Aldershot: Ashgate.

Reynolds, M. (1997) 'Learning styles: a critique', *Management Learning*, **28** (2), 115–33.

Rich, A. (1995) *What is Found There: Notebooks on Poetry and Politics*. London: Virago.

Richardson, L. (1992) 'The consequences of poetic representation: writing the other, rewriting the self', in C. Ellis and M.G. Flaherty (eds), *Investigating Subjectivity: Research on Lived Experience*. London: Sage. pp. 125–40.

Richardson, L. (2001) 'Getting personal: writing stories', *Qualitative Studies in Education*, **14** (1), 33–8.

Richardson, L. and Adams St Pierre, E. (2005) 'Writing: a method of inquiry', in N.K. Denzin and Y.S. Lincoln (eds), *Handbook of Qualitative Research*. 3rd edn. London: Sage. pp. 958–78.

Ricoeur, P. (1978) *The Rule of Metaphor: Multi-disciplinary Studies in the Creation of Meaning of Language*. Trans. R. Czerny. London: Routledge & Kegan Paul.

Rigano, D. and Edwards, J. (1998) 'Incorporating reflection into work practice'. *Management Learning*, **29** (4), 431–6.

Rilke, R.M. ([1934] 1993) *Letters to a Young Poet*. Trans. H. Norton. New York: W.W. Norton.

Robertson, P. (1999) Talk to King's Fund 'Arts in Hospital' forum, December.

Roche, R. (2012) 'Lost in translation: The dangers of using analogies in science', Wellcome Trust. Available at: http://blog.wellcome.ac.uk/2012/10/29/lost-in-translation (accessed 11 September 2013).

Roche, R. and, Commins, S. (eds) (2009) *Pioneering Studies in Cognitive Neuroscience*. Maidenhead: Open University Press.

Roffey-Barentsen, J. and Malthouse, R. (2013) *Reflective Practice in Education and Training*. London: Sage.

Rogers, C. (1967) *A Therapist's View of Psychotherapy*. London: Constable.

Rogers, C. (1969) *Freedom to Learn: A View of What Education Might Become*. Columbus, OH: Charles E. Merrill.

Rogers, J. (1991) *Mr Wroe's Virgins*. London: Faber & Faber.

Rolfe, G., Freshwater, D. and Jasper, M. (2001) *Critical Reflection in Nursing and the Helping Professions: A User's Guide*. Basingstoke: Palgrave Macmillan.

Rolfe, G. and Gardner L. (2006) 'Do not ask who I am: confession, emancipation and (self-) management through reflection', *Journal of Nursing Management*, **14** (8), 593–600.

Ross, J. (2011) 'Traces of self: online reflective practices and performances in higher education', *Teaching in Higher Education*, **16** (1), 113–26n.

Rowan, J. (1990) *Subpersonalities: The People Inside Us*. London: Routledge.

Rowe, J. and Halling, S. (1998) 'Psychology of forgiveness', in R.S. Valle (ed.), *Phenomenological Inquiry in Psychology: Existential and Transpersonal Dimensions*. New York: Plenum. pp. 227–46.

Rowe, J., Halling, S., Davies Leifer, M., Powers, D. and van Bronkhurst, J. (1989) 'The psychology of forgiving another: a dialogical research approach', in R.S. Valle and S. Halling (eds), *Existential-Phenomenological Perspectives in Psychology: Exploring the Breadth of Human Experience*. New York: Plenum.

Rowland, S. (1993) *The Enquiring Tutor*. Lewes: Falmer.

Rowland, S. (2000) *The Enquiring University Teacher*. Buckingham: Society for Research into Higher Education and Open University Press.

Rowland, S. and Barton, L. (1994) 'Making things difficult: developing a research approach to teaching in higher education', *Studies in Higher Education*, **19** (3), 367–74.

Ruch, G. (2009) *Post-qualifying Child Care Social Work: Developing Reflective Practice*. London: Sage.

Sacks, O. (1985) *The Man who Mistook his Wife for a Hat*. London: Picador, Macmillan.

Salvio, P. (1998) 'On using the literacy portfolio to prepare teachers for "willful world travelling"', in W.F. Pinar (ed.), *Curriculum: Towards New Identities*. New York and London: Taylor & Francis. pp. 41–75.

Saran, R. and Neisser, B. (2004) *Enquiring Minds: Socratic Dialogue in Education*. Stoke-on-Trent: Trentham Books.

Sartre, J.P. ([1938] 1963) *Nausea*. Harmondsworth: Penguin.

Sartre, J.P. ([1948] 1950) *What is Literature?* London: Methuen.

Scaife, J. (2009) *Supervision in Clinical Practice: A Practitioner's Guide*. Hove: Routledge.

Scaife, J. (2010) *Supervising the Reflective Practitioner: An Essential Guide to Theory and Practice*. Hove: Routledge.

Scaife, J. (2012) 'Soap box: reflections on evidence and the place of reflective practice', *Clinical Child Psychology and Psychiatry*, **17** (2), 208–11.

Schmidt, C. and Adkins, C. (2012) 'Understanding, valuing, and teaching reflection in counselor education: a phenomenological inquiry', *Reflective Practice: International and Multidisciplinary Perspectives*, **13** (1), 77–96.

Schön, D.A. (1983) *The Reflective Practitioner: How Professionals Think in Action*. New York: Basic Books.

Schön, D.A. (1987) *Educating the Reflective Practitioner*. San Francisco, CA: Jossey-Bass.

Schön, D. and Argyris, M. (1974) *Theory in Practice: Increasing Professional Effectiveness*. San Francisco, CA: Jossey-Bass.

Schwind, J.K. (2008) 'Accessing humanness: from experience to research, from classroom to praxis', in J.K. Schwind and G.M. Lindsay (eds), *From Experience to Relationships: Reconstructing Ourselves in Education and Healthcare*. Charlotte, NC: Information Age Publishing Inc.

Schwind, J., Zanchetta, M., Aksenchuk, K. and Gorospe, F. (2013) *Reflective Practice: International and Multidisciplinary Perspectives*. Nursing students' international placement experience: an arts-informed Narrative Inquiry. Published online July. Available at: http://dx.doi.org/10.1080/14623943.2013.810619 (accessed 30 December 2013).

Schwind, J.K., Cameron, D., Franks, J., Graham, C. and Robinson, T. (2011) 'Engaging in narrative reflective process to fine tune self-as-instrument-of-care', *Reflective Practice*, DOI:10 .1080/14623943.2011.626030.

Scott, T. (2005) 'Creating the subject of portfolios: reflective writing and the conveyance of institutional prerogatives', *Written Communication,* **22** (1), 3–35.

Segers, M., Nijhuis, J. and Gijselaers, W. (2006) 'Redesigning a learning and assessment environment: the influence on students' perceptions of assessment demands and their learning strategies', *Studies in Educational Evaluation*, **32** (3), 223–42.

Sellars, M. (2014) *Reflective Practice for Teachers*. London: Sage.

Senge, P. (2006) *The Fifth Discipline*. London: Random House Business Books.

Shafer, A. (1995) 'Metaphor and anaesthesia', *Anesthesiology*, **83** (6), 1331–42.

Sharkey, J. (2004) 'Lives stories don't tell: exploring the untold in autobiographies', *Curriculum Enquiry*, **34** (4), 495–512.

Sharpe, R. and Oliver, M. (2007) 'Designing courses for e-learning', in H. Beetham and R. Sharpe (eds), *Rethinking Pedagogy for a Digital Age: Designing and Delivering E-learning*. London: Routledge. pp. 41–51.

Shelley, M. ([1820] 1994) *Frankenstein*. Ware: Wordsworth.

Shem, S. (2002) 'Fiction as resistance (medical writings: physician-writers reflections on their work)', *Annals of Internal Medicine*, **137** (11), 934–7.

Shepherd, M. (2004) 'Reflections on developing a reflective journal as a management adviser', *Reflective Practice*, **5** (2), 199–208.

Shepherd, M. (2006) 'Using a learning journal to improve professional practice: a journey of personal and professional self-discovery', *Reflective Practice*, **7** (3), 333–48.

Shiel, C. and Jones, D. (2003) 'Reflective learning and assessment: a systematic study of reflective learning as evidenced in students' learning journals', in, LSTN BEST Annual Conference, 911 April 2003, Brighton. (Unpublished). Available at: http://eprints.bournemouth.ac.uk/1390/1/shiel_Output_1.pdf (accessed 13 April 2014).

Sidney, P. (1965) *The Poems of Sir Philip Sidney*. W.A. Ringler (ed.). London: Oxford University Press.

Simpson, D.J., Jackson, M.J.B. and Aycock, J.C. (2005) *John Dewey and the Art of Teaching: Toward Reflective and Imaginative Practice*. Thousand Oaks, CA: Sage Publications.

Sinclair, I. (2012) *Ghost Milk*. London: Penguin.

Sinclair-Penwarden, A. (2006) 'Listen up: we should not be made to disclose our personal feelings in reflection assignments', *Nursing Times*, **102** (37), 12.

Smith, D. (2009) 'I talk back to the voices in my head', *The Guardian Weekend*, 4 April, p. 10.

Smith, E. (2011) 'Teaching critical reflection', *Teaching in Higher Education*, **16** (2), 211–23.

Smith, L. and Winter, R. (2003) 'Applied epistemology for community nurses: evaluating the impact of the patchwork text', *Innovations in Education and Teaching International*, **40** (2), 161–72.

Sontag, S. (1991) *Illness as Metaphor: AIDS and its Metaphors*. London: Penguin.

Sophocles (1982) *Antigone*. Trans. R. Fagles. New York: Penguin.

Standal, Ø.F. and Moe, V.F. (2013) 'Reflective practice in physical education and physical teacher education: a review of the literature since 1995', *Quest*, **65**, 220–40.

Stefano, G. (2004) George Stefano quoted by Ian Simple, The new pleasure seekers, *The Guardian Life*, 16 December, pp. 4–5.

Steger, T. (2007) 'The stories metaphors tell: metaphors as a tool to decipher tacit aspects in narratives', *Field Methods*, **19** (1), 3–23.

Sterne, L. ([1760] 1980) *Tristram Shandy*. Vol. 2, ch. 11. London: W.W. Norton.

Stevens, D.D. and Cooper, J.E. (2009) *Journal Keeping: How to Use Reflective Writing for Learning, Teaching, Professional Insight, and Positive Change*. Sterling, VA: Stylus.

Stevenson, R.L. ([1886] 1984) *Dr Jekyll and Mr Hyde*. London: Penguin.

Stoker, B. ([1897] 1994) *Dracula*. London: Penguin.

Strawson, G. (2004) 'A fallacy of our age: not every life is a narrative', *Times Literary Supplement*, 15 October, pp. 13–15.

Summerscales, O. (2006) 'Reflective practice and reflective writing', unpublished MA dissertation, University of Birmingham.

Sutton, L., Townend, M. and Wright, J. (2007) 'The experiences of reflective learning journals by cognitive behavioural psychotherapy students', *Reflective Practice*, **8** (3), 387–404.

Svenberg, K., Wahlqvist, M. and Mattsson, B. (2007) 'A memorable consultation: writing reflective accounts articulates students' learning in general practice', *Scandinavian Journal of Primary Health Care*, **25** (2), 75–9.

Tarrant, P. (2013) *Reflective Practice and Professional Development*. London: Sage.

Taylor, E.W. (2009) 'Fostering transformative learning', in J. Mezirow, E.W. Taylor and Associates. *Transformative Learning in Practice: Insights from Community, Workplace and Higher Education*. San Francisco, CA: Jossey-Bass. pp. 3–17.

Taylor, E. W., Cranton, P. and Associates (2012) *The Handbook of Transformative Learning: theory, research and practice*. San Francisco, CA: John Wiley.

Tennyson, A. ([1886] 1932) 'The Lady of Shalott' in J. Wain (ed.), *The Oxford Library of English Poetry*. Oxford: Oxford University Press. pp. 79–83.

Thomas, P.A. and Goldberg, H. (2007) 'Tracking reflective practice-based learning by medical students during an ambulatory clerkship', *Journal of General Internal Medicine*, **22** (11), 1583–6.

Thomas, R.S. (1986) *Selected Poems*. 'Poetry for Supper'. Tarset, Northumberland: Bloodaxe.

Tóibín, C. (2009) Literature, *Guardian*, 3 March, p. 11.

Tolkein, J.R.R. (1937) *The Hobbit*. London: George Allen & Unwin.

Trelfa, J. (2005) 'Faith in reflective practice', *Reflective Practice*, **6** (2), 205–12.

Trotter, S. (1999) 'Journal writing to promote reflective practice in pre-service teachers', paper presented to the International Human Science Research Conference, Sheffield, July.

Tsai Chi Chung (1994) *Zen Speaks*. Trans. B. Bruya, London: HarperCollins.

Tummons, J. (2011) '"It sort of feels uncomfortable": problematising the assessment of reflective practice', *Studies in Higher Education*, **36** (4), 471–83.

Turnbull, W. and Mullins, P. (2007) 'Socratic dialogue as personal reflection', *Reflective Practice*, **8** (1), 93–108.

Tyler, S.A. (1986) 'Post–modern ethnography: from occult to occult document', in J. Clifford and G.E. Marcus (eds), *Writing Culture*. Berkeley, CA: University of California Press.

Usher, R. (1993) 'From process to practice: research reflexivity and writing in adult education', *Studies in Continuing Education*, **15** (2), 98–116.

Usher, R., Bryant, I. and Jones, R. (1997) *Adult Education and the Postmodern Challenge: Learning Beyond the Limits*. London: Routledge.

Van Manen, M. (1991) *The Tact Of Teaching: The Meaning of Pedagogical Thoughtfulness*. New York: The State University of New York Press.

Van Manen, M. (1995) 'On the epistemology of reflective practice', *Teachers and Teaching: Theory and Practice*, **1** (1), 33–49.

Varner, D. and Peck, S. (2003) 'Learning from learning journals: the benefits and challenges of using learning journal assignments', *Journal of Management Education*, **27** (1), 52–77.

Verghese, A. (2001) 'The physician as storyteller', *Annals of Internal Medicine*, **135** (11), 1012–17.

Vu, T.T. and Dall'Alba, G. (2007) 'Students' experience of peer assessment in a professional course', *Assessment and Evaluation in Higher Education*, **32** (5), 541–56.

Ward, J.R. and McCotter, S.S. (2004) 'Reflection as a visible outcome for preservice teachers', *Teaching and Teacher Education*, **20**, 243–57.

Warner, M. (1998) *No Go the Bogeyman: Scaring, Lulling and Making Mock*. London: Chatto & Windus.

Watson, C. (2006) 'Encounters and directions in research: pages from a simulacrum journal', *Qualitative Inquiry*, **12** (5), 865–85.

West, C. (2012) 'Developing reflective practitioners: using video-cases in music teacher education', *Journal of Music Teacher Education*, **22** (2), 11–19.

Whelan, J. and Gent, H. (2013) 'Viewings of deceased persons in a hospital mortuary: critical reflection of social work practice', *Australian Social Work*, **66** (1), 130–44.

Wiener, D.R. (2012) 'Enhancing critical reflection and writing skills in the HBSE classroom and beyond', *Journal of Teaching in Social Work*, **32** (5), 550–65.

Williams, A. (2002) 'Doing justice to human rights: the Human Rights Act and the UK law school', in R. Burridge, K. Hinett, A. Paliwala and T. Varnava (eds), *Effective Learning and Teaching in Law*. London: Routledge.

Williams, W.C. (1951) *Selected Poems*. London: Penguin.

Wills, K.V. and Clerkin, T.A. (2009) 'Incorporating reflective practice into team simulation projects for improved learning outcomes', *Business Communication Quarterly*, **72**, 221. DOI: 10.1177/1080569909334559.

Wilson, G. (2013) 'Evidencing reflective practice in social work education: theoretical uncertainties and practical challenges', *British Journal of Social Work*, **43** (1), 154–72.

Wilson, J.P. (2008) 'Reflecting-on-the-future: a chronological consideration of reflective practice', *Reflective Practice*, **9** (2), 177–84.

Winnicott, D.W. (1965) *The Maturational Process and the Facilitating Environment: Studies in the Theory of Emotional Development*. London: Karnac.

Winnicott, D.W. (1971) *Playing and Reality*. London: Tavistock Publications.

Winter, R. (1988) 'Fictional-critical writing', in J. Nias and S. Groundwater-Smith (eds), *The Enquiring Teacher*. London: Falmer. pp. 231–48.

Winter, R. (2003) 'Contextualising the patchwork text: problems of coursework assignment in higher education', *Innovations in Education and Teaching International*, **40** (2), 112–22.

Winter, R., Buck, A. and Sobiechowska, P. (1999) *Professional Experience and the Investigative Imagination: The Art of Reflective Writing*. London: Routledge.

Woolf, V. ([1928] 1992) *Orlando*. Oxford: Oxford University Press.

Woolf, V. (1969) 'Montaigne', in *Essays IV* (A. McNeillie: Ed), pp.71–81. London: Hogarth Press.

Woolf, V. (1977, 1978, 1980) *The Diary of Virginia Woolf*. 3 vols. London: Hogarth Press.

Woolf, V. (1979) *The Diary of Virginia Woolf (Jan 1919)*. Middlesex: Penguin.

Wordsworth, W. ([1802] 1992) Preface, in *The Lyrical Ballads*. Harlow: Longman, p. 82.

Wordsworth, W. ([1880] 2004) 'The Prelude', in *Selected Poems*. D. Walford Davies (ed.). London: Dent.

Wright, J.K. (2005) '"A discussion with myself on paper": counselling and psychotherapy masters student perceptions of keeping a learning log', *Reflective Practice*, **6** (4), 507–21.

Wright, J.K. and Bolton, G. (2012) *Reflective Writing in Counselling and Psychotherapy*. London: Sage.

www.hearing-voices.org (accessed 27 April 2009).

Yang, S. and Bautista, D.D. (2008) 'Reflection, arts, and self-inquiry: a letter to other for negotiating Korean English teacher identity', *Reflective Practice*, **9** (3), 293–305.

Yeats, W.B. (1962) *Selected Poetry*. London: Macmillan.

Yorke, J. (2013) *Into the Woods: A Five Act Journey into Story*. London: Penguin.

Zwozdiak-Myers, P. (2012) *The Teacher's Reflective Practice Handbook: Becoming an Extended Professional through Capturing Evidence-informed Practice*. Abingdon: Routledge.

AUTHOR INDEX

SUBJECT INDEX